COURAGE

COURAGE

Eight Portraits

GORDON BROWN

BLOOMSBURY

All royalties are being donated to the Jennifer Brown Research Laboratory
within the University of Edinburgh's Research Institute for Medical Cell Biology

Bloomsbury Publishing Plc
36 Soho Square
London W1D 3QY

www.bloomsbury.com

Bloomsbury Publishing, London, New York and Berlin

A CIP catalogue record for this book is available from the British Library

ISBN 978 07475 65321

10 9 8 7 6 5 4 3 2

Typeset by Hewer Text UK Ltd, Edinburgh
Printed by Clays Ltd, St Ives plc

The paper this book is printed on is certified by the © 1996 Forest Stewardship
Council A.C. (FSC). It is ancient-forest friendly. The printer holds
FSC chain of custody SGS-COC-2061

FSC
Mixed Sources
Product group from well-managed
forests and other controlled sources
Cert no. SGS-COC-2061
www.fsc.org
© 1996 Forest Stewardship Council

In memory of Jennifer

Courage is the first of human qualities because it is the quality which guarantees all others.

SIR WINSTON CHURCHILL

Contents

List of Illustrations

Edith Cavell (*Bettman/Corbis*)

Dietrich Bonhoeffer (*Walter Sanders/Time Life Pictures/Getty Images*)

Raoul Wallenberg (*Keystone/Getty Images*)

Martin Luther King (*Hulton-Deutsch Collection/Corbis*)

Robert Kennedy (*Steve Schapiro/Corbis*)

Nelson Mandela (*Reuters/Corbis*)

Cicely Saunders (*Robert Van Der Berge/Sygma/Corbis*)

Aung San Suu Kyi (*Reuters/Corbis*)

Acknowledgements

In researching this book I have had the privilege of talking to Nelson Mandela and his wife Graça Machel. I have also had the privilege of talking some years ago to Professor Michael Aris, the late husband of Aung San Suu Kyi. Fortunately, Cathy Koester was able to interview Cicely Saunders at length shortly before her death in 1995. And Cathy has met and talked in depth to Ernest Cromwell, a parishioner of Dietrich Bonhoeffer, and Raoul Wallenberg's half-sister Nina Lagergren. Cathy and I have also talked to Nelson Mandela's lawyer, Joel – now Lord – Joffe. Before writing my chapter on Robert Kennedy I was fortunate enough to visit Hyannisport and, there and in Washington and London, talk to Senator Edward Kennedy as well as other members of the Kennedy family. To all of them I am grateful.

I am particularly indebted to Cathy Koester for her meticulous research and advice, for tracking down the many quotations and references used in the book and for creating the bibliography, and for her insights into the lives of the characters I have studied.

Colin Currie has kept faith with the project, has advised, supported and added to it with his breadth of literary and historical knowledge, and I am grateful for all his suggestions and observations as we worked on shaping the material.

I have used many secondary sources, some great studies of the individuals I have portrayed, and I owe a huge debt of gratitude to these authors. At all points I have tried to acknowledge their work, and if I have failed to do so in any area I apologise.

I am grateful to Liz Calder of Bloomsbury, who first encouraged me to do this book, and to my editor Bill Swainson and the team at Bloomsbury, who have supported, assisted and encouraged me throughout.

There are many reasons why books are written. This started

as an offer to play my part in raising money for the Jennifer Brown Research Fund, and I have been inspired to use my summer holidays to complete the work by the encouragement and, most of all, the love of Sarah and our two boys, John and Fraser.

Introduction

As far back as I can remember I have been fascinated by men and women of courage. Stories of people who took brave decisions in the service of great causes enthralled me, especially when more comfortable and far less dangerous alternatives were open to them.

But what separates these people of courage from the rest of us and makes their lives and achievements so remarkable is that they were prepared to endure great sacrifices and persist, some of them for many years, against the odds and in the face of the greatest adversity. They are for us exemplars and icons, at once daunting and cherished. Their stories live on and inspire us.

They chose to act when others stood by, and made sacrifices that were worthwhile and noble. Social disapproval, danger, physical pain and even the risk of death mattered far less to them than personal belief and moral purpose. Quite simply, they seemed to be driven and sustained by higher ideals.

The kind of courage that fascinated me went beyond physical bravery, though almost always it did involve that admirable quality. It was not just risk-taking, and definitely not risk-taking in a doubtful cause. Here was altruistic courage: sacrifice and determination for a higher purpose; the courage that endures and prevails, and eventually dignifies all humanity. It was an expression of both strength of character and strength of belief.

In preparing to write this book I read widely about such heroism and learned much: sudden deeds of near-incredible valour by combat soldiers, some being recognised with a VC; the cool, selfless courage demanded of bomb-disposal officers almost routinely, as part of their daily task; the selfless heroism of individuals such as the passengers who took on the hijackers of United Airlines Flight 93; and the high courage displayed and the constant dangers and awful sacrifices endured by those who fought more covertly in Europe and Asia as members of the Special Operations Executive.

Hugh Seagrim served with the SOE in Burma from early 1943, and was awarded the George Cross posthumously. His remarkable story was summarised in the 'Action for which commended', which tells how an SOE party was ambushed, with only Seagrim and a Burmese colleague escaping, how the subsequent Japanese man-hunt involved brutal reprisals against the Karen hill people, and how Seagrim agreed to surrender simply to end the torture and the killing of the people who had sheltered him. When, with eight companions, he was sentenced to death, he argued that he alone should die since the rest were only obeying his orders. He failed in this, but comforted and sustained his men as they faced death and was steadfast to the end, which came in September 1944 in Rangoon.

All these heroes – civilians, soldiers and secret agents, called in sudden and unforeseeable circumstances to acts of bravery and even heroism – command our highest admiration and gratitude; already the wars and uncertainties of our still young century show these qualities are needed still, and are still there when they are needed.

Courage has fascinated me for many years now. I remember being given, when I was ten, an encyclopaedia of twentieth-century history. In it were recorded great deeds: the daring of Shackleton, the sheer determination and inspired improvisation that took his expedition across the Antarctic; the bravery and ill-fated amateurism of the Mallory and Irvine attempt on Everest in 1924; Scott's expedition to the South Pole in 1912, and Captain Oates and his last sacrifice. All of them I admired, but the page that I turned to again and again was the one that surprised me most: the story – and picture – of Nurse Edith Cavell. It made a deep impression on me.

Cavell, the daughter of a Norfolk vicar, was working in Brussels at the start of the First World War. She could have left but chose to stay, a British national in a country first threatened then overrun by German forces. Behind enemy lines, she set up secret routes home for escaping Allied prisoners but was eventually arrested, tried by court martial and executed. She had continued amid growing danger to tend the wounded and help prisoners on their way to freedom. She could have chosen not to, or she could have got away herself, but she did neither. She faced her trial and execution with dignity, courage and the words: 'I realise that patriotism is not enough. I must have no hatred or bitterness towards anyone.'

Many years later, and having read and seen much more of it, I am still in awe of that kind of courage – and that is how I came to write this book.

Of the people whose lives I have written about, the only one I have met and been fortunate enough to get to know is Nelson Mandela. Over a series of meetings I began to learn something of the nature, wisdom and courage of one of the greatest men of any century.

As I got to know him, the concept of courage – first glimpsed almost fifty years ago and elaborated on through my reading of history and a life in politics – came wonderfully alive in this wise and genial grandfather, now in his late eighties: a man who had faced death for his beliefs, survived an imprisonment that came to symbolise the injustice suffered by his people, and endured it to emerge to freedom and put an end to that injustice.

His long and often lonely struggle against apartheid, his defiance at his trial, his quiet dignity and growing authority even when still imprisoned, his ultimate vindication and his magnanimity – in office and retirement – amount to a towering record of courage in the best of causes: an achievement so great that it has allowed us to forget how catastrophically apartheid might have ended had it not been for his example, his work and his presence. I do not attempt to conceal my affection, indeed my reverence, for Nelson Mandela. Meeting him and his wife, Graça Machel – an unbelievably courageous woman – inspired me to write this book, and readers will, I hope, understand why the chapter about him has proved to be the longest.

I first came to know of Aung San Suu Kyi – the only other contemporary I write about in this book – when I met her husband, Professor Michael Aris, at a Labour Party conference in the early 1990s. I was aware of her struggle for human rights in Burma. What I did not know was the full human story behind what she did. Michael Aris told me he had not seen his wife for years, that even phone calls were becoming increasingly difficult, and that she had not seen her children for many years either.

Growing up in Burma after the Second World War, Aung San Suu Kyi admired her father's leadership in the struggle against Japanese occupation and his political and military achievements. She was abroad when her country's democracy was threatened by military dictatorship, but chose to return. As the military grip on Burma tightened, she turned down many opportunities to leave and rejoin her family, thus gradually acquiring the status of a political leader and her country's best hope for a better future. A Nobel laureate now, and still under house arrest after years of uncertainty, privation, bereavement and loss of family, she remains to this day the elected leader of her country – and the greatest and noblest symbol of the democratic aspirations of her people.

Martin Luther King was shot dead by a racist assassin in 1968. A scholarly third-generation Baptist minister, he resisted family pressures to succeed his father in a prestigious Atlanta parish and instead took up a pastoral charge in Montgomery, Alabama. He had hoped to finish his doctoral thesis and write, but as the Rosa Parks-inspired Montgomery Bus Boycott sprang up it was he – the charismatic young local pastor – who was called to a leadership role.

King was a reluctant leader, and courage was thrust upon him. He and his family faced death threats right from the start, but over the following thirteen years his leadership of the civil rights movement and his total commitment to non-violence succeeded in transforming the United States – freeing black Americans from the humiliation, injustice and political exclusion of segregation. 'The end we seek,' he said, 'is a society at peace with itself', and he knew that non-violence was the only possible means to that end.

It was his courageous choice of non-violent protest – which alienated him from blacks while not immediately endearing him to whites – that singled him out from other black leaders, but the courage and wisdom of that choice eventually prevailed. When, after centuries of entrenched injustice, legislation to establish civil rights for American blacks was passed in 1965, the single most important reason it succeeded was that it enjoyed the support of whites as well as blacks.

Despite pressure and threats from both white supremacists and Black Power activists, Martin Luther King had patiently created – through organisation, oratory and strategic vision – a majority, white and black, that ultimately prevailed. Tragically, he died for his cause, but bequeathed to the United States a better, fairer society.

Dietrich Bonhoeffer, who was executed by the Nazis just days before the end of the Second World War, took on a different kind of evil. As a young pastor and theologian in 1930s Germany, he abhorred anti-Semitism and opposed it when all too few of his colleagues wished or dared to. His Christianity was not theirs and his moral universe was not corrupted by racism: his respect for all human beings was absolute. He left Germany and returned, and then left and returned again at the most dangerous time to do so, gradually realising that to live out his Christian faith he must stay in his homeland and risk his life. As the ultimate evil and violence of fascism closed in on him he showed courage that was truly saintly, as priest and inspiration to his fellow prisoners right to the end. His selfless courage and endurance kept a flame of moral principle alight and, in a sense, contributed to the birth of a new post-war Germany.

In the same dark years in Europe, Raoul Wallenberg, a business-man from Sweden, which was neutral in the war, worked under diplomatic cover in Hungary, abandoning a life of privilege and safety that he was under no pressure to give up. Instead Wallenberg used his energy, ingenuity and charm to build an organisation that provided impressive if dubious documentation that allowed over

100,000 of Hungary's Jews with notional 'Swedish connections' to escape the Holocaust. As the war ended, he saved thousands more from Adolf Eichmann's death camps, before himself disappearing into a Soviet gulag, never to return.

I think of Robert F. Kennedy as the first modern political leader – prepared to break with old conventions and offer a wholly distinct message that transcended both the old right and the old left. Of course we think of his courage in risking his life in the full knowledge of his brother's and Martin Luther King's assassinations, and in thinking boldly about the future. When he broke with President Johnson on Vietnam he did so on ethical grounds, and when he broke with established democratic thinking on poverty and urban renewal he put forward a wholly different view of the responsible and empowered citizen and also a wholly different view of responsive and enabling government.

Cicely Saunders, who died in 2005 at the age of eighty-seven, is probably the least known of those I write about. Yet in her life she did more than anyone to come to terms with the greatest mystery of all: death. I believe she should be better known, because her long, courageous struggle transformed the way the dying are cared for, not only in Britain but across the world. After a sad childhood, she trained successively as a nurse, social worker and doctor because she saw how much dying patients suffered – physically and spiritually – as a result of being written off as 'failed cases', and she saw also how much had to be done to ease that suffering. She fought entrenched professional ignorance and indifference to the needs of the dying, but by the end of her long life had triumphed. I have chosen her because, through the hospice movement and the new medical speciality of palliative care, Cicely Saunders's life of service succeeded in changing attitudes, generating important new knowledge and transforming the care of the dying not only in Britain but across the world. In changing our view of death she has changed our view of life itself.

I believe the lives I have briefly summarised above and treat in more detail in subsequent chapters tell us much about courage: what it is, how it manifests itself and what a huge difference it can make in the most challenging and threatening of circumstances. The achievements of Edith Cavell, Dietrich Bonhoeffer, Raoul

Wallenberg, Martin Luther King Robert Kennedy, Nelson Mandela, Cicely Saunders and Aung San Suu Kyi are great and lasting, and very different. However, I believe that by attempting to understand more about the nature of that courage we can draw some lessons of real and enduring value, and I will return to that in the conclusion of this book.

But first their stories, which are about courage and much more. Eight people emerge with their human fallibilities, their doubts and hesitations, the choices they faced and how they faced them, yet all of them endured. The more I got to know about them the more fascinated I became, and the more I wanted to know, but within the limits of this series of short biographical essays I hope I can pass on to others something of the fascination courage held for me when I first learned about it at the age of ten – and how it can continue to transform our world today.

Edith Cavell

In every life there are moments when decisions taken set in train a sequence of events that ultimately seal a fate. Although most people who know anything about Edith Cavell know only about her fate and how she met it, the decisions she made at successive crossroads in her life show her already to have been a woman of great courage. At each testing time her sense of moral duty and her courage to act asserted themselves over fear, hesitation, concerns for her own safety, or any other consideration.

Edith Cavell's courage was not simply a matter of persever-ance, of making the best of difficult circumstances from which she could not escape; nor was it born of an instinctive reaction to a dramatic and unexpected emergency. Edith Cavell had choices and options throughout her life. There were easier choices and safer options. But she consistently and consciously acted in accordance with a strong sense of duty – a dedication to relieving the suffering of and helping, to the best of her ability, those in their darkest hours. And in the end she paid with her life.

Were it not for the outbreak of war Edith Cavell would have probably been best remembered for her services to nursing and for her pioneering work in its development as a respected profession in Belgium. But in the midst of war, her nurse's devotion to helping the sick and injured expanded to caring for the hunted and endangered. Miss Cavell, Matron of the Berkendael Institute in

Brussels, became Edith Cavell, rescuer and saviour of scores of Allied soldiers behind enemy lines.

The road that led from the English country vicarage where Edith Cavell was born in 1865 to her place of execution in Belgium fifty years later was a long and indirect one. What might have become of her, and the two hundred or so people whose lives and liberty were indebted to her, if only she had taken one of the easier, safer, turns along the way? Or had she stayed working as a governess for comfortably off English families instead of choosing to become a nurse; or pursued her vocation in English hospitals instead of accepting the challenge to foster professional nursing in Belgium; or even responded to her mother's urging to return to England when war broke out? What if she had simply chosen to turn away the first fugitive English soldiers who turned up at the door of her hospital on that first day? If only she had stopped there instead of offering, and then increasingly offering, her help to escaping troops long after German suspicions were aroused.

Each decision made at these crossroads tells something of Edith Cavell's remarkable character and steadfastness. Together and cumulatively, throughout her adulthood, they form a pattern of a truly great life: the pursuit of a nobler cause; danger coming before safety, hardship before comfort, isolation before the succour of strong family ties, and prison – and ultimately death – before liberty and life. Her courage at the moment of death, when she forgave her executioners, is perhaps the best-remembered aspect of her life, yet everything beforehand can be seen as a preparation for that one moment, her courage springing from a dignity and strength of character demonstrated again and again throughout a life lived in the service of her principles.

Edith Louisa Cavell was the eldest daughter of a Church of England vicar and grew up in the small Norfolk village of Swardeston. The testimonies of her siblings – two sisters – and neighbours reveal an early life framed by a sense of both duty and freedom. Edith Cavell's father is remembered as devout and committed in his ministry, her mother as generous and warm, and her family life as close and supportive. The vicarage was close to Swardeston Common and the Cavell children spent a great deal of time outdoors on the common and in the vicarage garden.

As well as being at liberty to roam, the Cavell household diligently supported the vicar in his duties. Several biographers make reference to the family custom of taking a portion of their Sunday dinner to share with local families most in need. Edith would have been aware from the earliest days of her childhood that the world's abundance is not equally bestowed and that she had it within her means to soften some of the sharpness of other people's suffering through her own actions. Edith also taught at the local Sunday school and dutifully attended every one of her father's church services, a duty all too familiar to the families of the clergy. As an adolescent she wrote to a cousin: 'I would love to have you with us, but not on a Sunday. It's too dreadful, Sunday school, Church services, family devotions morning and evening.'

As the eldest child of the vicar, Edith bore witness to the suffering of the people in her father's parish when she accompanied her mother and father on pastoral visits to villagers in their times of need: birth and death, sickness, poverty and grief. Such proximity to death and to other people's suffering would become even more familiar to her during her nursing years and the war. Indeed, by the time she came to face her own death she would claim it had lost some of its sting. As she told the vicar who visited her on the eve of her execution: 'I have seen death so often that it is not strange or fearful to me.'

But being witness to the suffering of others does not necessarily bring compassion. Repeated exposure to misery can just as easily lead to a hardening of the heart – desensitisation, disengagement and withdrawal – or an even less helpful mindset that blames misfortune on its victims, as divine punishment for an unknown deed. And compassion, even when stirred, does not necessarily translate into action. Edith Cavell saw suffering, was deeply moved by it, and was prepared to do much to mitigate it. As a young woman she wrote again to the cousin to whom she had expressed her frustration at her father's long Sunday services and this time spoke of her desire to do more to relieve the pain she saw in others: 'Being a governess is only temporary, but someday, somehow, I am going to do something useful. I don't know what it will be. I only know that it will be something for people. They are, most of them, so helpless, so hurt, and so unhappy.'

From an early age, when confronted with unsatisfied need, Edith Cavell chose the course of action over inaction. An event in her youth, recalled by her siblings, is one of the first recorded instances of Edith's readiness to act in a lifetime devoted to duty. Her father's parish was not particularly wealthy, and the church, St Mary's, could not afford to build a separate hall for the Sunday school. Edith, probably then a young teenager, took it upon herself to write to the Bishop of Norwich, without her parents' knowledge, explaining the situation and asking for his help. The Bishop replied to the effect that he would match whatever funding the parish could raise. So Edith set about using her significant drawing and painting skills to mass-produce greeting cards to sell to parishioners and around the village. Once she had raised enough money she called upon the Bishop to keep his side of the bargain and the church hall was built.

Edith remained at the vicarage until around the age of sixteen when she left Swardeston to embark on her formal education, first in London, then near Bristol, then finally in Peterborough. By the time she completed her schooling and returned to Norfolk she was twenty. She then took a post as a governess and worked for the same family for three years.

In 1888, when Edith was twenty-two, she inherited a small legacy which she used to travel to the Continent, primarily to Bavaria and Austria. In Bavaria she discovered the Bavaria Free Hospital and became a frequent visitor. An anonymous, and somewhat hagiographical, biography, written in 1915, records that those in the hospital referred to her as 'The English Angel'. She is also said to have given part of her inheritance to the hospital so that it could buy surgical instruments, specifically indicating how the money should be used – much to the annoyance of the chief doctor who thought the decision should be left to him. It is possible that the connection with the Free Hospital was the beginning of Edith's interest in nursing. The 1915 biography also records that Edith Cavell became very fond of the German people during her stay and spoke of her admiration for their generosity and gentle manners.

After her travels Edith returned to England and to working as a governess. A turning point came in 1890 when she was twenty-five. On the recommendation of the principal of her former school, Edith was offered the opportunity to act as governess to the François family in Brussels. She accepted the position and remained in it for five years. Her time in Brussels appears to have been a happy one, and it laid the foundations for her return twelve years later to take charge of the Berkendael Institute. One of the François children in her charge recalled that Edith organised mock dinner parties, plays and performances, taught them drawing and painting, and took them on long walks through the countryside. 'It was an intelligent way of bringing up children,' she said. But it was also during this period that Edith wrote to her cousin of her determination to find a way of doing something more useful for 'helpless, hurt and unhappy' people.

In 1895, Edith received news that her father was seriously ill and she returned to Swardeston to tend to him. He made a full recovery, but Edith did not return to the François family or to working as a governess. Instead she applied to train as a nurse at the Fountains Fever Hospital in London. What led to her decision to change the direction of her life and train as a nurse at the age of thirty is not recorded. Full training would take many years and she would be in her mid-thirties before she could fully practise. She would experience a fall in income and the conditions of her training would be a stark contrast to her work as a governess, with exhausting hours in a far less comfortable environment, surrounded by injury, sickness, disease and death. Biographers surmise that nursing her father through his illness inspired Edith to pursue nursing as the 'something useful . . . for people' that she had longed for.

On her application form to train as a nurse she wrote: 'I have had no hospital training nor any nursing engagement whatever'; nonetheless she was accepted and trained for seven months before applying for a general nursing training at the London Hospital. Her formative years of general training were under the authority of its matron, Eva Lückes, who was for some time in correspondence with Florence Nightingale, and who strove to maintain the newly acquired professional status of the nursing profession. The intensity of the training and exacting demands fostered a bond between the probationers that Edith Cavell never forgot. In particular, she admired the dedication the matron inspired in her students and the high standards of discipline and care she demanded.

When Edith Cavell became a matron herself, she sought to replicate those exacting standards and instil an equally uncompromising dedication to duty, vocation, and pride into her student nurses. Of particular importance were the regular informal talks the matron would have with her students in the evenings. These were broad in scope, exploring nursing and positioning it in a much broader philosophical context of service, vocation, duty, pride, honour, and professionalism.

In 1897, an epidemic of typhoid fever broke out in Maidstone, and the local hospital was overwhelmed. Emergency help from other hospitals was requested. Edith Cavell was sent as part of a delegation of six from the London Hospital. About 250 nurses in total joined the effort to fight the epidemic, which had affected around 1,700 people – 132 of whom died. Once the epidemic waned, a great dinner was held for all the nurses and the Mayor of Maidstone presented each nurse with a medal: this would prove to be the only medal Edith Cavell ever received from her compatriots.

A report on Edith Cavell's traineeship by Matron Eva Lückes acknowledged her good work in Maidstone, but was otherwise unflattering. Nevertheless, Edith earned her hospital certificate in 1898 and corresponded with Eva Lückes for many years thereafter, asking her advice and, once she became a matron herself, reporting on progress in Brussels. Eva Lückes may have been a formidable matron not much given to easy compliments, but Edith Cavell clearly admired her and valued her instruction. 'You will, I think, be pleased to hear that I was elected yesterday to the post of assistant matron at the Shoreditch Infirmary,' she wrote to Matron Lückes in November 1903, 'but no place will ever be to me what the London was, nor any matron like the one under whom I trained.'

For ten years Edith worked in a succession of senior nursing positions. She also made numerous job applications, eager to take on greater responsibility and authority. In 1904 she wrote to her sister: 'I am beginning to think of a new appointment and am putting in for the matronship of the Consumption Hospital at Ventnor – but again with little hope of success – so many are always in for these posts.' And two years later, in a letter to Eva Lückes: 'I have been trying for some time to obtain a post of trust as Matron or Superintendent in an Institution, but so far without success.'

Edith was clearly ambitious, and restless. But her letters, particularly those written in later years, point towards an ambition not motivated by self-advancement, but rather by a knowledge of her capacity to help others. She recognised that she had more to give and embarked on an energetic and relentless quest to give expression to her strong sense of duty. In the last solitary moments of her life, under the shadow of execution, she reflected on this aspect in a letter addressed to her nurses at Berkendael: 'I have told you that devotion will give you real happiness, and the thought that you have done, before God and yourselves, your whole duty and with a good heart will be your greatest support in the hard moments of life and in the face of death.'

In 1907 Edith Cavell was presented with the opportunity she so craved. Dr Antoine Depage, one of the most respected surgeons in Europe at the time, was looking for a matron to run a progressive new teaching hospital on the outskirts of Brussels, the Berkendael Institute. In Belgium nursing still lacked respectability and the limited duties of nurses were performed either by nuns or by lay women who had no other means of income – neither group having trained in medical knowledge or being much concerned with hygiene.

Depage wanted to professionalise nursing in Belgium to the level already being achieved by the likes of Florence Nightingale and Eva Lückes in England. He sought an English nurse who was familiar with Belgium and its culture, who could speak French, and who could help him with his groundbreaking mission: Edith Cavell, whom Depage already knew, could hardly have been better suited. In this remarkable phase of her life, the ideals that had motivated Edith Cavell thus far flowered and matured. She could put into practice her fierce devotion to nursing and to the relief of suffering. As matron she finally had the authority she required to breathe life and power into the profession and to enable it to realise the good she knew it could accomplish. This would prove to be the height of Edith Cavell's career, and her resolve and resourcefulness during this period seemed boundless.

In June 1907 she wrote of her 'mission' to Miss Lückes:

My dear Matron, I am writing to tell you that I have just accepted a permanent appointment in Brussels. I had a letter some time ago asking me if I would consent to become the Matron of the first training school of nurses out there, which is to be opened in October. Up to the present they have only had nuns to nurse the sick, and they are often ignorant and the lay nurses always dirty. They have formed two committees – one of ladies and the other of well-known doctors and lawyers – so that I think it should be a success, particularly as some of the best-known names there are connected with them. They are anxious that the school should be carried on in English lines, and that the head of it should be an Englishwoman, knowing their language and manner of life. We shall begin with a few pupils (I have made a point of educated women as the first trained nurses will become the teachers ultimately) and a few patients, and it will, I hope, develop rapidly into a fair-sized training school. Looking forward I hope that in time both private and district nursing may spring from this beginning as the need for both is, I believe, greatly felt, and people are no longer to put up with the old class of nurse . . . I am going over to Brussels in August to get everything in readiness, and hope that I shall be allowed to engage a trained nurse as night superintendent. For no one will know anything about the care of the sick who could be left in charge. Thank you very much for sending me your welcome annual letter. I always keep the last one until the new one arrives, and never fail to read any little bits of news about the dear old hospital which appear in the papers. With very best wishes, dear Matron,

Yours affectionately.

The magnitude of the task that Edith Cavell had accepted was immense. Not only would she be in charge as matron, but she would have to create the hospital and the nursing school from scratch, and prevail over both a sceptical public and ill-disciplined recruits, to achieve the respectability and esteem that was necessary to establish the profession and ensure its potential for good. A further letter to Eva Lückes upon her arrival in Brussels in September 1907 gives a sense of what she was up against:

> I arrived two days ago and found the four houses, which had been made to communicate, only partly furnished and in much confusion. The Council were all absent on holiday, except the Secretary and the President who returned for a day or two to welcome me. No servants – only a portress – and nothing furnished but my sitting-room! And we have to open on October 1st!

Her courage at taking on such a task – so great an opportunity but so great a risk of failure – repeats again the pattern in her life of action aligned to conviction. For now, it would help revolutionlise nursing in Belgium. Later, it would save hundreds from certain imprisonment and likely death.

In an article written for the *Nursing Mirror*, Edith Cavell explained in her own terms what she was trying to achieve: not merely the organisational and managerial challenge of setting up and running an organisation, but a radical transformation of nursing. Like Dr Depage, Eva Lückes and Florence Nightingale, Edith Cavell had the vision of a pioneer:

> One house had been fitted up as a home for twelve nurses . . . Five pupils have had the courage to come forward, and they are already settling down to their new life and seem happy at their work. Each one has five patients to look after. They breakfast at 7 a.m. Then they wash their patients and give them their breakfasts. During the morning they accompany the doctor on his rounds and carry out the treatments he orders . . . The probationers wear blue dresses with white aprons and white collars.

White linen sleeves cover the forearm which is bare beneath. Their caps are of the plain Sister Dora type without strings. The contrast which they present to the nuns, in their heavy stiff robes, and to the lay nurses, in their grimy apparel, is the contrast of the unhygienic past with the enlightened present . . . These first nurses of ours will in the years which lie ahead teach, as no others have ever had the opportunity of doing, the laws of health and the methods of treating disease. They will also prove to their countrymen that education and position do not constitute a bar to an independent life for a woman, as so many seem to suppose over here. Indeed, they will show them that education and position are in point of fact good and solid foundations on which to build a career which demands the best and highest qualities that womanhood can offer.

For eight years under Edith's direction, the Berkendael Institute fought against the tide to earn itself a respectable reputation. Edith was at her busiest. As well as running the school, teaching and training her probationers, and managing the supply of nurses to hospitals and schools, she also took personal care of Grace Jemmett, an English friend's daughter who had become addicted to morphine and for whom she cared as if she were her own.

Edith Cavell's successes at Berkendael came only with huge effort and many setbacks. Despite the difficulties, Berkendael's standing grew, and received a significant boost when Queen Elisabeth of Belgium, having broken her arm, sent for a trained nurse from Miss Cavell's school. By 1913 she had gone some way to realising the ambitious vision she had set out in the *Nursing Mirror* so many years ago and a letter to Eva Lückes is full of hope and expectation:

Our hospital, I am thankful to say, has made progress and will, I hope, be a model in point of view of good order, cleanliness and good nursing for all the other hospitals of Belgium. My Council are very good and kind, and I always feel now that I have their support in any difficulty. They have the work very much at heart, and have raised the necessary funds to build us a new school which will be worthy of the object.

The years at Berkendael richly satisfied Edith Cavell's sense of vocation. Here she was a leader, a teacher and a pioneer: an agent of change and progress. Her work made a discernible difference at both an individual and a more general level: tending to the injuries and illnesses of patients, and at the same time raising the standard of nursing and helping to establish it as a profession across the country.

Edith Cavell's dedication to duty, and to nursing, was whole-hearted and total. But to explain her life, and death, simply as the tenacious pursuit of duty would be to ignore much of her commit-ment and courage. Hard and conscientious work was not enough. Edith Cavell wanted her work to be directed towards something worthy of the extreme effort she was prepared to make. Nursing met that test. There is a danger, however, of defining Edith Cavell's courage simply as the courage to perform her duty as a nurse no matter what the circumstances. The idea of a slavish dedication to duty – even to the high ideals of nursing – suggests either a retreat from personal responsibility or a blind passivity that cannot fully account for her subsequent actions. Edith Cavell was active, creative, in her work and in her life. If the only ideal she was prepared to recognise was the profession of nursing, then she might well have turned the first fugitive soldiers away in order to main-tain her profession's – and her hospital's – neutrality.

Instead, her life's work gave expression to her innate humani-tarianism. She had the courage to attempt to fulfil her potential, to continually extend her efforts, as part of an obligation to use, rather than squander, her talents to ease human suffering and to help those in their hour of greatest need. In her letters and her trial testimony, and finally, in the words she uttered before execution, she explained her life's meaning and purpose. 'It is not enough to love one's own people,' she said, 'one must love all men and hate none.' Nursing and her clandestine wartime activities proved to be arenas in which she could put these greater ideals into practice.

When news of the outbreak of war came, Edith was in England visiting her mother, who had been recently widowed and had moved to Norwich. Edith decided to immediately cut her visit short and return to the Institute. But travel was chaotic, with ports and railway stations almost overwhelmed with panicstricken people rushing to reach home and safety. Yet Edith Cavell travelled against the current, leaving the shelter and protection of her home for a more dangerous and uncertain future. The dedication and resolve that led her to nursing in the first place, the same sense of duty that she tried to instil in her student nurses in times of peace, drove her to return to her hospital to tend to the victims war would inevitably bring.

Edith Cavell was never to return to England or see her family again. Britain declared war against Germany on 4 August 1914 and shortly afterwards she and her nurses watched the German army enter Brussels. Alarming stories abounded of massacres and atrocities visited upon the civilian population of other Belgian cities at the hands of the German invaders. A letter Edith Cavell wrote to her family in anticipation of the impending occupation shows her great fortitude in the face of terror:

My darling mother and family, If you open this, it will be because that which we fear now has happened, and Brussels has fallen into the hands of the enemy. They are very near now and it is doubtful if the Allied armies can stop them. We are prepared for the worse. I have given dear Gracie and the Sisters a chance to go home, but none of them will leave. I appreciate their courage and I want now to let the Jemmetts know that I did my best to send Gracie home, but she refused firmly to leave me – she is very quiet and brave. I have nothing to leave but £160 in the Pension Fund, which has never been touched and is mine to leave. I wish mother to have it with my dearest love. It will supply the place of my little quarterly allowance to her. If I can send my few jewels over will you divide them between Flor and Lil [her sisters], and please send Mrs McDonnell my long gold chain which she gave me, and a keepsake to Marion Hall. I shall think of you to the last, and you may be sure we shall do our duty here and die as women of our race should die. My dear, dear love to mother and Flor, Lil, Jack, Longworth and children; also to Eveline McDonnell. God bless and keep you safe.

This letter in fact never reached her family. It fell into the hands of a German officer and only came to light on his death twenty years later. It is scarcely possible to imagine the fear that must have gripped Edith Cavell and her nurses as the German army advanced. They had all heard of 'sinister tales of burned and shattered houses, villages razed to the ground; of women and children murdered, of drunken soldiers and of rapine, looting and mutilation', as Edith Cavell wrote in the *Nursing Mirror*. And she had written to her mother that the 'wildest rumours are current – we know for certain that there is fighting near at hand for we can hear the cannon & not far away the smoke can be seen with field glasses'.

But even more striking than the terror is the bravery Edith Cavell and her nurses showed in their decision to stay rather than flee, as they so naturally might have done, as the sound of the approaching guns grew louder and nearer. Something of the courage that Edith Cavell inspired is recorded in the memoirs of Jacqueline van Til, a nurse who was resident at the Berkendael Institute at the outbreak of war:

> I shall never forget the evening before the Prussians entered. We went up to the roof of the clinic and saw the sky towards the east fiery red while clouds of thick black smoke rolled in our direction. It was an awe-inspiring sight, its effect greatly enhanced by the thunder of the guns, the concussion of which was so great that windows were broken round us. We were all trembling with fear, and Madame found me sitting on the landing weeping. She peered into my face with that powerful gaze of hers, with something mild in it, yet full of firm reproach, and bade me not to give way to my feelings, telling me that my life no longer belonged to myself alone but also to my duty as a nurse. And she finally succeeded in calming me, as she did all the others. For, whenever there was an occasion to use persuasion, she always seemed to know the proper thing to say. So I went the very next day to the ambulance where I had been detailed to work.

They had expected and prepared for the worst, but rumours and reports of German atrocities had been exaggerated. But even as the soldiers marched, Edith Cavell's patriotism did not reduce her empathy towards her fellow human beings, no matter how hateful the enemy might seem. Her description was published in the *Nursing Mirror*:

In the afternoon with much pomp and circumstance of war, the German troops marched into Brussels, and to the Town Hall, where the brave tricolour came down and the German stripes of black and white and red took its place . . . On August 21 many more troops came through; from our road we could see the long procession, and when the halt was called at midday and carts came up with supplies, some were too weary to eat and slept on the pavement of the street. We were divided between pity for these poor fellows, far from their country and their people suffering the weariness and fatigue of an arduous campaign, and hate of a cruel and vindictive foe, bringing ruin and desolation on hundreds of happy homes and to a prosperous and peaceful land. Some of the Belgians spoke to the invaders in German, and found they were very vague as to their whereabouts, and imagined they were already in Paris; they were surprised to be speaking to Belgians and could not understand what quarrel they had with them. I saw several of the men pick up little children and give them chocolate or seat them on their horses.

The initial terror of occupation gave way to a grim adjustment to life behind enemy lines. In occupied Brussels, the Berkendael Institute was turned into a Red Cross hospital. Edith Cavell instructed her nurses that their first duty was to help the wounded no matter which army they came from, and both German and Allied soldiers received equally devoted care at the Institute.

As the fighting moved further away from Brussels, and soldiers were treated closer to the front line, nursing work at the Institute tailed off; those German soldiers remaining in the city were now being treated in German-staffed hospitals and civilian patients continued to attend the communal hospitals. The staff of the Institute was cut back and most nurses were posted to other Brussels hospitals, to private clinics, or closer to the front.

During these months Edith Cavell wrote home often to reassure her family that she was safe and well. Despite the Institute's lack of patients, she and her nursing staff were kept busy with other work. Food and other supplies were becoming increasingly scarce and refugees from the fighting were pouring into Brussels without any means of support. Edith Cavell and her nurses became engaged in charitable works on their behalf. In one letter to her mother she wrote: 'We are busy making garments for the poor, there will be great need of them this winter – there are many refugees and so many homeless.' In the following months she wrote to her mother of 'scarcity in the poor quarters & [there] will be much misery all through the winter – we are engaged in making up all the stuff we can get into garments for the children of the refugees and the other poor'.

But there was a patriotic as well as a charitable impetus to the work done by Edith Cavell and her staff, and by the many Belgian families busy gathering up clothes and food to supply to the refugees. Among their number were Belgian and other Allied soldiers who had escaped German imprisonment and who now needed to be disguised as civilians if they were to have any hope of survival. A neighbour of Edith Cavell's kept a diary during the first months of occupation. In September 1914 he wrote:

> Germans all over the place guarding avenue Hautpoint & rue de la Culture [the street in which the Berkendael Institute was located] . . . Today they are examining all the covered carts & women's market baskets to see if they are carrying clothes for the Belgian soldiers to escape from the hospitals and where they are imprisoned.

Edith Cavell may have already anticipated how her hospital might come to their aid. Jacqueline van Til's memoirs record that

> on September 26th Madame called us into her office to explain to us that at this moment many soldiers were without food and shelter and that it would be a very worthy and charitable act for us to give up our salaries to these destitute and hungry men. At

first we were surprised at this request, and were reluctant to part
with the few five and ten franc pieces, the meagre wages that we
received, but seeing our hesitancy she persuaded us. It would be
a grand way to show devotion to our unhappy country. She
would take charge of the fund, she said, and relieve us of all the
worry that this good work would entail.

Despite the gloom and despondency of the first months of
occupation, Edith Cavell never betrayed any signs of despair to
her nurses and she kept them busy and in a constant state of
readiness. Jacqueline van Til wrote of her: 'To us it seemed that
darkness and horror had taken up a dwelling in our souls. Madame
alone was as calm as ever, and continued tranquilly to direct us in
all our duties.'

But the calm was not to last. On 23 August 1914, not far from
Brussels, General Alexander von Kluck, in charge of the German
First Army's advance towards Paris, met unexpected resistance
from the British Expeditionary Force under Field Marshal Sir John
French. The Battle of Mons ensued. The BEF was heavily outnumbered and began a fighting withdrawal. In the general confusion of battle soldiers were cut off from their units and sought
shelter: in the forest, in homes of sympathetic Belgians, anywhere
where they could avoid the German army. The Germans posted
notices advising that Allied soldiers who did not give themselves up
would be shot, and that those who harboured them would face an
equally severe punishment.

An emergency ambulance worker called Madame Liebiez took
in two wounded English soldiers who had managed to evade
capture. The soldiers stayed with her for two months until the
Germans received a tip-off that she was sheltering fugitives. Despite
several searches of Madame Liebiez's home the soldiers were not
discovered but, with German suspicions aroused, they needed to
leave the area fast. Two nuns guided them to the shelter of a
convent where they remained until Herman Capiau, a Belgian
engineer, arrived to help. He took their photographs for false
identity cards, gave them food and a map that showed them
how to reach the home of Albert Liebiez, the son of their first

guardian. Albert then guided them to the home of Louis Dervaire, where they received their fake ID, and then on to central Brussels to seek concealment and sanctuary amid the anonymity of the city. There they were introduced to Madame Depage, wife of Dr Antoine Depage of the Berkendael Institute, who in turn directed them to Edith Cavell.

According to the account given by the assistant matron, who survived the war, the two soldiers arrived dressed in civilian clothes looking dirty and tired, and were accompanied by a third person who appeared well dressed and respectable. She showed all three of them into Edith Cavell's office where they remained with her in conversation for a little while. Then the well-dressed man left abruptly. A little later, the assistant matron was called into the office and Edith Cavell explained to her that the two men were fugitive soldiers, and directed her to give them beds in the surgical house.

The wounded English soldiers stayed in the Institute for about two weeks until rumours came that the Institute was likely to be searched by the Germans. Edith Cavell had to move them and found a vacant house in the district; but continuing searches left them in constant danger. Eventually they decided to make a run for the border and escape to Holland. With the help of civilian clothes, false documents, money, and a guide, they set off – and made it to safety.

Thus began Edith Cavell's introduction to the underground movement in the autumn of 1914. The core network of contacts soon widened to include many more – around seventy people were eventually arrested on suspicion of being implicated in it. From the arrival of the first two soldiers until her arrest the following July, Edith Cavell would help as many as two hundred people to escape.

After the success of the first escapes, more and more soldiers came to the Institute seeking help. Many fugitives arrived wounded and in need of medical care; but others who arrived were in good health, and still others were Belgian and French civilians who simply wanted to escape in order to join the Allied forces as soldiers. Thus there developed, from sheer necessity, a network of safe-houses, guides, and escape routes across the border.

The 'confession' Edith Cavell signed in prison describes her role in the operation:

At first I hid the Englishmen, sometimes for a fortnight or three weeks in my house, as I was not sufficiently familiar with the means of transport on the roads which they should follow to the frontier. When later, with the help of Capiau and of a certain Baucq . . . guides for the French and Belgians of military age were put at my disposal, I concealed the men brought to me until favourable opportunity arose for their departure which during this period might be one day to a week. I usually took the soldiers and men of military age to the following places myself . . . Guides sent by Capiau, Baucq and Severin waited for me in these places on days arranged beforehand, between five and seven in the morning, and on the day before a departure the guide would come to my house to give me particulars. In a few cases the guides actually came to my house. All men started on the journey with twenty-five francs as I made whatever they possessed up to that amount. Some were entirely without resources when they came, and the funds out of which these men were provided were supplied to me by engineer Capiau, 1000; by Prince Reginald, 500; by Severin, as a loan, 400 francs. I gave them 300 francs out of my own resources, and collected 200–300 francs for them ostensibly for philanthropic purposes . . .

Edith Cavell became fairly well acquainted with those soldiers who stayed the longest, and made particular efforts to befriend any originating from her home county of Norfolk. She asked many of them to write to her mother once they reached England to assure her of her safety. Some of the letters survive, telling Mrs Cavell of her daughter's bravery and courage and attributing their survival to her actions.

Sergeant Jesse Tunmore wrote to Mrs Cavell on 20 January 1915:

I am writing to you to say that your daughter the Matron of the Nurses' School in Brussels, Belgium, is quite well. I am a soldier of the 1st Norfolks . . . I was a prisoner in the hands of the

Germans near Mons. I managed to get away and reached Brussels, where your daughter worked very hard for me as regards to get me money, finding chances for me. One chance was by going off as Roumanian, but I had not got a passport, but got as far as St Nicholas near Antwerp. I cannot express enough thanks for all she done for me, she worked very hard for us indeed, but the 12th of this month all French, Russians, Japanese, etc in Brussels had to report themselves to the Germans but I left Brussels on 12th so I do not know what really happened. She told me to tell you she was quite well. She told me it was some time [since] she received a letter from England . . . I spent Xmas & the New Year with your daughter.

And in February 1915 Mrs Cavell received the following letter from Lance-Corporal J. Doman:

I am a wounded soldier and was taken prisoner in Belgium where I escaped from. I was passing through Brussels & your daughter kept us in hiding from the Germans for fifteen days & treated us very kindly. She got us a guide to bring us through to Holland, and we arrived in England safely. Your daughter wishes you to write to her and let her know we arrived here safe, as you must not let anyone know or they may visit her home in Brussels. I thought it best to let you know this in case you have not been able to get a letter from her.

Edith Cavell was to become a leading member of this loosely bound organisation, which had sprung up originally in response to immediate and unexpected circumstances. The network would later develop into a reasonably sophisticated, audacious and effective resistance operation. Over the months, Edith and many of her associates in the resistance risked much, under extremely dangerous conditions, to help the Allied cause. The bravery she witnessed bolstered her own strength and resolve, just as her courage in turn inspired others. She wrote to her mother:

What do you think of these brave Belgian people? They have suffered (& are suffering) a martyrdom & in silence – their

attitude is wonderful in reserve and dignity – not a word of hate
or reproach or despair – the attitude of a people who have
suffered through generations the same fate over & over again &
have it in them to struggle and endure – I did not believe it
possible, tho' I have known them many years now.

As the escape route became better established, those Edith
Cavell sheltered tended to move on more quickly. She never
refused help to anyone in need, even after the Germans' suspicions
had been aroused. Some of those she helped put her own life at
considerable risk by careless, drunken or rowdy behaviour. A
testimony of one member of the group records that:

> Indeed, at this time Miss Cavell's house became publicly known
> as a refuge for fugitive soldiers. So I became worried, and went to
> try to induce her to keep free of all relations with this group of
> guides, telling her that the work itself was imperilled and must be
> diverted into other channels. But she would not listen. 'Nothing
> but physical impossibility, lack of space and money,' she said,
> 'would make me close my doors to allied refugees.'

What special quality did Edith Cavell possess that numbered
her among those who act when roused to anger, pity or empathy
in the face of injustice or suffering – among those who don't just
seethe until their righteous indignation burns itself out – or who
don't absolve themselves from responsibility to act because they
feel there is nothing they can really do? What was it about Edith
Cavell that opened her eyes to suffering so that she felt it so
keenly? And what inspired her to do something about it with a
resourcefulness and energy that changed the course of many
lives?

Edith Cavell's entire life was one of action over inaction: leaving
her work as a governess and turning to nursing; applying repeatedly for more senior nursing positions, establishing a teaching
hospital – and a profession within a nation – from scratch, despite
repeated setbacks; not simply accepting fugitive soldiers under her
shelter, but helping them secure false documents, money, and

guides to reach safety. Edith never seemed to lack the courage to act, even when such action put her own life at risk.

By June 1915 the activities of the local resistance movement were under closer German scrutiny, and the Institute was under increasing suspicion. On Monday, 14 June Edith wrote what would be her last letter ever to reach England. It hinted at her fear of discovery and the implications that might follow:

My darling Mother, Very many happy returns of your birthday & my best love & good wishes – I have always made a point of being at home for July 6, but this year it will not be possible . . . Do not forget if anything very serious should happen you could probably send me a message thro' the American Ambassador in London (not a letter) . . .

One of the other leading members of the resistance, Marie de Croy, visited her at the end of June to warn her that their activities must stop; that it was too dangerous to continue. Marie recalled that Edith Cavell asked: 'Are there any more hidden men?' And when Marie replied there were, she said: 'Then we cannot stop, because if a single one of those men were taken and shot, that would be our fault.' So they made emergency arrangements for their safe passage.

Around that time two soldiers presented themselves to the Institute, one of whom was George Gason Quien. It is now thought that he was an agent for the Germans and that he provided the prime source of information that led to Edith Cavell's arrest. After German officers conducted surprise searches of the Institute, she became increasingly concerned to rid the premises of all traces of her activity, destroying the carefully hidden records she kept. On 31 July, she learned that two of the leaders of their operation had been arrested. Despite frantic warnings to the rest of those involved in their movement, it was too late. On 5 August, German officers arrived for Edith Cavell.

They ransacked her office and arrested her and her assistant matron, Sister Elizabeth Wilkins. They were separately interrogated. Sister Wilkins denied having any knowledge of anything and

was released. Her ignorance was her protection. While she undoubtedly knew of Edith Cavell's involvement and how the Institute had been used as part of the escape network, Edith Cavell
had kept her in the dark about details of the operation. She in turn
attempted to protect her matron by refusing to admit to what she
did know.

For Edith Cavell there was no such luck. She was interviewed at
length on three occasions and eventually signed a statement confessing her guilt. Surviving members of the movement spoke of the
tactics used to elicit confessions: the interrogators would present
their suspicions as confirmed evidence based on other members'
confessions, and urge the prisoner to cooperate by signing the
confession as the best way to ensure leniency for all those involved.
Furthermore, Edith Cavell gave her statements in French, which
were then translated into German, and it is the German translation
of her 'confession' she signed. Biographers speculate that Edith
Cavell's captors greatly manipulated her interviews during the
translation into a more frank and explicit confession.

The day after her arrest Edith Cavell was allowed to send a letter
to her charge, Grace Jemmett. In it she appeared to be in good
enough spirits and tried to offer her reassurance and hope:

> My dearest Gracie, Let's hope you are not worrying about me –
> tell everybody that I am quite all right here. I suppose from what
> I hear that I shall be questioned one of these days, and when they
> have all they desire I shall know what they mean to do with me.
> We are numerous here and there is no chance of being lonely . . .
> if Jackie [her dog] is sad, tell him I will be back soon . . . I will
> write again when there is anything to tell. Don't – don't worry.
> We must hope for the best. Tell them all to go on as usual.

Edith Cavell remained in prison for ten weeks until the date of
her trial. She was eventually permitted to receive occasional visits
from Sister Wilkins and to write letters to her. Those business-like
letters – in which she gave administrative and book-keeping
instructions – suggest that Edith Cavell was still very much focused
on the work of the Institute and the progress of the new school,

though the book-keeping instructions may have been connected to the money she raised from various sources to supply fugitive soldiers. She also wrote anxiously to secure the continued care of Grace Jemmett, who had been totally reliant on her.

In a letter to Sister Wilkins on 23 August she wrote:

> My dear old Jack! Please brush him sometimes and look after him. I am quite well – more worried about the Sch. than my own fate. Tell the girls to be good and work well and be tidy. I am sure you have many worries. Are all my things put away safely? With camphor? Don't buy anything for me, I do very well with what I have. My love to you . . . Please see the nurses going for their exam for the 2nd time in October study regularly.

But her next letter to Sister Wilkins was less hopeful and indicated that she knew her time at the prison was running out – whether she anticipated trial and imprisonment in Germany or a worse fate is unclear. She again wrote book-keeping instructions, adding: 'The money from M.J. 800 frs please keep in hand till I tell you how to place it. I hope you will get it soon as I want to arrange all before I go . . . Love to you all. I hope to see you again soon as time may be short.'

She asked for a few specific belongings to be brought to her, including the Bible and a beloved devotional work, Thomas à Kempis's *The Imitation of Christ*, which had been given to her by one of the families she worked for as a governess. She also requested the clothes she would wear for her trial, and execution. Her days in prison must have been a time of extreme duress, yet far removed from the frantic pace of life to which she had grown accustomed. She seemed to use the time to prepare herself mentally for whatever might lie ahead with equanimity and resolve.

After six weeks in prison she wrote again to her nurses:

> Your delightful letter gave me great pleasure, and your lovely flowers have made my cell gay, the roses are still fresh, but the chrysanthemums did not like prison any more than I do – hence they did not live very long. I am happy to know that you are

working well, that you are devoted to your patients and that you are happy in your service. It is necessary that you should study well, for some of you must shortly sit for your examinations and I want you very much to succeed. The year's course will commence shortly, try to profit from it, and be punctual at lectures so that your professor need not be kept waiting. In everything one can learn new lessons of life, and if you were in my place, you would realise how precious liberty is, and would certainly undertake never to abuse it. To be a good nurse one must have lots of patience – here one learns to have that quality, I assure you. It appears that the new school is advanced – I hope to see it again one of these days, as well as all of you. Au revoir, be really good.

Your devoted Matron

Edith Cavell was court-martialled along with her collaborators on 7 and 8 October 1915. She did not deny her role in helping Allied soldiers reach the frontier and for this the prosecution demanded death. Three excruciating days passed between the end of the trial and formal sentencing. She turned to the Bible and other religious books in her possession, marking and dating passages of particular relevance and poignancy to her. In the Book of Revelation, she marked one passage strongly with three downstrokes, dating it 'St Gilles, 11 Oct.'. It was the last day of her life. The passage reads:

> I indeed labour in the sweat of my brows. I am racked with grief of heart, I am burdened with sins, I am troubled with temptations; I am entangled and oppressed with many evil passions; and there is none to help me, none to deliver and save me, but thou, O Lord God my Saviour, to whom I commit myself and all that is mine, that thou mayest keep watch over me, and bring me safe to life everlasting.

And she also turned to passages in *The Imitation of Christ*:

> How happy and prudent is he who tries now in life to be what he wants to be found in death. Perfect contempt of the world, a

lively desire to advance in virtue, a love for discipline, the works of penance, readiness to obey, self-denial, and the endurance of every hardship for the love of Christ, these will give a man great expectations of a happy death.

On her last evening, just hours before she was led to her death, Edith Cavell was visited by the English chaplain, Stirling Gahan, whose church she regularly attended in Brussels. He later recalled their final hour:

> She presented herself at her cell door as calm as ever, just as I had known her when last at liberty. When we were alone she began quietly to speak of things which concerned her most as one who saw the nearness of eternity. Then she assured me, in answer to my questions, that she trusted in the finished work of Christ for her soul's salvation and was fully at rest.

She then added that she 'wished all her friends to know that she willingly gave her life for her country' and said:

> I have no fear or shrinking. I have seen death so often that it is not strange or fearful to me. I thank God for this ten week quiet before the end. Life has always been hurried and full of difficulty. This time of rest has been a great mercy. They have all been very kind to me here. But this I would say, standing as I do in view of God and eternity: I realise that patriotism is not enough; I must have no hatred or bitterness towards anyone.

After the chaplain left, Edith Cavell wrote her final letters to her loved ones. The letter to her mother was not amongst those collected after her execution and it is presumed it was confiscated by her captors; but the one she wrote to her nurses survives. In it she wrote:

> My dear sisters, It is a very sad moment for me now that I write to you to bid you farewell. If, during the past year, our work has diminished, the cause is to be found in the sad times through

which we are passing. When brighter days come our work will resume its growth, and all its power for doing good. I have told you that devotion will give you real happiness, and the thought that you have done, before God and yourselves, your whole duty and with a good heart will be your greatest support in the hard moments of life and in the face of death. There are two or three of you who will recollect the little conversations we have had together; do not forget them . . . If there is one of you who has a grievance against me I ask you to forgive me . . . I have loved you all much more than you thought. My wishes for the happiness of all my girls . . . and thanks for the kindness you have always shown me.

Her last words to Grace Jemmett were:

My dear girl, how shall I write to you this last day? I worried about you at first, but I know God will do for you abundantly . . . I do earnestly beseech you to try to live as I would have you live. Nothing matters when one comes to the last hour but a clear conscience, and life looks so wasted and full of wrong-doing and things left undone. You have helped me often, and in ways you little dreamed of . . . I want you to go to England at once now and ask Dr Wainwright to put you where you can be cured. Don't mind how hard it is. Do it for my sake, and then try to find something useful to do, something to make you forget yourself while making others happy. If God permits, I shall watch over you and wait for you on the other side. Be sure to get ready for then. I want you to know that I am neither afraid, nor unhappy, but quite ready to give my life for England.

Frantic, last-minute diplomatic efforts were made on Edith's behalf, although unknown to her, to delay the sentence being carried out so that an appeal could be launched. But to no avail. Early in the morning on 12 October 1915, Edith Cavell was driven to the Tir Nationale where a firing squad awaited her.

The German pastor who accompanied prisoners to their deaths reported the final minutes:

I thought I had to make what I said as brief as possible. So I took Miss Cavell's hand and repeated, of course in English, the Grace of the Anglican Church. She pressed my hand in return, and answered in these words. 'Ask Mr Gahan to tell my loved ones that I believe my soul is safe, and that I am glad to die for my country.' Then I led her to the pole, to which she was lightly bound, and a bandage tied over her eyes which, as the soldier who put it on told me later, were full of tears.

The command was given, and she was killed.

Edith Cavell was a patriot to the last. It would be easy to try to define her legacy as that of an English patriot in wartime Europe. She spoke of her readiness to 'die as women of our race should die'. She wrote of her hatred of 'a cruel and vindictive foe' and referred frequently to 'the enemy'. Her language was the language of war. But to the *Nursing Mirror* she wrote:

> I am but a looker-on after all. It is not my country whose soul is desecrated and whose sacred places are laid to waste. I can only feel the pity of the stranger within the gates. They have grown thin and silent under the strain. They walk about the city shoulder to shoulder with the foe but never see or make a sign to them. They live their lives a long way off apart. A German officer in a tram asked a Belgian gentleman for a light. He handed him his cigar without a word, but, on receiving it back, flung it into the gutter with a gesture of disgust . . .

Of course Edith Cavell was patriotic, and outraged by the destruction and misery wreaked upon her neighbours by an invading enemy intent upon conquest. To act out of patriotism for a country whose cause is just is beyond reproach and needs no apology. And Edith Cavell was not blind or innocent to the implications of her underground work to help Allied soldiers escape. Indeed, her execution was seized upon and used as an effective instrument of propaganda during the war, and after the war her body was exhumed, brought back to England, and trumpeted through the streets as that of a war heroine.

But as Edith Cavell insisted herself, patriotism is 'not enough'. She recognised also values that transcended nationalism. Her anger at the German invasion was equally mixed with empathy for those German soldiers – the enemy – who appeared to her to be tired and bewildered. Her skilful care of the wounded was administered just as conscientiously to German as to Allied soldiers. Her ministry did not discriminate. Her compassion knew no nationality.

Patriotic she certainly was, but those who seek to define Edith Cavell narrowly as an icon of chauvinism will always be disappointed. At her court martial, she was asked by the judge: 'Why have you committed these acts of which you are accused?' While others who were arrested with her retorted that they acted because they were patriots, Edith Cavell answered: 'At the beginning I was confronted by two English soldiers who were in danger of their lives.' And when the judge asked her: 'Do you realise that in recruiting men you have hindered the German cause and helped our enemies?' she replied: 'My aim has not been to assist your enemies, but to help these men gain the frontier. Once across they were free to do what they liked.'

Her patriotism was not the sole motivating factor – her aim was to help people whose lives were in immediate danger. Though proud to die for her country, her final words, uttered moments before she faced a firing squad, were these: 'I realise that patriotism is not enough. I must have no hatred or bitterness towards anyone.'

Edith Cavell's life was not just the sum of chance and accident, but of purposeful resolve at each crossroads in her life. It was a search to give expression to her vocation to minister. As a child of the vicar, as daughter to an ailing father, as governess, nurse, teacher, matron, and as part of a resistance movement in time of war, Edith Cavell's duty was to humanity, and her legacy is its triumph.

2

Dietrich Bonhoeffer

There are people who regard it as frivolous, and some Christians think it impious, for anyone to hope and prepare for a better earthly future. They think that the meaning of present events is chaos, disorder and catastrophe; and in resignation or pious escapism they surrender all responsibility for reconstruction and for future generations. It may be that the day of judgement will dawn tomorrow; in that case, we shall gladly stop working for a better future. But not before.

Dietrich Bonhoeffer, *Letters and Papers from Prison*

Dietrich Bonhoeffer was just thirty-nine when he was executed. For over a decade he had lived under the shadow of Nazism. He was one of a small number of German churchmen, whose number included the theologians Martin Niemöller and Karl Barth, to consistently and steadfastly speak out against Nazi anti-Semitism, and also one of the few to actively participate in the resistance movement. His own Church would ostracise him for his stance and he would grow to know well the meaning of the aphorism: 'If the test of tolerance is when you are in the majority, the test of courage is when you are in a minority.'

Bonhoeffer's own personal courage contrasted starkly with what he saw as a collective loss of courage on the part of his fellow countrymen. For him, Germany had not only given in to Hitler; it had been brutalised by totalitarianism and overrun by anti-Semitism. Someone had to stand up for 'civilised values' and point the way to the future. Bonhoeffer's stance, his courage and his resistance, would ultimately prove to be an essential starting point in the rebuilding of a post-war Germany.

Yet there was little in Bonhoeffer's childhood to suggest that he would pursue such a path or leave such a legacy. Nor was there later a sudden road-to-Damascus moment, a blinding-light conversion to Christianity. The youngest son of eight children, he was educated at home by his mother and was expected to follow his brothers and father into medicine or science. His family was shocked therefore when he declared, aged fourteen, that he wanted to become a minister of the Church. Perhaps he was influenced by his brother's death in the First World War; perhaps, like so many of that immediate post-war generation in Germany, he had become interested in understanding and explaining mortality.

So, from a professional family background, Bonhoeffer trained for the clergy: the courageous choices that would later define his life undoubtedly sprang from the strong sense of personal and social responsibility developed during his upbringing – from the broad social engagement of a family steeped in professional service in the law, the Church and medicine. The young Bonhoeffer acquired a broad theological education: he first enrolled at Tübingen University and then in seminaries and colleges round the world, including New York and Oxford; he visited Africa and travelled widely in Europe.

By the early 1930s the full horror of the Nazi Party's racial policies was becoming clear. The young Bonhoeffer was quick to recognise the sheer injustice of anti-Semitism. In his view the Church could not withdraw and retreat from such a moral issue, or even try to continue to claim, as it did, that it represented an ideal society with no need to reform. Nor, he argued, could the Church assert that it was simply an assembly of an elite of the just: it had a duty to identify with those who suffered.

It was at this point that the twenty-eight-year-old Bonhoeffer made his first choice. He was in London at the time of Hitler's rise to power and could so easily have stayed in relative safety so far away. However, he immediately returned to his homeland with a determination to campaign and speak out against Nazism. The day after Hitler assumed office, in January 1933, Bonhoeffer gave a radio broadcast directly challenging him and lambasting a concept of leadership in which, he claimed, people 'set themselves up as gods'.

And this is the courage I most admire in Bonhoeffer: the strength of character that meant that, time after time, when he could have taken the easier course, he chose the more challenging one. It was a strength of belief matched by a strength of will that singled him out and defined him. He did not simply broadcast his lecture. Since it had been partially censored in advance, he published the full version and circulated it to his friends and colleagues. True leadership, he said, was not totalitarianism practised against the people but proper democratic respect for the people.

> If the leader allows himself to be persuaded by those he leads who want to turn him into their idol – and those who are led will always hope for this – then the image of the leader will degenerate into that of the 'misleader'. The leader who makes an idol of himself and his office makes a mockery of God.

Bonhoeffer's sermon was a reasoned and audacious attack on Hitler. But if he expected any praise, or even support from the Church, he was to be disappointed. His fellow clergymen thought him foolhardy. At a time when the rise of Hitler and Nazism troubled even moderate members, Bonhoeffer's clear defiance brought risks of a serious split in the Church.

One of Hitler's first acts when he came to power was to introduce a law that gave Germany's Jews separate legal status on racial grounds, establishing the basis for their later wholesale, quasi-legitimised persecution. Bonhoeffer was outraged: half of his classmates at school in Berlin had been Jewish; his twin sister was now forced to flee Germany with her Jewish husband, and his best friend – a fellow minister – was effectively barred from the Church because he had a Jewish grandparent.

Of course, Bonhoeffer's outrage at the persecution of Jews reflected a far deeper intolerance – both moral and intellectual – of injustice. Yet in the 1930s the accepted sentiment of Protestant Christianity towards Jews, particularly in Germany, was at best ambivalent and at worst anti-Semitic. Bonhoeffer argued that any persecution of the Jews was utterly incompatible with Christianity. He rejected from the outset all attempts to justify the Church's acquiescence to such policies, whether on moral, intellectual, or simply pragmatic grounds. 'Only he who cries out for the Jews may sing Gregorian chant,' he said. An 'Aryan clause' in the law explicitly excluded anyone of Jewish descent from working in the civil service; and later, in any profession, including the Church.

It was this latter law that provoked Bonhoeffer into writing his essay, 'The Church and the Jewish Question', which he had printed and distributed to other ministers. In it he argued unequivocally that: 'The Church has an unconditional obligation to the victims of any ordering of society, even if they do not belong to the Christian community.' Of course, he argued, the Church had responsibilities to the state, but where there was gross misrule – as was the case with the Third Reich – then, as a last resort, the Church had a duty to act. And that obligation, he insisted, might also require the individual to 'jam a spoke in the wheel', that is: to take direct political action.

This statement shocked Bonhoeffer's colleagues and foreshadowed his own later decision to take direct action by joining an anti-Nazi group operating covertly from within the German military intelligence organisation, the Abwehr, during the war. But in the mid-1930s all Bonhoeffer was asking of the Church was that it abandon its 'prudent' distance from the political, secular world in order to prevent a much more fatal error: that of failing to uphold the sanctity of human life at a time when the voices of moderation and compassion had all but been silenced. He had the vision to see that the Church risked a far worse fate if it failed to act.

Bonhoeffer went further still. He set a challenge for the Church to move beyond its privileged, sanitised detachment from secular concerns: the Church must honour Christ through engaged ministry in the world rather than by spiritual withdrawal from it. In this way Bonhoeffer's theology cleared a way for the Church to redefine itself in the aftermath of war and defeat. As James Mark writes: 'What happened to him in the last phase of his life is at once a tragedy and a priceless and providential gift to the whole Church, wherever its boundaries may be drawn.'

Despite Bonhoeffer's energetic campaigning, the Prussian Synod of German Protestant clergy opted to adopt the Aryan clause in 1933. It was a decisive moment. Though the majority of the clergy capitulated to Hitler at that synod, some Christian leaders had become increasingly alarmed and wary of the attempts by the Nazis to interfere with the autonomy of the Church. The next year, a significant minority of clergy formed the Pastors' Emergency League to counterbalance the centralising control of the Nazis. This in turn led to a split from the established Protestant Church of the 'Confessing Church', which Bonhoeffer attempted to galvanise into a concerted opposition movement to Nazism.

Initially the Confessing Church approximated to a German Christian anti-Nazi movement. But Bonhoeffer found that it lacked decisiveness and moral purpose and that it seemed more concerned with protecting its independence from the state rather than defending Christian ideals. As war approached, Bonhoeffer became increasingly dissatisfied and disappointed by the Confessing Church's timidity in the face of intensifying Jewish persecution. He had hoped that the Confessing Church would position itself confidently against Nazism as a powerful and unified body of clergy. It failed to do so, and left him without an institution from which to mount opposition. In the end he would have to act alone.

Bonhoeffer's battle against Nazism can be seen as all the more courageous because so few people were willing to stand with him. As the author Marilynne Robinson writes of Bonhoeffer and his fellow dissenters: 'If these tempests among the churchmen seem marginal to the events of the time, it should be remembered how alone they were. Bonhoeffer's article was the first such defence of the Jewish people.'

Bonhoeffer's moral courage – to speak when he could have remained silent – is fascinating. Its impact is broad and subtle too. His words were clearly directed against his enemies, but his voice, distinctive and alone, could be heard in clear contrast to the silence of his friends. Harry Truman said: 'It takes courage to face a duellist with a pistol and it takes courage to face a British general with an army. But it takes still greater and far higher courage to face friends with a grievance.' Dietrich Bonhoeffer had this kind of courage – the courage to stand up against self-interest and timidity. Unlike the daring of the rogue, or courage on the battlefield, the moral courage needed to make and sustain a stand against the vested interests of friends can be a lonelier and more bitter battle.

Bonhoeffer insisted that it was the duty of the Christian Church to intervene. The Church, however, was reluctant to pose the 'Jewish question', never mind answer it. Senior clergy argued that it was a political matter in which the Church had no role or standing. Others foresaw the potential danger of the state over-extending its reach with the 'Aryan clause', but braced themselves for a battle in defence of Church autonomy rather than one of fundamental moral principle.

The risk that Bonhoeffer was prepared to take in clearly setting himself up in open opposition to the legitimate and increasingly powerful political leadership of his country shows the depth of his convictions and the strength of his courage. Bonhoeffer was pre-pared to address the issue head on and demand that the Church open its eyes to reality. In doing so, he risked the censure of his friends, his profession and the privileged class of which he was part. The Bonhoeffer family was eminent in German society and very much a part of the establishment. Bonhoeffer himself was seen as having excellent prospects in the Church. Instead he chose to diverge from the safety of the prevailing mood and place himself in a volatile and increasingly dangerous political climate – one that would inevitably make him enemies and put him in personal danger.

The loneliness of his stance troubled him and led him to question, repeatedly, the correctness of his conviction. Bonhoeffer was not so ideologically driven that he acted without experiencing moral dilemma. He did not possess the harsh, blinding certainty of the zealot. Both his thought and action changed direction over the course of his life as the turn of events exposed the limitations of his position. He tried wherever possible to accommodate conventional ideology, whether on the role of the nation state, the destiny of the German race, or on the status of Jews, until such ideas clashed irreversibly with his uncompromising commitment to justice, fair-ness, and compassion. The Church's repeated failure to take the moral lead caused Bonhoeffer, a man of far greater courage and conviction than the institution of which he was a part, to pay the price of its failure with his own life.

Bonhoeffer did not set out to be a lone voice or a martyr, and rebellion did not come naturally to him. He wanted the Church to speak with one voice, in its legitimate capacity and defending Christian principles, rather than to lead a rebellion himself. He was interested in a theological debate on the purpose of the Church and the ideals of Christian ministry. But the rise of Nazism paradoxically both overwhelmed his more general theological concerns and charged them with an urgency and clarity they might otherwise have never known. Whereas Bonhoeffer had initially concentrated on an ecclesiastical formulation of discipleship, the turmoil of war broadened his theology to a wider analysis of ethical responsibility and led him to redraw the boundaries between Church, state and the individual.

Bitterly disappointed by the Church's weakness, Dietrich Bonhoeffer left Germany for England in 1933, to serve as pastor to two German congregations in London. Letters from that time show that he had doubted the wisdom of his decision to leave Germany, and questioned his own impatience at the Church's inaction. One letter to Karl Barth shows him battling with a troubled conscience:

I am at last writing you the letter that I meant to send you six weeks ago that would perhaps have resulted in a totally different turn in my personal life . . . I wanted to ask you whether I ought to go to the London parish or not. I would simply have believed that you would tell me the right thing. The London offer was made to me in July . . . At the time I was offered a parish in the east, there was no doubt about my choice. Then came the Aryan clause in Prussia and I knew that I could not take the parish I had longed for in this very district, unless I wanted to give up my total opposition to this church, unless I wanted to lose all credibility in the eyes of my congregation right from the start, and unless I wanted to abandon my solidarity with the Jewish Christian ministers – my best friend is one and is faced at the moment with nothing; he is coming to me in England now. So there remained the alternative of being a university lecturer or a minister, although not a minister in Prussia . . . I felt that I was in conflict quite radically with all my friends and I did not understand why. I felt more and more isolated from them by my views, although I still had, and kept, a close personal relationship with them – and all this made me worried and unsure of myself, and I was fearful of being led astray by dogmatism – and I saw no real reason why I should be able to understand things better or be more right than so many good and able pastors whom I respect – so I thought it was perhaps time to go into the wilderness for a while and simply do parish work as unobtrusively as possible. The danger of making a gesture seemed to me greater at the moment than that of retreating into silence.

In this frank examination of his inner motives there is a Gethsemane-like anguish. Was he doing the right thing? And how could he be sure? If older, wiser members of the Church remained silent, was it not sheer arrogance for him to speak out? Was he right to retreat from Germany to work in England, or was this simply a retreat from the crisis facing Christianity in Germany? Ernest Cromwell, a London parishioner who knew Bonhoeffer during that period, recalls this anguish:

Bonhoeffer was very concerned over the world situation. He pined for *The Times* every morning the same way in which an addicted smoker wants his first cigarette.

He found the Nazi regime totally incompatible with his religious beliefs. He was diametrically opposed to any form of discrimination against Jews or otherwise. He found it impossible to live with his conscience to take an oath of allegiance to Hitler.

He spoke a lot about the dilemma he felt for himself, whether to stay out and keep away from all this, or to go back, as he felt there really weren't enough people to train to follow on in the ministry of the church in Germany. He suffered agony and indecision over this. He wanted to sort out his own thoughts on the matter, whether to go to any extremes or not. That was one of the reasons why he accepted this post in London.

Bonhoeffer's equivocation and internal struggle make his courage all the more remarkable. Horace Walpole once said: 'Perhaps those, who, trembling most, maintain a dignity in their fate, are the bravest: resolution on reflection is real courage.' Bonhoeffer's courage was not born of certainty and fearlessness. His courage was resolve after reflection, and after fear and uncertainty too.

For two years Bonhoeffer remained in London, working on behalf of the Confessing Church to recruit German pastors in England, and helping German Jews arriving as refugees. Meanwhile, with the support of wealthy members of its congregation, the Confessing Church set up seminaries to train men opposed to Nazism and to minister in parishes around Germany.

In 1935, the Gestapo declared the Confessing Church and its seminaries illegal. Shortly after, Bonhoeffer was offered the opportunity to run one of the illegal seminaries, and he left London to return to Germany. '[In going back] he knew he would be entering on a collision course with the Gestapo,' said Ernest Cromwell. But it was a challenge that suited him well. Working with like-minded friends and students, he prepared them for a life of active discipleship in parish life – a discipleship that would engage with the secular, political world around it. The work he was able to do through his ministry and in the seminaries was a realisation of his emerging theology of 'Christology'. At the end of the year he published 'The Cost of Discipleship', a work born out of the intense experience of bearing witness to Christ in a community of fellowship in dangerous times.

By 1937 the Gestapo again turned its attention to the Confessing Church and in particular to the illegal seminaries. That year Bonhoeffer's seminary in Finkenwalde was ordered to shut down and twenty-seven of his students were arrested. He responded by moving the seminary to two remote sites in the countryside and secretly continuing his work. The courage he had shown in returning to Germany was tested again, and prevailed. He defied the Gestapo, carried on with his mission, and risked the wrath of an increasingly hostile and dangerous regime.

But the Gestapo continued to pursue Bonhoeffer and he was forced to flee Germany. Increasingly frustrated and disillusioned with the timidity of the Confessing Church in the face of intensifying persecution of the Jews, it was around this time that he made contact with figures in the political resistance to Hitler. A brother-in-law, Hans von Dohnanyi, was already a member of the Abwehr – paradoxically and in great secrecy increasingly the focus of dissidence within Germany. This contact opened the door to Bonhoeffer's own eventual involvement.

By 1938, most of the seminarians who had remained in his illegally run seminary had been drafted into military service. There were no exemptions, and Bonhoeffer faced another dilemma. In the event, he refused to be drafted to serve a regime he found morally repugnant and decided on pre-emptive action. Using his friends and contacts, he arranged that he should be invited to New York to tour America – preaching, teaching and ministering to German refugees – and left his homeland once again in 1939.

If Bonhoeffer had agonised over his decision to leave Germany and work in London when Hitler first came to power, his decision to leave Germany and work in America as war approached was even more anguished. Eberhard Bethge had been one of Bonhoeffer's seminarians; he later became his close friend and, posthumously, his biographer. He wrote of the crisis of responsibility that beset Bonhoeffer both in London and New York:

> The retreat in 1933 was undertaken because he would no longer serve a church corrupted by new privileges; but he came back to serve an unprivileged, outcast church. The retreat in 1939 was undertaken because he would not serve a fatherland heading towards war; but he came back to serve a fatherland of the past and of the future.

The diary Bonhoeffer kept during his first few days in New York shows his mental torment at having left Germany at such a decisive moment:

> Above all I miss Germany and the brethren. The first lonely hours are difficult. I do not understand why I am here, whether it was wise, whether it will prove worthwhile . . . Nearly two weeks

have passed without any news of what is happening over there. It is almost unbearable . . . No news from Germany all day, waited in vain from one post to the next. No point in becoming angry . . . I wish I knew how the work is going over there, whether everything is going well or whether I am needed.

In New York, Bonhoeffer found he could not follow through with his plans. Ignoring the entreaties of those who warned him he was forsaking safety for possible death, he decided to return to Germany and accept whatever fate might await him there. His diary records both his agony and his eventual relief:

The decision has been taken . . . it has wider implications for me than I can foresee at the moment. Only God can know. It is extraordinary how I am never certain of my motives in any of my decisions. Is this a sign of confusion, or an inner dishonesty, or is it a sign that we are being guided beyond what we can understand or is it perhaps both? We cannot escape our destiny; least of all out here . . . The last day Paul Lehmann tried to keep me here. To no avail. Journey to the boat with Paul. Said goodbye at half-past eleven. My travels are over. I am happy I went and happy to be going home . . . at least I have had valuable insights which will help me in my future personal decisions. I have probably yet to feel the true influence the trip has had on me. Since I came on board, my inner uncertainties about the future have ceased. I can think about my shortened stay in America without regrets.

For Bonhoeffer, the battle unfolding in Germany and Europe was for the survival of Christianity and it was not a battle he could fight from the safety of New York. In a letter to a friend in which he explained his decision to return, he wrote:

It was a mistake for me to come to America. I have to live through this difficult period in our nation's history with Christians in Germany. I have no right to participate in the reconstruction of Christian life in Germany after the war if I do not share the tribulations of this time with my people . . . Christians in Germany are faced with the fearful alternatives either of willing their country's defeat so that Christian civilisation may survive, or of willing its victory and destroying our civilisation. I know which of the two alternatives I have to choose but I cannot make the choice from a position of safety.

So within only a few weeks of his arrival in New York, he had taken the decision to leave the United States, where his personal safety was guaranteed, and return to a Germany now at war, and where he had already identified himself as an enemy of the government and had become an outcast even among his own friends and colleagues. Just as thousands of people were frantically fleeing the oncoming war, Bonhoeffer turned and headed straight towards its centre. In Robert Frost's words, he saw 'two roads diverged' and 'took the one less travelled'. But he took it with a purpose: Bonhoeffer had the courage to leave a safe situation for a perilous one because living life as a witness for Christ was more important to him than simply living; he was impelled by his faith in a greater cause.

Once back in Germany, Bonhoeffer was still faced with the prospect of conscription. But this time, instead of evading military service, he joined his brother-in-law in the service of the Abwehr. Once there he managed to convince the authorities that he could reliably work as a double agent for Hitler's Germany – travelling to neutral and hostile countries to meet with clergy there and galvanise support for the Nazi cause. In fact, he would do just the opposite. From 1940 to his arrest in April 1943, he visited Switzerland, Norway, and Sweden and met influential clerical leaders to exchange information to help strengthen religious opposition to Nazism. In 1942 Bonhoeffer and his brother-in-law, Hans, also took part in a rescue operation, referred to as 'Operation 7', to help Jews escape to Switzerland.

Within the Abwehr many were convinced that Hitler was a murderous tyrant and that it was their duty as patriots to get rid of him. They planned to orchestrate simultaneous coups throughout Europe to bring down Nazism and halt the spread of fascism, and hoped to convince Allied forces to suspend their attacks once the coup took place so that Germany could be rebuilt by Germans rather than conquered by foreign forces.

While in Switzerland, Bonhoeffer arranged a top-secret meeting with the Bishop of Chichester, George Bell, with whom he had been friends while working in London. Through him he passed information to the Allied forces in Britain about the Abwehr's planned coup against Hitler, including names and specific proposals. But it seems the Allies were lukewarm about such a plan. Bonhoeffer never, in fact, received a reply from the Allied leaders.

Astonishingly, amid the heat of war and resistance and when he was purportedly working for the military, Bonhoeffer wrote his great work on ethics. In its pages, he took on Nazism by drawing a clear distinction between the villain and the saint, writing:

> It is easy for the tyrannical despiser of men to exploit the baseness of the human heart, nurturing it and calling it by other names. Fear he calls responsibility. Desire he calls keenness. Dependency becomes solidarity. Brutality becomes masterfulness. Human weaknesses are played upon with unchaste seductiveness, so that meanness and baseness are reproduced and multiplied ever anew . . . As the base man grows baser, he becomes an ever more willing and adaptable tool in the hand of the tyrant. The small band of the upright are reviled. Their bravery is called revolt; their discipline is called pharisaism; their independence arbitrariness and their masterfulness arrogance. For the tyrannical despiser of men popularity is the token of the highest love of mankind. His secret profound mistrust for all human beings he conceals behind words stolen from a true community . . . He thinks people stupid, and they become stupid. He thinks them weak, and they become weak. He thinks them criminal, and they become criminal . . . In his profound contempt for his fellow-men he seeks the favour of those whom he despises, and the more he does so the more certainly he promotes the deification of his own person by the mob.

This extraordinary time, as a double agent within the Nazi machine and as a theologian working out an approach to Christology, was the most intense, creative period of Bonhoeffer's life. In the preceding years he had initiated the first steps in his theological and personal journey of defining modern discipleship. His concern had been for the Church and how it should prepare and support its clergy in ministry. Until he began to work for the Abwehr, Bonhoeffer had struggled with how to most truly express obedience to Christ's teachings in relation to the non-religious world, for it was the non-religious world where Christ himself had moved. But as he became more disengaged from the Church as an institution, his theological ideas on the future role for the Church in society became increasingly bold and challenging, and his own witness to Christ as a conspirator against the state more necessary. Bonhoeffer's theology had come of age.

During this transition he had been torn between reflective withdrawal from the compromising, suffering world and engagement with and responsibility towards it. At different points in his life he had been equivocal. In urging the Church to take a stand against Jewish persecution, was he urging the Church towards its own oblivion? Should he retreat from the hotbed of Germany and accept a pastoral role in the relative calm of England or America, rather than risk action prompted on an unsound theology? Confronted with conflicting loyalties to different masters, Bonhoeffer knew he could serve only one God. And for him, obedience to God demanded not just silent resistance to that which is un-Godly, but active opposition to confront it. Through much anguish and doubt, Bonhoeffer had forged a theology of action, whereby Christians could bear witness to Christ through deed and example. Ultimately this meant for Bonhoeffer a rejection of the tidy demarcation between religious and secular life, and in due course it led to his death.

Eberhard Bethge describes the progression of Bonhoeffer's understanding of the role of Church and state, and consequently the role of individual members within the Church and state:

As a good Lutheran [Bonhoeffer] acknowledged the State's right to settle even the Jewish question legitimately. This was nothing new for his audience and counted as good theology at the time. But then he demanded – and this was considered bad theology – that within this framework the Church must, first, ask the State 'whether it could answer for its action as legitimate political action . . .'; secondly, the Church has an unconditional obligation to the victims of any social order, regardless of whether they belong to the Christian community or not; thirdly, when the Church sees the State exercising too little or too much law and order, it is its task not simply to bind the wounds of the victims beneath the wheel, but also to put a spoke in the wheel itself.

Events in Germany had become so fierce and brutal that silence and withdrawal implied complicity. Likewise, involvement necessarily became opposition, resistance, and conspiracy. Bonhoeffer did not originally intend the third possibility – that of direct political opposition – to be left to individual choice; it was to be carried out and authorised by an 'Evangelical Council'. But he was disappointed to find that he had overestimated the capabilities of the ecumenical movement. And Bonhoeffer had made the decision that he had, without any corporate help from the Church or Council, to put 'a spoke in the wheel' himself.

In the midst of war, his work on ethics and activities with the resistance, Bonhoeffer fell in love. When not working for the Abwehr, he spent a great deal of time at the home of his friend Ruth von Kleist-Retzow, who had been a great patron of the illegal seminary he had run in the 1930s. Now he used her home as a base to work on his book, and it was during this time that he became acquainted with members of her extended family, and in particular her granddaughter, Maria von Wedemeyer.

Maria recalled the early months of their romance: 'During the next fall I was in Berlin taking care of my grandmother, and Dietrich had ample opportunity to visit and talk. It amused him to take me to lunch at a small restaurant close to the hospital which was owned by Hitler's brother. He claimed there was no safer place to talk.'

The two grew increasingly intimate. Bonhoeffer comforted Maria when within a year her father, brother and close cousins were killed in the war; and in January 1943 they became secretly engaged. But there was never to be a wedding. A few weeks later, the Gestapo arrested Bonhoeffer over suspicions aroused by irregularities connected to the activities of the Abwehr and incarcerated him in Tegel prison in Berlin. But his arrest was considered more a show of strength as the Gestapo sought to exert more direct control over the work of the Abwehr. The Gestapo still had no idea of much of the Abwehr's – or Bonhoeffer's – true work, and Bonhoeffer, his family, and his fiancée were confidently optimistic of his eventual release.

Finding himself in prison so soon after becoming engaged was a blow. The authorities did not permit him to write to Maria until after the first phase of their investigation was concluded and so for several months he had to rely on communicating with her through his parents. In his first letter from prison to his parents, he wrote:

> You can imagine that I'm most particularly anxious about my fiancée at the moment. It's a great deal for her to bear, especially when she has only recently lost her father and brother in the East. As the daughter of an officer, she will perhaps find my imprisonment especially hard to take. If only I could have a few words with her! Now you will have to do it.

Though the weeks passed and Dietrich became more accustomed to life in prison, he always believed he would be released to marry and enjoy a life with Maria. He wrote with certainty to his parents that: 'She will be a very good daughter-in-law to you, and will surely soon feel as at home in our family as I have for years in her own.'

After a few months, Maria was allowed to visit him regularly, and he to write her a one-page letter every eight days – though other letters were smuggled out through sympathetic guards. Maria recalled how

> Dietrich often mentioned his reluctance to express his feelings. He pondered the differences between our two families and his own feelings of propriety and privacy. Yet when he felt the need to express them in a smuggled letter (or on those few times during

my visits when the attending officer would tactfully leave the room), he did so with an intensity that surprised him more than it did me.

Maria decided to move in with Dietrich's parents in order to be closer to him. His love for her does not seem to have been diminished by separation and imprisonment. A year after his arrest, he wrote to her:

My dear, dear Maria. It's no use. I have to write to you at last and talk to you with no one else listening. I have to let you see into my heart without someone else, whom it doesn't concern, looking on. I have to talk to you about that which belongs to no one else in the world but us, and which becomes desecrated when exposed to the hearing of an outsider. I refuse to let anyone else share what belongs to you alone; I think that would be impermissible, unwholesome, uninhibited, and devoid of dignity, from your point of view. The thing that draws and binds me to you in my unspoken thoughts and dreams cannot be revealed, dearest Maria, until I'm able to fold you in my arms. That time will come, and it will be more blissful and genuine the less we seek to anticipate it and the more faithfully and genuinely we wait for each other.

Bonhoeffer wrote mostly of the blessedness of their relationship and how much happiness it brought him, but there were moments when he revealed the agony of his separation from her just at the time when their mutual love had been openly declared. In one letter he wrote:

Both of us have lost infinitely much during the past months; time today is a costly commodity, for who knows how much more time is given to us . . . Your life would have been quite different, easier, clearer, simpler had not our paths crossed a year ago. But there are only short moments when this thought bothers me . . . I believe that happiness lies for both of us at a different and hidden place which is incomprehensible to many.

Maria recalled that Bonhoeffer encouraged her to plan the practical aspects of their future together: 'It helped him to envision a specific piece of furniture in our future apartment, a particular walk through the fields, a familiar spot on the beach . . .' They managed to share some happy times together during her prison visits. At Christmas, 1943, she brought him a large Christmas tree for his cell. 'The fact that I brought a sizable Christmas tree all the way from home created great hilarity with both the guards and Dietrich,' Maria wrote. 'He remarked that maybe if he moved his cot out of his cell and stood up for the Christmas season he could accommodate the tree comfortably.' There were also some light-hearted exchanges in letters: 'We made a bet about whether I would be able to teach him to dance: he thought I could while I considered him a hopeless case.' But he also wrote to Maria: 'Isn't it so that even when we are laughing, we are a bit sad?'

Bonhoeffer had the courage to endure the confinement and humiliation of prison, separated from his friends, family and fiancée, isolated from the events with which he was so deeply and passionately engaged, without succumbing either to reckless-ness or to despair and resignation. From solitary confinement he wrote:

It is wiser to be pessimistic; it is a way of avoiding disappointment and ridicule, and so wise people condemn optimism. The essence of optimism is not its view of the present, but the fact that it is the inspiration of life and hope when others give in; it enables a man to hold his head high when everything seems to be going wrong; it gives him strength to sustain reverses and yet to claim the future for himself instead of abandoning it to his opponent. It is true that there is a silly, cowardly kind of optimism, which we must condemn. But the optimism that is a will for the future should never be despised, even if it is proved wrong a hundred times; it is health and vitality, and the sick man has no business to impugn it.

The ancient Roman philosopher Seneca wrote: 'There is nothing in the world so much admired as a man who knows how to bear unhappiness with courage.' Evidence from prison guards and inmates give testament to the fact that Bonhoeffer retained his humour and optimism from behind the prison walls. The ease with which he was able to enlist the help of sympathetic guards to smuggle letters indicates they might have recognised Thomas Paine's sentiments when he said: 'I love the man that can smile in trouble, that can gather strength from distress, and grow brave by reflections.'

Bonhoeffer, with the help of his family, had begun to plan his escape from prison. But in September 1944 the Gestapo discovered incriminating documents linking him to the resistance. His brother Klaus, brother-in-law Hans and other members of his family were also arrested and imprisoned. This made it impossible for Bonhoeffer to press ahead with his plan to escape for fear of the repercussions for his relatives. He was forced to give up the hope for freedom through escape.

In October 1944, Bonhoeffer was moved to the Gestapo bunker in Berlin. There he underwent a new series of interrogations. He was permitted to send a letter to his mother on her birthday on 28 December and chose to write words of comfort and praise to her:

> All I really want to do is to help cheer you a little in these days that you must be finding so bleak. Dear mother, I want you to know that I am constantly thinking of you and father every day, and that I thank God for all that you are to me and the whole family. I know you've always lived for us and haven't lived a life of your own.

In February 1945 he was transferred to Buchenwald where he stayed until being transported to another concentration camp, Flossenburg, which would be the place of his death. No letters from Bonhoeffer exist from his final months, and the main source of information about him comes from the recollections of Captain Payne Best, a British army officer and fellow prisoner.

Captain Best's memoirs show Bonhoeffer to have been courageous to the very end, even when all hope had been extinguished. He was, according to Best:

cheerful and ready to join in any joke. Bonhoeffer was all
humility and sweetness; he always seemed to diffuse an atmosphere of happiness, of joy in every smallest event in life, and of
deep gratitude for the mere fact that he was alive. He was one of
the very few men I have ever met to whom his God was real and
ever close to him.

Incredibly, Bonhoeffer delivered a sermon a few days before his
execution. Captain Best recalled that he and Bonhoeffer were being
transferred along with other prisoners to Flossenburg, when the
prison van broke down. The prisoners were kept in a little school-
house while they waited to continue the journey. During their wait,
Bonhoeffer was asked to conduct a prayer service where he contemplated the hope of a new birth through the resurrection of
Christ from the dead.

Bonhoeffer's last recorded words were to Captain Best. He asked
him to send a message to the English Bishop George Bell telling him
that he believed 'in the principle of our universal Christian brotherhood which rises above national interests, and that our victory is
certain'. Then he said: 'This is the end – for me, the beginning of
life.'

Courage, it is said, is something you always have until you need
it. Bonhoeffer's courage in facing death was undisputed – witnessed
by an SS doctor who later wrote: 'In nearly fifty years as a doctor I
never saw another man go to his death so possessed of the spirit of
God'.

Dietrich Bonhoeffer was hanged only a few days before war
ended, on 9 April 1945. At this stage in the war the Nazi
authorities were more concerned with their own fate than that
of their prisoners and news of his death travelled slowly: neither
his fiancée nor his parents knew until weeks after he had been
killed.

Some of his most profound and far-reaching theological work
had been produced while he was in prison, and he never lost hope
that he would survive the war, marry his fiancée, and help rebuild
the Christian Church in Germany. And even when death was
inevitable he did not retreat into his inner self or rail against his

fate; he remained engaged with events and ministered to those around him until the very end.

But I think of Bonhoeffer's courage not just in terms of the dignity with which he faced execution – the 'two o'clock in the morning courage' that Napoleon spoke of – but rather of his whole lifetime of courage.

Long before his execution, Bonhoeffer had contemplated the meaning and value of life at a time when death had become all too familiar. The mass destruction of war threatened the gross devaluation of all human life. No rational assessment of human value seemed credible amid the mass carnage that was the war. German men disappeared into conscription to die all over the world, and once-stable families, including Bonhoeffer's own, fled ignobly from place to place. In the face of the absurdity of meaningless, relentless violence, Bonhoeffer was aware of the danger of succumbing to either dissociation and detachment or spiritual desolation. He knew that once life loses its value, all morality collapses. The human spirit cannot weather the onslaught of repeated days under duress and continue to live ethically unless it is supported by the solidity of profoundly held belief.

From prison he wrote an essay called 'Insecurity and Death'. In it he said:

In recent years we have become increasingly familiar with the thought of death. We surprise ourselves by the calmness with which we hear of the death of one of our contemporaries. We cannot hate it as we used to, for we have discovered some good in it, and have almost come to terms with it. Fundamentally we feel that we really belong to death already, and that every new day is a miracle. It would probably not be true to say that we welcome death (although we all know that weariness which we ought to avoid like the plague); we are too inquisitive for that – or, to put it more seriously, we should like to see something more of the meaning of our life's broken fragments. Nor do we try to romanticise death, for life is too great and too precious. Still less do we suppose that danger is the meaning of life – we are not desperate enough for that, and we know too much about the good things that life has to offer, though on the other hand we are only too familiar with life's anxieties and with all the other destructive effects of prolonged personal insecurity. We still love life, but I do not think that death can take us by surprise now. After what we have been through during the war, we hardly dare admit that we should like death to come to us, not accidentally and suddenly through some trivial cause, but in the fullness of life and with everything at stake. It is we ourselves, and not outward circumstances, who make death what it can be, a death freely and voluntarily accepted.

Bonhoeffer died courageously, but – far more importantly – he lived courageously. How much easier it would have been for him to loosen his grip on notions of good and evil. How much safer it would have been for him to abandon responsibility for himself and his neighbour. But Bonhoeffer never shirked from answering for his life. He never shrugged or pointed the finger to extraordinary circumstances as an excuse for taking leave of his call to duty as a human being.

We think of acts of courage in wartime, personal moments of bravery that we can applaud. These are often acts of daring that win recognition and medals for valour and for leadership. Bonhoeffer's courage was very different. He was brave in becoming part of the resistance movement to Nazi Germany. But he showed himself to be courageous not in one act of daring but over nearly fifteen years of considered, growing and ever more dangerous defiance. His perseverance in resisting Hitler was part of his life; it was the manifestation of his steadfast intolerance to injustice and an instinctive compassion so inimical to Nazism.

Even from his early student days, Bonhoeffer reached out across the gulf that separated his class from society's excluded – to the ghettoes in New York, to disaffected youth growing up in poverty in Berlin. But reaching out to these groups through his ministry never jeopardised his own standing in society in the way that his solidarity with the Jews alienated him from his colleagues and friends in the run up to the war.

Bonhoeffer effectively excluded himself from his own secure position in society by standing up against Nazism when he could

have remained silent – as so many others did. The inner turmoil
Bonhoeffer and his conspirators felt – effectively acting as traitors to
their country – should not be underestimated, nor should the initial
feelings of shame of arrest and imprisonment to a man of such high
social standing. An early letter to Bonhoeffer from his mother
conveys the sense of social disgrace: 'Who would have thought
it possible that such a thing could happen to you! We are trying to
get rid of our old idea that being in prison is a disgrace; it makes life
unnecessarily difficult.'

But if, as he grew up, Bonhoeffer was comfortable in society and
felt a sense of belonging and ease with the world around him, by the
time he was in prison he would reflect on how his experience in
adulthood had given him insight into the 'view from below' – how
the world appears from the perspective of the outcast, the persecuted, the excluded, the despised – those on the margins and fringes
of society. Bonhoeffer himself saw his fall from grace as a blessing
and extended the metaphor to the Church, seeing it as a means by
which the Church, by also falling from grace and its privileged
position in society, could better serve those who suffer. He wrote of
this from prison:

> There remains an experience of incomparable value. We have for
> once learnt to see the great events of world history from below,
> from the perspective of the outcast, the suspects, the maltreated,
> the powerless, the oppressed, the reviled – in short, from the
> perspective of those who suffer. The important thing is that
> neither bitterness nor envy should have gnawed at the heart
> during this time, that we should have come to look with new eyes
> at matters great and small, sorrow and joy, strength and weak-
> ness, that our perception of generosity, humanity, justice and
> mercy should have become clearer, freer, less corruptible. We
> have to learn that personal suffering is a more effective key, a
> more rewarding principle for exploring the world in thought and
> action than personal good fortune. This perspective from below
> must not become the partisan possession of those who are
> eternally dissatisfied; rather, we must do justice to life in all
> its dimensions from a higher satisfaction, whose foundation is

beyond any talk of 'from below' or 'from above'. This is the way in which we may affirm it.

From the confinement of his cell Bonhoeffer charted a way towards freedom and rebirth, not just for himself but for the Church. Here was the opportunity for the Church to claim a new legitimacy. It would have to let go of privilege and move among the suffering. Instead of salving the wounds of those who entered its doors, it would have to take its healing power out and offer it even to those who would never think to seek it. But the evangelicalism promoted by Bonhoeffer was far more than just preaching the Word; it was living the Word through example in service, and through extreme difficulty and danger. 'The Church must share in the secular problems of ordinary human life, not dominating it, but helping and serving. It must tell men of every calling what it means to live in Christ, to exist for others,' Bonhoeffer exhorted. But he added: 'It is not abstract argument, but example, that gives its word emphasis and power.'

Deeds, not words. The source of strength lies in the doing, by action and example. Ernest Cromwell, the parishioner who knew Bonhoeffer when he was in London, recalls him seeing a traffic sign at a crossroads that read 'Safety First'. Bonhoeffer considered it one of the worst signs because it 'was contrary to his philosophy of life'. For Bonhoeffer, according to Cromwell,

Life was not a question of safety first and making ourselves comfortable. It was a question of adventure and risk for things that are worthwhile, because his whole philosophy of life and religion and belief was that life was a period of development, it wasn't static; it was something that you had to create, in your context, with other people.

It is the 'he who dares' courage that Theodore Roosevelt celebrated when he wrote:

It is not the critic who counts; not the man who points out how the strong man stumbles or where the doer of deeds could have done better. The credit belongs to the man who is actually in the arena, whose face is marred by dust and sweat and blood; who strives valiantly, who errs and comes short again and again, who errs and comes up short again, but who knows great enthusiasms, the great devotions, who spends himself in a worthy cause; who, at the best, knows, in the end, the triumph of high achievement, and who, at the worst, if he fails, at least fails while daring greatly, so that his place shall never be with those timid souls who know neither victory nor defeat.

But mere activity is not enough. Action for the sake of action does not make a hero, and the foolhardy are not hailed as courageous. Just as Pythagoras and Aristotle warned against blind action made independent of a broader philosophical context in which such action would be consistent, Bonhoeffer warned against untargeted, thoughtless action where 'like a bull he rushes at the red cloak instead of the person who is holding it; he exhausts himself and is beaten'.

Bonhoeffer instead pleaded for 'responsible action in a bold venture of faith'. It is through responsible action itself that Bonhoeffer believed God's will is enacted on earth. Bethge insisted that: 'At no point is it possible to understand Bonhoeffer's theological work without reference to the actual here and now. His theology draws its vitality from the risks inherent in action.'

Even when the consequences were dire, Bonhoeffer never retreated from his belief that the path to spiritual freedom is through action. After hearing of the execution of some of his companions, he composed a prose poem in prison which he called 'Stations on the Road to Freedom':

(Discipline)
If you set out to seek freedom, then learn above all things to govern your soul and your senses, for fear that your passions and longings may lead you away from the path you should follow.

Chaste be your mind and your body, and both in subjection, obediently, steadfastly seeking the aim set before them; only through discipline may a man learn to be free.

(Action)

Daring to do what is right, not what fancy may tell you valiantly grasping occasions, not cravenly doubting – freedom comes only through deeds, not through thoughts taking wing. Faint not nor fear, but go out to the storm and the action. Trusting in God whose commandment you faithfully follow; freedom exultant will welcome your spirit with joy.

(Suffering)

A change has come indeed. Your hands, so strong and active, are bound; in helplessness now you see your action is ended; you sigh in relief, you cause committing to stronger hands; so now you may rest contented. Only for one blissful moment could you draw near to touch freedom; then that it might be perfected in glory, you gave it to God.

(Death)

Come now thou greatest of feasts on the journey to freedom eternal; death, cast aside all the burdensome chains, and demolish the walls of our temporal body, the walls of our souls that are blinded, so that at last we may see that which here remains hidden. Freedom how long we have sought thee in discipline, action and suffering; dying we now may behold thee revealed in the Lord.

If the particulars of Bonhoeffer's life provided a template for individual responsible action, they also offered the Church a way to salvation from the ruination of war. Bonhoeffer's life was an illumination of his theology, not just as an individual but as an exemplar for the Church as an institution.

The significance of Bonhoeffer's theological legacy is still debated amongst ecumenical leaders. The fragmentary – and some would argue contradictory – nature of his work means he has been reinterpreted and re-evaluated many times over since his death. He has been both hailed as a martyr and dismissed as a traitor. Certainly Bonhoeffer did not play lightly the role of the saboteur in his country's war. The path he chose led him to lie, betray trust, undermine his own country, and ultimately plot murder. But he

had said at the outset of war that the battle was between his
country's success in war and the survival of Christianity in his
country. He knew they could not both survive; each was the other's
antithesis, and he knew which side he was on. The responsibility to
act in such a way as to prevent the annihilation of Christian
civilisation was more important than preserving the purity of an
uncompromised personal piety. 'Civil courage,' Bonhoeffer wrote,

> can grow only out of the free responsibility of free men. Only now
> are the Germans beginning to discover the meaning of free
> responsibility. It depends on a God who demands responsible
> action in a bold venture of faith, and who promises forgiveness
> and consolation to the man who becomes a sinner in that
> venture.

Bethge charted the stages of Bonhoeffer's theological progression
which developed in parallel to Bonhoeffer's own life – first as a
pacifist, then through his ministry, then as conspirator, then finally
as a prisoner looking beyond the war to the reconstruction of
German Christianity:

> Jesus, the man for others, is expressed in three different forms in
> Bonhoeffer's life. A new form appears at each point when the old
> form can no longer cope with new historical challenges. First of all,
> it was the cause of peace against nationalistic militarism; then, the
> fight against anti-Semitic racism; finally, the 'being below' of the
> Church. Each stage meant he had to question his Church's way of
> existence anew; finding an answer became each time more pre-
> carious. Each new step was unpopular and threatening – as it still is
> today. The part Bonhoeffer played in the struggle for peace made
> him, a follower of Christ, an ally of the few pacifists, who were then
> very unpopular. His resistance to Nazi racism – which could no
> longer be countered by a pacifist sermon on peace, because a
> sermon could not prevent complicity in murder – turned the
> preacher of peace into an ally of conspirators plotting to rid their
> country of the murderers. In his own painful process of learning
> Bonhoeffer discovered the vision of a transformation process for

Christianity: the liberation of his own Church through a return to poverty, through a rejection of the position of hierarchical dominance which has developed theologically as well as historically, legally and economically, through a return down to Christ's way among men.

Bonhoeffer's belief that Christ is revealed through the responsible action of modern disciples was a challenge not just for him as an individual but for the whole Church. Paradoxically, in castigating the Church for the collapse of its moral leadership before and during the war, Bonhoeffer also helped salvage its moral authority afterwards, particularly in Eastern Germany where the Church sought more readily to accept its share of the blame for the crimes of fascism. Bonhoeffer's sacrifice enabled others to move forward. By opposing Hitler and seeking to overthrow him, Bonhoeffer went a long way to ensuring the survival of German Christianity through one of the darkest periods in its history.

Amid the cataclysm of the Second World War it took the courage of a Bonhoeffer not just to stand up to the evil of the day but to restore a sense that Germany had a future. In an essay written in prison about his ten years of protest, Bonhoeffer was honest in his description of 'the death of civil courage' in Germany. He wrote:

in recent years we have seen a great deal of bravery and self sacrifice but civil courage hardly anywhere, even among ourselves . . . to attribute this simply to personal cowardice is too facile a psychology. Its background is quite different . . . Luther did not realise that submissiveness and self-sacrifice could be exploited for evil ends . . . civil courage can in fact grow only out of the free responsibility of free men . . . only now are the Germans beginning to discover the meaning of free responsibility . . . it depends upon a god who demands responsible action in a valid venture of faith . . . talk of going down fighting like heroes in the face of certain defeat is not really heroic at all but merely a refusal to face the future.

And he added: 'The ultimate question a responsible man asks is not how he is to extricate himself heroically . . . but how the coming generation is to live.'

Gerhard Liebholz, a brother-in-law, wrote that Dietrich Bonhoeffer's life and death

> belong to the annals of Christian martyrdom. His life and death have given us a great hope for the future. He has set a model for a new type of true leadership inspired by the gospel, daily ready for martyrdom and death and imbued by a new spirit of Christian humanism and a creative sense of civic duty. The victory which he has won was a victory for all of us, a conquest never to be undone, of love, light and liberty.

But most of all Bonhoeffer's life shows that strength of belief is not enough: it needs to be matched by strength of character. Strong belief and weak character can all too easily amount to nothing more than moral cowardice: the condition of the Nazi-dominated Germany of the 1930s, too weak to stand up to Hitler. But in that time of national trauma Bonhoeffer – by his life, his actions and his writings – showed a whole nation that with moral courage its people could move forward.

3

Raoul Wallenberg

He remains the hero without a grave. But as long as humanity
remembers those days, his name will live as a symbol of courage
in the face of seemingly invincible evil. He stood firm; he refused
to be intimidated; he resisted, knowing that in dark times, what
we do makes a difference. The good we do lives after us, and it's
the greatest thing that does.

Two thousand years ago the sages said a single human life is
like a universe. Save a life, and you save a world. Change a life
and you begin to change the world. That was Raoul Wallenberg.

Chief Rabbi Dr Jonathan Sacks

Raoul Wallenberg was a man who chose to enter into one of the
darkest corners of Nazi-occupied Europe for the sole purpose of saving
Jewish lives. He operated largely alone and unaided; he had no army,
no weapons and he was never a spy. His own country was not at war.
He was not even Jewish. Indeed he had few powers at his disposal
beyond his own initiative, courage and conviction. But by using his
inner resources he was able to summon the means to frustrate
substantially Nazi plans to annihilate all Hungary's remaining Jews.

Wallenberg's mission in the final months of the Second World War
took place in one of the most violent and chaotic places on the earth,
where human life had become virtually worthless. Calm and in-
genious amid the cold and orderly brutality of the Nazi regime and
the frenzied violence of the mob, he outmanoeuvred the authorities
with tactical brilliance, flair and bravery in order to save Jews in
Hungary from concentration and extermination camps.

Yet Wallenberg – whose story fascinated me as soon as I came across it as a boy growing up in Scotland in the 1950s – was the most unlikely of war heroes. He was a mild-mannered civilian from a privileged background in a neutral country. The lives of his friends and family were barely affected by the mass killings of the war. His family's wealth and position were not at risk from the war. His homeland was not being desecrated. And he had no previous history as a man of courage. Indeed at just thirty-one years old he would have more likely been called a playboy than a hero of the resistance and subverter of the Holocaust.

Until he went to Budapest, in the summer of 1944, the events in Raoul Wallenberg's life do not appear to be any more remarkable than other young men of his privileged background. He was single, wealthy and a member of one of Sweden's most prominent banking and diplomatic dynasties. He divided his time between business trips around Europe and something approaching an aristocratic lifestyle. The rest of Europe may have been on its knees but the comfortable lives of well-off families in neutral countries went on almost uninterrupted.

So, from the safety, security and luxury of his surroundings, Raoul Wallenberg placed himself at the heart of one of the worst places in Europe at one of the worst times in its history. And what is remarkable is that he not only risked all, but that at every stage when, as the challenge intensified and he could have justified standing back, he took yet more risks with his life.

Initially, Wallenberg used his diplomatic status as a member of the Swedish legation in Budapest to issue Jews with protective Swedish passports. As the situation there became more desperate, he bribed, cajoled, threatened those who got in his way, and even raided German convoys. He went as far as to arrange face-to-face meetings with high-ranking officials, including the infamous SS officer Adolf Eichmann, whom he informed that Germany had no chance of winning the war. Yet all the time he operated in Hungary he had no real official power.

What is all the more remarkable is that such fearlessness did not come naturally to Raoul Wallenberg. Lars Berg, a friend and colleague at the Swedish legation in Budapest, recalled that his daring was all the more admirable, as 'Raoul was not a brave man by nature . . . during the air raids he was always the first to seek shelter and he was sometimes affected when the bombs fell too close'. Indeed Wallenberg had told another friend that he had packed a small revolver in the backpack of belongings he brought to Budapest, 'not because I ever intended to use it but to give myself courage'.

Yet the events of the war would transform Wallenberg into a hero of great courage.

Was it simply bravado? Or the actions of a thrill-seeking aristocrat in search of adventure? No, because we know that when the bombs fell his first instinctive response was to want to run away. And bravado alone does not explain the personal risks Wallenberg was prepared to take. The answer lies much deeper, in a set of beliefs that grew so strong and so powerful that it gave him the willpower to risk all. Quite simply, Raoul Wallenberg was outraged at the persecution of the Jewish race; he saw it as an affront to humanity.

We now know that his support for the Jews preceded his work in Hungary. In 1936, when he was twenty-three years old, Wallenberg's grandfather found him a job at a Dutch bank in Haifa and he lived for some months in a kosher boarding house with young Jews who had fled Hitler's Germany. There he learned of the terrible personal cost of anti-Semitic persecution and heard details of Jewish livelihoods, homes and families being torn apart. Raoul's half-sister Nina Lagergren recalls his experiences in Haifa:

He had come up against the Jewish Problem, as it was in 1936 [in Haifa], where there were many Jewish immigrants from Germany. He was amazed that they were so enthusiastic about their new future, and didn't want to linger on the catastrophe that had made them flee from Germany. In a letter he wrote in 1939 he said he had read *Mein Kampf*. You could foresee what Hitler bluntly told the world he was going to do about the 'Jewish question'.

Then when the war came: 'Raoul felt he wanted to achieve something for a cause. He knew so many people in Hungary. He felt he could do something wholeheartedly.'

Letters written while he was staying in Palestine suggest Wallenberg was moved also by a strong admiration of the Jewish people: 'Poor people, they evidently have to adjust to being in a minority wherever they go,' he wrote. 'They have boundless enthusiasm and idealism and these immediately strike you as the most common characteristic of Zionism.'

So, while Wallenberg's courage lay untested before Budapest, it was underpinned by a strength of belief and willpower that surprised all around him. As one of his Budapest colleagues noticed the day Wallenberg arrived on his rescue mission, he had 'only one source of power: an unfaltering faith in himself buttressed by the justness of his cause'.

Such was Wallenberg's drive in wartime Hungary that he is supposed to have targeted young people for rescue, explaining apologetically that he was on a mission to save the Jewish nation and had to rescue those with the best chance of keeping the 'Jewish nation' alive.

When pressed by his colleagues to save himself he replied: 'But I have no choice. I have taken upon myself this mission and I would never be able to return to Stockholm without knowing that I've done everything that stands in a man's power to rescue as many Jews as possible.'

However, Raoul Wallenberg's involvement in the rescue mission to save Hungary's Jews happened almost by accident. In response to the desperate plight of the remaining Jews still within reach of the Nazis' grasp, President Roosevelt had belatedly set up the War Refugee Board, in January 1944. Its purpose was to try to save Jews and other potential victims of Nazi persecution.

Until early 1944, in contrast to Jews in other occupied areas, the Jews in Hungary had remained relatively safe. Indeed many Jewish refugees had fled from Germany, Poland and Czechoslovakia to the 'safe-haven' of Hungary, swelling the Jewish population there to approximately 750,000. Despite widespread anti-Semitic sentiment and policies, Hungary had proved to be an unreliable ally in the Nazis' orchestration of the Final Solution. The country's regent, Miklós Horthy, was on good terms with some of the wealthy Hungarian Jews and its prime minister, Miklós Kallay, resented German demands for the deportation of his country's Jews.

Nazi Germany grew increasingly impatient with what it considered to be Hungarian insubordination. In March 1944, under the pretext of protecting their southern border, it moved to occupy part of Hungary. Regent Horthy was summoned to meet Hitler, and during his absence, German forces poured into Hungary. Prime Minister Kallay was replaced with the pro-Nazi Dome Sztojay. Plans to eliminate the rest of Hungary's Jews could, it seemed, now proceed unhindered.

At the head of these operations was Adolf Eichmann. Eichmann – the Reich's pre-eminent expert on 'Jewish affairs' – had set up the efficient killing furnaces of Auschwitz. He had masterminded the deportation of Jews from other occupied territories and was obsessed with the extermination programme. But for Eichmann, Hungary's large Jewish population would become his biggest personal challenge. In just a few weeks, between May and June 1944, he personally oversaw the deportation of almost half a million of them – 437,000 – to Auschwitz and to other death camps. The remainder of Hungary's Jews were herded into Budapest from where he planned one final liquidation.

That was the unfolding tragedy in July 1944. Hungary became the most urgent priority of Roosevelt's War Refugee Board. Its whole strategy was a belief that the presence of foreigners in official capacities would deter such atrocities. So the Board urged international aid organisations, the Church hierarchy, and Europe's neutral nations to send representatives to Budapest, imploring them to use whatever means they could to dissuade the Hungarians from permitting the slaughter to take place.

But only one neutral European country agreed to the War Refugee Board's request to expand their diplomatic presence in Hungary. Back in Stockholm, its representative, Ivar Olsen, called on prominent Swedish Jews to advise him on the best means of using Sweden's diplomatic cover to help Hungary's Jews. One summoned to advise was Koloman Lauer, Wallenberg's business partner and close friend – himself a Hungarian Jew. The plan was to recruit a non-Jew to travel on a rescue mission to Budapest. He would do so under the auspices of being a special envoy to the Swedish government and in Budapest he would issue Swedish passports with the aim of getting as many Jews as possible to Sweden.

Thus it was that through this unlikely chain of events – and the desperate but unpromising eleventh-hour manoeuvres to save lives – that Raoul Wallenberg's life took a dramatic turn, as he was propelled from aristocratic comfort to occupied Hungary.

No record exists of the conversations that took place between Wallenberg and Lauer as the rescue plan was being hatched. The first Swede chosen to lead the rescue operation had been rejected by the Hungarian government and it was only then that Lauer had pushed Wallenberg's name to the fore. The War Refugee Board's Ivar Olsen was deeply sceptical of Wallenberg's suitability because of his youth and inexperience. He did however agree to meet him. In fact this introductory meeting on 9 June 1944 lasted all night. By dawn of the next day, Wallenberg had convinced Olsen that he was the right man for the job.

En route to Hungary, Wallenburg stopped off briefly to visit his half-sister Nina:

> He told me about his plans and his appointment, and we understood that it was very dangerous, but we didn't know at that point quite how dangerous it was going to be. He insisted on total freedom to do anything possible to save people; nothing should stop him. He knew bureaucracy could prevent young secretaries in the embassies from doing anything independently, so he asked for permission for complete freedom to speak to or make representations on behalf of the government and Crown to whomever he needed, which was absolutely unknown. It was an unbelievable request for a very young, newly appointed secretary. But in his last letter he points out that he has been a thousand times to different ministers to ask for help and to get to the people that he needed. So he really made use of that.

Wallenberg arrived in Budapest on 9 July. By then most of Hungary's rural Jews had already fallen victim to Eichmann. Crammed into airless compartments on freight trains, many died before they even reached the extermination camps. Some were sent to work as slave labourers before being shot by the guards. So even before Wallenberg arrived 70 per cent of Hungary's Jews had already been murdered.

The remainder, concentrated in ghettoes in Budapest, were sealed away from the rest of the city but were perilously vulnerable as Eichmann intended to push ahead with his grand plan of a massive deportation to Auschwitz at the earliest opportunity.

Wallenberg's mission, meanwhile, was to set up and run a humanitarian department at the Swedish legation in the city. By issuing protective passes to any Jew with the vaguest of links with Sweden, he would extend the protection of the Swedish Crown to the largest possible number of Jews in Hungary.

Neutral legations had been able to issue protective passes for some time, and the Catholic Church had begun issuing baptismal certificates to protect Jews from the Germans. But these efforts were disjointed and sometimes half-hearted. Nothing had yet succeeded in forging well-meaning humanitarianism into a coordinated rescue mission. Indeed Budapest was in the grip of a grim hopelessness. So bleak was it that in one of his early reports to Stockholm, Wallenberg wrote: 'We have to rid the Jews of the feeling that they have been forgotten.'

And so he did. Lars Berg, already stationed at the Budapest legation, recalled Wallenberg's arrival and the scale of the challenge he faced:

Raoul Wallenberg began from such a hopeless starting-point, with such small resources and with such a lack of actual force to back him up. When he arrived to organise help for the Hungarian Jews, he was nothing but a blank page. He was not a career diplomat. His knowledge of the Hungarian language was limited. He knew no one of importance in Budapest.

Hungary was to become a battleground between Adolf Eichmann's malevolent determination to kill its Jews and Raoul Wallenberg's courageous efforts to save them. Were it not for the personalities of Eichmann and Wallenberg, the drama that was to unfold in Hungary might well have been played out on a lesser

stage. But Eichmann was fixated with the idea of ridding Hungary
of its Jews. It had become, for him, the cause above all causes:
success in masterminding the deaths of so many thousands of people
quickly and efficiently would be his crowning achievement.

In the course of the fight Raoul Wallenberg grew in stature.
Very quickly he grew into an inspired leader whose strength of
character summoned others to his cause and whose bravery defied
all the logic of self-preservation. 'He had a job to do,' Berg recalled,

> to stop the already initiated deportations of the Hungarian Jews,
> to give them food and shelter, and, above all, to save their lives.
> The most remarkable thing about his work was that it was not
> based on any legal rights whatsoever. His task was not to protect
> any Swedish subjects, nor Allied prisoners of war, nor wounded,
> nor sick people. Neither he nor the Swedish Legation had any
> right at all to interfere with the manner in which the Hungarian
> authorities chose to handle their internal problems – in this
> instance the Jews. Nor was Wallenberg supported by physical
> force. Neither weapons nor soldiers gave weight to his words.

While Per Anger, Secretary of the Swedish legation, and other
legation colleagues, including Minister Carl Ivar Danielsson and
also the head of the Swedish Red Cross, Valdemar Langlet, laid the
groundwork for Raoul Wallenberg's work in Budapest in the months
before his arrival in July 1944, and thereafter worked alongside him,
becoming, in the words of US senator Tom Lantos, 'radiant sparks of
humanity that glowed in the darkest of midnight', it was Wallenberg
who made the important early decision to raise the status of the
Swedish pass. Exploiting the Nazis' instinct for bureaucratic recti-
tude, a forgettable slip of paper was transformed into a document
resembling a passport, called a *Schutzpass* (protective pass). It was
now emblazoned with the official colours of Sweden, the triple royal
Swedish crown, and with various gaudy seals, stamps, and signa-
tures. The effect was to imbue the pass with an air of officialdom and
authority, and at the same time give the passholders a sense they were
under the shield of a strong and protective nation state.

The Hungarian authorities agreed to print an agreed quota of

Schutzpasse based on the number of persons thought likely to meet the criteria of having substantive connections with Sweden. The passes themselves were then to be issued by Wallenberg at the Swedish legation.

It was a remarkable achievement that Wallenberg convinced the Hungarian Foreign Ministry to increase the official quota of *Schutzpasse* from, at first, several hundred to ultimately several thousand. Bribery helped add an estimated 13,000 more. Later, when he could get no more official *Schutzpasse* printed, Wallenberg counterfeited and signed thousands more in person. Wallenberg took risk after risk. Survivors describe how he kept a typewriter in his car so he could issue a *Schutzpass* immediately to anyone he saw in danger. In any group of Jews he found being transported by the Nazis to concentration camps or being rounded up from their homes, he would simply enter the crowd, weave his way through and thrust passes into people's hands in a desperate bid to save them. In total Wallenberg is thought to have issued 25,000 *Schutzpasse*.

The proliferation of so many illegitimate passes was not without its own risks. Colleagues in the Swedish legation worried about a collapse of the entire *Schutzpass* system if the documents were to lose their legitimacy. But Wallenberg gambled. He believed that the possession of a *Schutzpass*, even a fraudulent one, would make the bureaucratic Nazis think twice about pushing a Jew into a death march or into slave labour. At the very least it might buy the holder precious time, something that could often make the difference between life and death.

For Wallenberg it meant added danger. Aware of the proliferation of Swedish passports, the Gestapo kept a constant watch over him. Sometimes they tested him, confronting him with a Jewish person they knew to be carrying a false document and asking him to examine the document for its validity – him knowing all the while that he would have to choose between the life of the individual Jew, or the integrity of the entire *Schutzpass* system.

The distribution of *Schutzpasse* saved the lives of thousands of Jews who queued at the Swedish legation. But Wallenberg's achievement was far greater. Within weeks of his arrival in Budapest he also set up hospitals, then a nursery and an orphanage, and then emergency soup kitchens. With incredible foresight he bought – and secretly stored – medical supplies, food and other survival essentials.

Wallenberg's own department at the Swedish legation grew from an initial staff of one – himself – to several hundred including many medics. And all of them were Jews. Wallenberg rightly reasoned that their employment at the legation would provide them with some protection in itself. In shifts, Wallenberg's staff worked round the clock to issue *Schutzpasse*, tend to sick and hungry Jews, secure and distribute vital supplies, and find safehouses. Indeed, Wallenberg himself is said to have worked almost constantly without rest.

As his colleague Per Anger wrote, Wallenberg's despatches from Budapest had 'a matter-of-fact style but between the lines you feel his compassion for and engagement in the fate of these people'. In one Wallenberg reported that: 'For many months now I have witnessed the suffering of the Hungarian people. And, if it is not too presumptuous to say so, I think I have participated in it spiritually to such an extent that it has now become my suffering.'

Spurred on by his early success, Wallenberg took yet more risks. The Nazis now required all Hungary's Jews to identify themselves as such by wearing a yellow star. Their movement was heavily restricted, and most were confined to living in specially marked Jewish ghettoes, making them particularly vulnerable. But using his position as a representative of the government of Sweden, Wallenberg won for his own legation staff an exemption from wearing the yellow star. In effect, he won their freedom.

He then took another bold step. Wallenberg negotiated with Regent Horthy to move those Jews in possession of *Schutzpasse* into a group of safehouses under the protection of Sweden, the Red Cross, and other neutral organisations. The occupants of these homes would be considered to be under the jurisdiction of the international organisations whose insignia they bore. In effect, Wallenberg succeeded in extending diplomatic immunity to the thousands of Jews who carried protective passes. Each night more and more Jews crammed themselves into what became known as the 'International Ghetto' where they could be fed, clothed, and protected.

Quickly the number of buildings used as safehouses in the International Ghetto rose to thirty-two; up to 25,000 Jews were sheltered in such houses.

With the Soviets gaining in the East and the Allies pushing in from the West, the implementation of the Final Solution became even more urgent for Adolf Eichmann. But in this race against time, Wallenberg's *Schutzpass* system and his protected International Ghetto meant thousands were escaping Eichmann's grasp. Within Hungary, Wallenberg and others were piling new pressure upon Regent Horthy – bombarding him with pleas to resist Eichmann's planned deportation of Budapest's Jews.

Still Eichmann tried to push ahead with his plan for the final deportation to Auschwitz, setting new dates for the mass round-up. Each time Wallenberg learned of the plans through informants and mounted a furious counter-campaign to have the deportation orders blocked. Among the inducements Wallenberg offered to Regent Horthy was the promise of favourable treatment by the Allied powers for saving Jewish lives once an Allied victory was secured.

Frustrated, Eichmann sought to remove Horthy. But besieged by greater problems, Hitler refused to grant Eichmann permission to topple the regent. With the fall of Romania in September, Eichmann was recalled to Berlin. Wallenberg wrongly believed his mission would soon be over and scaled down the work of his department.

When Regent Horthy announced his secret armistice with the Russians on national radio in October, scenes of wild jubilation swept across Budapest. But things would grow worse not better. The Red Army was not yet within reach of Budapest. In the meantime the Nazis connived with Hungary's extreme-right, militantly anti-Semitic fascist party, the Arrow Cross. Regent Horthy was deposed and sent to Bavaria and the Arrow Cross took control of the government.

The Arrow Cross was made up of thugs, mercenaries, thieves, bandits and low-level criminals; their random attacks upon Jews were of almost unparalleled savagery. With Horthy gone, Eichmann returned from Berlin intent on executing his grand plan.

With the Arrow Cross in charge, Wallenberg's diplomatic status now counted for little. The situation had become so dangerous that all neutral delegations moved their headquarters across the river to the Buda side of the Danube. Because of their previous success in protecting Jews, the Swedes were a particular target of the Arrow Cross regime and 'wanted' posters promising a reward for Wallenberg's capture were posted around the city. Hit men stalked him, yet, never sleeping in the same place on consecutive nights, Wallenberg somehow managed to stay one step ahead.

Under pressure, his response was to take even more risks. Using his authority as a representative of the Crown of Sweden, he now sought to deal with, bully or bribe Arrow Cross and Gestapo officials, including the newly returned Eichmann.

Wallenberg invited Eichmann to dinner at his private apartment. Aides to Wallenberg have recorded that momentous evening. Apparently Wallenberg had forgotten about his guests, arriving home as their car was drawing to a halt outside his house. Quickly he phoned Lars Berg, who lived nearby in a grand house rented from a nobleman, which had come complete with servants and a splendid dinner service. A meal was quickly and successfully devised.

After dinner Wallenberg showed Eichmann into the living room. There he turned out the lights, drew back the curtains from the windows and revealed a horizon with the sky ablaze from Russian gunfire on the Eastern Front as the Red Army closed in on Budapest. He then launched into a discussion about the likely outcome of the war. It is said that the discomfited Eichmann flinched, recognising the Nazis' weakening position. Wallenberg then moved on, seeking to discredit the Nazi ideology with an intellectual force that left Eichmann floundering.

'Eichmann could scarcely conceal his amazement that anyone should dare attack him and criticise the Führer,' a colleague from the legation wrote. 'But he soon seemed to realise that he was getting the worst of the argument. His propaganda phrases sounded hollow compared with Raoul's intelligent reasoning.'

It is said that Eichmann sounded defeated in argument, but belligerent in his threats:

For me there will be no escape, but if I obey my orders from Berlin and exercise my power harshly enough I may prolong my respite for some time here in Budapest. I warn you, therefore, Herr Legationssekretar, that I will do my best to stop you, and your Swedish diplomatic passport will not help you if I find it necessary to have you removed. Accidents do happen, even to a neutral diplomat.

Later Eichmann was overheard shouting out in a rage that he would have Wallenberg killed. The threat was reported to the Swedish legation, and an official complaint was lodged by the Swedish ambassador in Berlin. Wallenberg knew he was vulnerable. In the chaos of wartime Budapest, he could easily fall victim to a 'stray bullet' or be 'accidentally' injured in all the commotion. Indeed, shortly after the dinner his car was crushed by a heavy military truck, though Wallenberg was not in it at the time. But there would be greater dangers to come.

The Arrow Cross had declared that anyone seen to be assisting the Jews would be deemed an enemy. They also refused to honour any existing agreement for the protection of Jews. In such a threatening atmosphere, Eichmann's plan to deport Budapest's Jews could proceed. All Jewish men were rounded up and taken to the Eastern Front to be put in the path of the advancing Russians. The women and children, meanwhile, were to be shipped to the death camps. But this time, rather than be crammed into freight trains, they had to make the journey on foot. All trains were employed in the war effort and could not be spared to transport Jews.

While Hungary's Jews needed Wallenberg more than ever before, he had less power than ever before. Now he was hunted himself; his own life was in danger. But once again he not only refused to abandon the Jews but, seemingly immune to personal danger, he took even greater risks. If the new regime would grant exemption to some Jews, no matter how few, he knew he could exploit the exemption to save many more. So Wallenberg sought out an unlikely ally – the young wife of the Foreign Affairs Secretary of the Arrow Cross. She was pregnant with her first child, more compassionate in her own views than her husband, and anxious to protect her husband's position as an insurance policy for the post-war world. Wallenberg persuaded her to convince her husband to announce that protective passes would be honoured. Incredibly he succeeded – and with the protective pass now once again recognised, Wallenberg and his colleagues made daring rescue raids on Eichmann's death march.

Loading up vehicles with food, blankets and medical supplies, Wallenberg and his team showed immense courage. Pulling up alongside columns of women and children, they demanded that anyone in possession of a *Schutzpass* should return at once with them to Budapest. Flustering the guards with bluff and false authority, Wallenberg loaded up a fleet of vehicles with Jewish women and children. In a despatch to Stockholm in December 1944, Wallenberg reported in his typical matter-of-fact way: 'it was possible to rescue some two thousand persons from deportation through intervention for some reason or another'.

And using a similar display of authority to rescue men as well as women and children, he secured the return of 15,000 Jews on labour service. Eyewitness accounts of Wallenberg's rescue missions repeatedly refer to his presence – and to his calm authority. One survivor recalled how:

> He stood out there in the street, probably feeling the loneliest man in the world, trying to pretend there was something behind him. They could have shot him there and then in the street and nobody would have known about it. Instead, they relented . . .
> He must have had incredible charisma, some great personal authority, because there was absolutely nothing behind him, nothing to back him up.

Desperate to buy time, Wallenberg played yet another card. He met face to face with the head of the Arrow Cross and, bargaining with the food he had secretly purchased, he negotiated a delay in the transfer of Jews out of the protected International Ghetto into the unprotected Common Ghetto. Just meeting the Arrow Cross meant that he ran the risk of being assassinated or taken prisoner and tortured, but such was the demand for food supplies that he was able to sign a deal and record it in writing with diplomatic formality. Per Anger feared for Wallenberg's life and urged him to shelter in the diplomatic quarters across the Danube until the Russians arrived. In his memoirs Per Anger wrote:

> I urgently asked him to discontinue his activities and stay with us on the Buda side of the Danube. The Arrow Cross were obviously after him and he took great risks by continuing these rescue activities. However, Wallenberg refused to listen.
>
> While bombs were exploding all around us, we set out on a visit to SS headquarters, where, among things, I was to request some kind of shelter for the embassy members. We had to stop the car repeatedly because the road was blocked with dead people, horses, burnt-out trucks, and debris from bombed houses. But danger did not stop Wallenberg. I asked him whether he was afraid. 'It's frightening at times,' he said, 'but I have no choice. I have taken upon myself this mission and I would never be able to return to Stockholm without knowing that I've done everything that stands in a man's power to rescue as many Jews as possible.'

Eichmann's final defiant act of evil before the fall of Budapest was to plan the mass execution of all remaining Jews in the city. But the night before the day designated for the massacre Eichmann was forced to flee Budapest as the last escape route out closed up. As Budapest descended into complete chaos, Wallenberg learned that Eichmann's orders for a massacre were still to be carried out by the remaining Nazis. Tens of thousands of vulnerable Jews, with no one to protect them, were to be gunned down. Wallenberg was powerless. If he protested to the Nazi command he would be shot or taken prisoner. If he didn't act, there would be a massacre. So, just moments before the mass killing was to take place, Wallenberg took it upon himself to send one of his Arrow Cross informants to the overall commander of the SS troops with the message that if the massacre went ahead, Wallenberg would see to it that he would be held personally responsible and hanged as a war criminal. The threat worked. With no time to spare, a command was sent that the massacre must not take place. Thousands of Jewish lives were saved.

Two days later, the Soviets entered Budapest. They found 69,000 Jews alive in the Common Ghetto. In the International Ghetto there were another 25,000 survivors. A further 25,000 emerged from hiding places in gentile homes, convents, and monasteries. Wallenberg had succeeded in his mission 'to rescue as many Jews as possible'.

But what drove the aristocrat Wallenberg to risk his life on so many occasions to save another country's citizens when he could have continued to live a life of luxury and ease? And do we know what really made him go so far beyond the call of duty, beyond the terms of his assignment, beyond anything anyone could have ever expected of him?

We know that Wallenberg's courage was not fearlessness. He knew he was in danger from the beginning. After all, he had packed in his belongings a small revolver 'to give myself courage'. And Lars Berg recalled how Wallenberg was always the first to run and seek shelter during the air raids, but 'when it was a question of saving the lives of his protégés, he never hesitated a second. He acted with a challenging boldness and bravery, though his life then mostly hung by much thinner than a thread during the air raids.'

And none of the testimonies of Wallenberg either before his Budapest mission or during it suggest that he was a natural-born hero. Friends and colleagues who knew him before Budapest described him as a bit of a dreamer, not particularly dashing, and even weak. Colleagues who worked with him in Budapest speak of his courage as quiet and unexpected.

Yet his moral courage shines through so strongly that it lights up our lives. He had seen the fate that hundreds of Jews had already suffered. Their mutilated bodies littered the streets and bore the evidence of the torture that had been inflicted upon them before death ended their torment. Already one of Europe's most dangerous places, by late 1944 Budapest under the Arrow Cross was a nightmare of unbridled savagery, with no moderating forces to check the sadistic desires of marauding mobs. Shortly after the Arrow Cross coup, Wallenberg sent a report to Stockholm:

During the first night of the putsch, numerous arrests and many pogroms took place and between a hundred and two hundred people are believed to have been killed. Moreover, a number of Jewish houses were emptied of their occupants by members of the Arrow Cross. Some hundreds have disappeared.

In such chaos most people with the means to flee to safety would have done so. His own staff were amongst the victims of the Arrow Cross gangs. In a letter to his business partner Lauer he wrote:

> The work is unbelievably absorbing but the situation in town is extremely hazardous. The bandits are chasing people in the street, beating, killing and torturing them. Even among my own staff I have had 40 cases where people were abducted and tortured.

Consider the circumstances. Unlike the Jews on whose behalf he was working, Wallenberg's fate was not sealed. Safety was available to him without a personal price. He did not need to trample over other human beings to get out of Budapest. His country was neutral and there was no expectation of him, as there would be of a soldier, to continue to fight. He had a way out. He could have left. He had already exceeded his remit. He had already won praise for what he had accomplished. He risked no censure or shame for removing himself from an impossible situation. And he had so little power.

Yet still Wallenberg exposed himself to the risk of death, even going into hiding in order to save others from death. What compelled him to set concerns for his own safety to one side, especially when the violence to which he exposed himself was so horrific? Why did he choose to stay?

It could be claimed that Wallenberg now sought out danger. It is maybe tempting to caricature him as a daredevil, living off the adrenalin of his actions; dicing with danger. Did he imagine himself a hero and crave the plaudits? Was he motivated by a desire for greatness? An attempt to explain Wallenberg's motives as ultimately self-serving could pitch him as an arrogant, haughty, reckless young man. Wallenberg's half-sister recalls an evening in 1942, two years before his assignment to Budapest, when they saw a private screening of *Pimpernel Smith* – an updated version of *The Scarlet Pimpernel* – in which a university professor outwits the Nazis and rescues Jews. On the way home from the film, Wallenberg told his sister that he wanted to do something just like Pimpernel Smith.

There was, indeed, a sense that Wallenberg wanted to make his name, to prove himself. Per Anger said when he arrived in Budapest: 'To start with, he shocked some of us professional diplomats by his unconventional methods.' A month after his arrival at the city's legation, the War Refugee Board's Ivar Olsen wrote to his superior in Washington: 'I get the impression indirectly that the Swedish Foreign Office is somewhat uneasy about Wallenberg's activities in Budapest and perhaps feel that he has jumped in with too big a splash.'

Letters home to his family betray an almost adolescent satisfaction at having achieved a new status. In one of his first letters to his mother, Wallenberg reported:

> My birthday was great fun. By chance my secretary, Countess Nako, got to know about it, and two hours later on my desk there appeared a writing case, an almanac, an inkstand, flowers, and champagne. I have rented a very beautiful house from the eighteenth century on the castle hill, with beautiful furniture and with a lovely small garden and beautiful view. Now and then I have official dinners there.

Months later, when the situation had deteriorated, he wrote again to his mother:

> For the moment we are sitting at candlelight and trying to get the courier ready. The light is not working, and that is the only thing missing in this chaos. If you could only see me. There are a dozen people standing around me, everyone with urgent questions. I don't know to whom I shall give an answer or advice first.

And in December 1944, when Budapest was gripped by the Arrow Cross, he wrote:

> We hear the artillery thunder day and night from the approaching Russians. The diplomatic frenzy began after the arrival of Szalasi.

I alone do all the legation work relating to the government. So far I have met 10 times with the Foreign Minister, twice with the Deputy Minister, twice with the Interior Minister, once with the Security Minister, and once with the Finance Minister. I had become quite friendly with the wife of the Foreign Minister. Unfortunately, she now has left for Meran . . . Dear mother. I am sending you two recently taken photographs. I am in a circle with my aids and workers, at my desk. Because of all the work, time passes very quickly. And it often happens that I am invited to dinner, where there are steaks and Hungarian specialties.

Perhaps Wallenberg did feel proud to have been recognised for the first time to have an authority that matched his aristocratic background. And perhaps he did feel that his social standing and status made him less likely to be the victim of physical attacks and more able to withstand pressure from the Nazis.

Yet this same aristocratic confidence – arrogance even – was put to good use as Wallenberg deployed threats, bribery, bluff and all the panoply of his status to ride roughshod over conventional diplomatic channels.

So it is tempting to try to portray Wallenberg as a daredevil looking for the chance to prove his greatness, who never really believed he would fall victim to the danger around him but who nonetheless thrived on the adrenalin it produced. But this portrayal of Wallenberg as a reckless adventure-seeker is a travesty of the real Wallenberg and what he succeeded in accomplishing. To recapitulate his achievements: the innovation of the Swedish *Schutzpass*; the creation of the International Ghetto; the stockpiling and distribution of food, shelter, and medicine to desperate Jews; the repeated raids on Eichmann's death march and the resulting rescues; the volumes of diplomatic letters he wrote as a formal and public protest at the treatment of the Jews; the deals he brokered to halt deportations and buy time for the Jews; the repeated risks he accepted in order to save lives. At every stage Raoul Wallenberg could have withdrawn, satisfied he had done something. But at every stage he was prepared to do even more and put his own life at even greater risk.

Wallenberg was one-sixteenth Jewish, though he often exaggerated the extent of his Jewishness: his great-great-grandfather on his mother's side was Jewish, but had converted to Christianity and married a Christian. Professor Ingemar Hedenius, a leading Swedish academic, knew Wallenberg when they were both working in an army hospital in the early 1930s to fulfil national service. He said that Wallenberg was very proud of his Jewish ancestry and boasted: 'A person like me, who is both a Wallenberg and half-Jewish, can never be defeated.'

This weak line of Jewish blood became a focal point in the family in the mid-1930s when the Wallenbergs got a small taste of anti-Semitic prejudice themselves. One of Raoul Wallenberg's maternal cousins became engaged to a German nobleman, but before the couple could marry, the Nazis investigated her background for proof of her Aryan purity. During their investigations they discovered the Jewish link. The marriage was permitted, so the Wallenberg family was clearly considered by the Nazis to be 'purely Aryan', but Wallenberg's sister recalled that it sparked a lot of impassioned discussion in the family.

But what motivated Wallenberg was not being part-Jewish but his anger at Nazi persecution. Tibor Baranski, a fellow gentile who worked alongside Wallenberg in Budapest, recalled that Raoul once asked him if he was Jewish, implying that he must be Jewish to be so committed to trying to save Jews. Baranski in turn asked Wallenberg about his own dedication to saving Jews. 'He told me that he had a Jewish ancestor, but that had little influence on his motivation. He did say that he spent some time in Palestine and met refugees who fled from German persecution. At that time he made a commitment to help such victims if he ever got the opportunity.'

A great deal has been written about what motivated people in the resistance to help Jews escape persecution. Samuel Oliner has written of gentiles who rescued Jews. Many were, of course, led to act by face-to-face contact with a victim with whom they sympathised; so their main impulse was a sense of empathy. But some felt more than sympathy; they felt anger and rage at the injustice being done. They did not need to wait to meet a Jew before acting.

They began by looking for Jews to help. Many were not part of organised groups. Many simply showed as individuals a high degree of social responsibility. Finding it hard to walk by on the other side in the face of the injustices they saw, many were ready to sacrifice something for their principles.

Of course even the work of the Good Samaritan could be caricatured as an exercise in reputation-building and glory-seeking. But with Wallenberg what we find is the delivery in action of what he had said he would do. A letter to his grandfather, in which he rejected the life of a banker that had been expected of him, exposes an instinctive generosity which he felt was incompatible with his grandfather's choice of profession. 'To tell the truth I don't feel particularly bankish,' he wrote:

> a bank president should have something judgelike and calm about him and moreover be cool and cynical. Freund and Jacob are no doubt typical and I myself feel as different from them as I possibly could. I think it is more in my nature to work positively for something than to sit around telling people 'no'.

The letter, and particularly the last sentence, is revealing. In it Wallenberg constructs a polarity between a career spent defending something that has already been acquired from those clamouring to make a claim on it, and a career spent in pursuit of a cause.

And a fuller insight into Wallenberg's character and what he admired can be found in the introductory text he wrote to the recovery plan he commissioned for post-war Hungary. In it he praised the people who worked alongside him, and named the qualities he sought out in them. 'I have come to know my collaborators during the most testing times. I picked them for their qualities of compassion, honesty, and initiative.'

Compassion, honesty and initiative – he could have been describing the qualities that gave him, first, his strength of belief and, secondly, the strength of willpower to achieve what he did. Faced with danger, not all decent people have the courage of their convictions. And not all have the character that leads them to act. Yet there was nothing theoretical in the passes he issued, the food he distributed, or the rescue raids he carried out. Each success meant a liberty defended, an individual protected, a life saved.

Wallenberg did not need to volunteer but he did. As a citizen of Sweden he was neutral but he fought Nazism. As a diplomat his weapons were usually words, but he risked real physical danger. And he did all of this and more because his strength of conviction of teh rightness of his cause overwhelmed everything else – even fear of death itself.

Raoul Wallenberg disappeared for ever just as the war ended – perhaps entombed in the Soviet Gulag, as is most credibly believed. Early in 1945, he set out for Debrecan and the Soviet military headquarters, east of Budapest – possibly to present the occupying Soviets with his detailed plans for the financial support of the city's remaining Jews. He told friends that he would be back in about a week but neither he, nor his driver, ever returned.

Wallenberg's family dedicated the rest of their days to trying to find out what happened to him, grieving over the loss of their loved one. 'Raoul meant so much to us,' says his half-sister Nina. 'We adored him. He stood out.' In particular she laments the loss of his talents, which would very likely have been put to great humanitarian use in the aftermath of war: 'With all the gifts he had, and all his good heart and empathy, he could have been instrumental in the troubled times after the war. All his experiences from Budapest would have been well used. He was not a blue-eyed idealist, he was really a doer. His imprisonment was a disaster in every way.'

It may have been his aristocratic air of confidence that accounted for his disappearance into the Soviet Gulag. No verifiable accounts survive of Wallenberg's dealings with the Soviets. But biographers imagine the circumstances pieced together from rumour and precedent. In them Wallenberg presents himself to the advancing Russian command with customary confidence; makes sweeping claims for his position and his links with both the Swedish Crown and the American government; speaks with a determination and authority they might find arrogant; is found with implausible amounts of money on him; tells terrific tales of why he had come to Budapest and why he had now come to seek their cooperation in supporting his recovery plan for Hungary.

To the Red Army command he might have seemed the embodiment of the values they despised most: loaded with cash, arrogantly claiming the spoils of Hungary in the name of Sweden and America, ostentatiously operating under the cover of a humanitarian mission that to them must have seemed wholly unbelievable. Far more likely he appeared to the Russians as a likely spy, or racketeer, or indeed a diplomat who had strayed beyond his brief in order to line his own pockets in the murky opportunities created by war. All the confident charisma that had protected him against the fascists might have become his greatest weakness in the hands of the communists.

Wallenberg's family, friends, the thousands of people indebted to him, and the millions of people inspired by him still keep his memory alive. Nina is often invited by schools to tell his story:

> I think it so important to tell young people so that they can be inspired by his actions. In a way, I owe it to Raoul, so that he should not have done what he did in vain. At least it is important for young people to learn about empathy and courage and that one man can make a difference. That is what I always tell young people. That whatever your capacities, you have enormous possibilities within you.

And there is still hope that the secret of his fate will yet be relinquished, wherever it lies. A joint report by Sweden and the Soviet Union into his fate, published early in 2002, failed to discover exactly what befell him but conceded that the man who disappeared at the age of thirty-three is likely to have died in isolation in a Russian prison.

But the man who could not in the end save himself saved tens of thousands of his fellow human beings from extermination. 'He was definitely not the square-jawed hero type, more of an anti-hero,' Wallenberg's sister said of him. Yet as one of the Jews he saved wrote: 'He was more of a hero than the heroes of old.' And why? Because he 'did good for the sake of doing good. He never made any demands and he never expected any thanks.' By the sheer strength of his belief that the persecution of Jews was wrong and by the sheer strength of his willpower, the good that he did has lived on after him.

4

Martin Luther King

More than any other individual, politician or president, Martin Luther King was responsible for delivering civil rights to America's black community. In a career spanning only thirteen years he achieved something that statesmen, preachers, organisers, agitators, demonstrators and prisoners of conscience had not managed to do for over two centuries. He convinced the white majority to accept the principle of racial equality. He changed the laws and – although the dream is still not fully realised – the life of an America where, by 2008, an African-American could be a prime contender for the presidency. And the momentum of his movement has overflowed the banks of race and flowed on to equal rights for women and an end to discrimination against gays.

His transformative greatness was to achieve all this with a philosophy and a language designed to persuade and unify his listeners both black and white: the philosophy was non-violence, and the language was religion.

Martin Luther King was vilified. His phones were tapped, and he was physically attacked and imprisoned. The odds against him seemed to mount steadily as his life proceeded; the adversities he had to overcome did not diminish with time, but became successively harder to bear.

The question we must ask is what gave Dr King the strength of character to change almost overnight from a young, academically minded pastor into the national leader of America's civil rights revolution?

And what gave him the strength of will, in the face of all opposition to his philosophy of non-violence, to stay faithful to that ideal, even in the face of isolation? It was said that on all sides, even his own, there were those who wanted to fight King, abuse King, sideline King, or succeed or supplant King; but – denigrated, punched, dismissed as yesterday's man by younger firebrands – he continued to reject violence even as a last resort. His commitment was total and enduring. As he himself said: 'If a man hasn't discovered something he will die for, he isn't fit to live.'

When the young Martin Luther King finished his theological studies in 1955 and then took up the relatively comfortable pastoral charge of Montgomery, Alabama, he did so against the advice of his father. A towering and sometimes overbearing presence in his son's life, the Rev. Martin Luther King Sr wanted his namesake to assist him at Ebenezer Baptist Church in Atlanta. But the son wished to break free, to study, to develop and perhaps leave behind the dogmatic reputation and expectations of his father, a distinguished preacher. But, perhaps in spite of himself and his background, he had already inherited something else that was enduring. Like his father and grandfather, both Baptist ministers, he was from an early age a member of the local chapter of the National Association for the Advancement of Colored People (NAACP). The whole King family boycotted public institutions that practised segregation. The young Martin felt the sting and shame of segregation as he reached school age, when the paths of white and black children abruptly parted. He recalled his mother telling him why he was suddenly barred from playing with his close boyhood friend:

I will never forget what a great shock this was to me . . . Here for the first time I was made aware of the existence of a race problem . . . My mother confronted the age-old problem of the Negro parent in America: how to explain discrimination and segregation to a small child. She taught me that I should feel a sense of 'somebodiness' but that on the other hand I had to go out

and face a system that stared me in the face every day saying you
are 'less than', you are 'not equal to' . . . Then she said the words
that almost every Negro hears before he can yet understand the
injustice that makes them necessary: 'You are as good as anyone.'

That was not a view widely valued in Atlanta before the Second
World War. At the 1939 gala premiere of *Gone with the Wind*,
attended by Confederate veterans of the civil war, civic dignitaries
and many of the stars, a 'negro boys choir' from the Ebenezer
Baptist Church participated, but only within limits. The boys,
including the seven-year-old Martin Luther King, came and sang,
but they were not invited to stay and join in the wider celebrations:
they were for whites only.

Yet despite formative experiences, King's leadership in the civil
rights movement was by no means inevitable. As historian Peter
Ling pointed out in an essay on King's leadership: 'The African
American church has been central to both accommodation and
resistance, and King would have joined the ranks of the majority if
he had been a more circumspect preacher.'

As he started his ministry, King was sheltered to an extent by his
own prestigious education and good connections, while his well-
paid position as pastor of the affluent Dexter Avenue Baptist
Church in Montgomery could have permitted him to live through
troubled times in relatively untroubled comfort.

Just as some successful blacks, after attaining a degree of security
or affluence, dissociated themselves from the slums and held back
from the civil rights agitators, King, too, could have enjoyed the
benefits that intellect, success and opportunity had brought him.
He had grown up against the backdrop of discrimination, but in an
established family. He had sought to prove himself educationally in
a white world, and had prevailed. In a sense, he had already fought
his fight. He could easily have left others in his community to fight
battles for individual advancement on their own. He was not
compelled to turn and face the storm of injustice. He could have
chosen safety first. Instead he chose to take on a great challenge,
enlarged it by his leadership, and redirected history itself.

Late in 1955, a seamstress named Rosa Parks refused to give up her seat on a Montgomery bus to a white passenger, and her arrest sparked a city-wide bus boycott by the African-American community. At the age of only twenty-six, and as a new pastor in the town, King was not the obvious choice to chair the movement. After only a year in Montgomery, he was not well known. His qualifications were mostly academic. He had no great record as a civil rights activist in school, no special history of leading on civil rights at college and university, and, though a member of the NAACP and the Alabama Council on Human Relations, he had just refused the presidency of his local NAACP chapter to focus on his doctoral thesis and parish duties. He had already decided not to take on any more community responsibilities.

So he did not step forward; events pushed him forward. And while King did accept the leadership of the Montgomery Bus Boycott, he confessed in his autobiography that 'the action had caught me unawares. It had happened so quickly that I did not even have time to think it through. It is probable that if I had, I would have declined the nomination.'

Yet within an hour of his appointment he had to reassure and rally a several-thousand-strong audience that was defying age-old barriers and taboos. From the moment when he memorably told that crowd, 'There comes a time when people get tired of being trampled over by the iron feet of oppression,' the word began to go out, across the city, the south, and then the nation, that here was a great and inspiring leader. That speech revealed him as more than the tribune of one segment of society, and instead as a prophet and peaceful protagonist for America's best ideals.

He expressed a resolve rooted first of all in a deep comprehension and soaring capacity to express the anger of the black community; yet – more than that, and perhaps uniquely – he also showed what was needed to bring white America to see and share that anger, and the urgent need for justice.

King knew the routine evils of racism. He could recall the first time a bus driver had forced him to give up his seat for whites, and how in his presence his father, a senior clergyman, had been humiliated by a white policeman who addressed him as 'boy'. As he wrote later: 'From that moment on I was determined to hate every white person. As I grew older and older this feeling continued to grow . . . some of the experiences that I encountered made it very difficult for me to believe in the essential goodness of man.'

The economic injustice, the countless denials of human dignity, the lynchings and the cross-burnings were all of a piece. But it was what happened on a bus, the only transport most blacks could afford, that set in motion the march for sweeping change. And it was the memories of one young minister, genuinely appalled by the gratuitous humiliation heaped upon blacks by white bus drivers and conductors, that made this the thread that would unravel the seamless garment of segregation. In his autobiography, King described what a visitor coming to Montgomery before the bus boycott would have heard: bus operators referring to passengers as 'niggers', 'black apes' and 'black cows'. He would have noticed black passengers getting on at the front door, paying their fares, and then being forced to get off and go to the back of the bus to board. He would witness how, at times, before the black passenger could get to the back door, the bus drove off with his fare already in the box.

But even more, that visitor would have noticed black passengers standing up even beside seats that were empty. It did not matter whether a white person got on or not; if the bus filled up with black passengers they were prohibited from sitting in the first four rows of seats because these were reserved for whites only. The apartheid went beyond even this boundary: if the section reserved for whites was full and other whites boarded the bus, black passengers sitting in the unreserved section were told to give up their seats.

The boycott of Montgomery's buses would run for over a year, until November 1956, when the Supreme Court upheld the federal district court's ruling that Alabama's racial segregation rules were unconstitutional and the Montgomery Bus Company yielded to pressure and allowed the complete integration of black and white passengers. Along the long road of that year, more and more attention had focused on King, and the choices he faced became harder by the day. One journalist who met him at the peak of the boycott wrote: 'Why does God lay such a burden on one so young, so inexperienced, so good? King can be a Negro Gandhi or he can be made into an unfortunate demagogue destined to swing from a lynch mob's tree.'

As King himself admitted, he suffered and struggled greatly as he and his family were subjected to intimidation and violence, and even death threats, including the firebombing of their home. That sense of struggle, of moral crisis, hit King early on during the boycott, late one night in January of 1956. He was sitting alone at his kitchen table, after midnight, having just received another sinister phone call warning him to get out of town or he or his family would be killed. Suddenly he found that his courage had deserted him.

'So often our experience of courage must be cobbled together by negative inference from those miserable moments in which we wished we had it and found it wanting,' writes William Miller in *The Mystery of Courage*. So it now threatened to be with Martin Luther King, who would remember that night of crisis, of courage lost, many times later in his life. He would tell church congregations about the terror that possessed him, and would write about the panicked conversation with God he had in prayer – and his own words to justify his temptation to quit and retreat into the safety of inaction.

> With my cup of coffee sitting untouched before me, I tried to think of a way to move out of the picture without appearing a coward. I sat there and thought about a beautiful little daughter who had just been born. I'd come in night after night and see that little gentle smile. I started thinking about a dedicated and loyal wife, who was over there asleep. And she could be taken from me, or I could be taken from her. And I got to the point that I couldn't take it any longer. I was weak . . . The words I spoke to God that midnight are still vivid in my memory: 'Lord, I must confess that I'm weak now, I'm faltering. I'm losing my courage. Now, I am afraid.'

So here was King close to losing his courage, a man in crisis, a moral coward or at least a bystander, perhaps, in the making. Thomas Carlyle wrote:

They err greatly who imagine that man's courage was ferocity, mere coarse disobedient obstinacy and savagery, as many do. Far from that. There may be an absence of fear which arises from the absence of thought or affection, from the presence of hatred and stupid fury. We do not value the courage of the tiger highly!

If evidence is needed that courage is not the absence of fear but the mastery of it, then King's temptation that fateful night provides the proof. So unguarded, so exposed, his cause for alarm so terrifyingly real that he felt he had to consider not only his own safety but that of his family. Cast down by fear and loneliness, he had to clarify for himself how, for a seat on a city bus, it was worth putting at risk the fragile innocence of his sleeping daughter and her young mother.

Alone with his agonising thoughts that night, King recalled how, even as he trembled, he summoned a courage that would never again abandon him. In his autobiography he wrote of 'the quiet assurance of an inner voice saying, ' "Martin Luther, stand up for righteousness. Stand up for justice. Stand up for truth. . . ." At that moment I experienced the presence of the Divine as I had never experienced Him before. Almost at once my fears began to go.'

As King's fears receded, his courage carried him on and his vision widened. He found the confidence to take his case to white Americans, too, and to convince them that, in the truest sense, it was also their cause. It would not be quick and easy; indeed, it was often dispiriting. 'Disappointment is part of the moral life,' he admitted. 'This is my grief and I must just bear it.'

He did, and in the pain and goodness of his now unflagging purpose he drew on deepened, powerful sources of wisdom. King was widely read and highly educated, with his theology doctorate still in progress at the time of the bus boycott, and he was more academically oriented than most of his peers in comparable churches in the South. Historians have documented three philosophical influences that shaped him as the thinker and social activist he eventually became.

From the theologian Walter Rauschenbusch, whose work he studied closely, King learned that the Church should be the servant of society, and that central to its mission was the creation of a just

society. From Reinhold Niebuhr he learned the theological implications of man's inhumanity to man and the strength of evil. But
if he had stopped at Rauschenbusch and Niebuhr he might have
doubted whether, in an evil world, we could ever succeed in
creating a good society.

What squared the circle for King was the thinking of Paul
Tillich, whose theology was the subject of his doctoral dissertation.
King was profoundly influenced by Tillich's description of unconditional love. So while he accepted man's inhumanity to man –
indeed the widespread Southern experience of racial prejudice
made clear to him the potential of evil in human nature – he
came to believe strongly in the redemptive power of a Christian
love not given in return, not 'deserved' in any conventional sense,
but truly and fully given even in the face of hate.

Despite the evils perpetrated by individuals of principalities and
powers, King insisted, the Church could still build a good society.
Unconditional love – what the ancient Greeks called *agape* – could
overcome the sinfulness of humanity, and it was this idea of
unconditional love that led him inexorably to non-violent action
as the way forward.

In his essay 'Pilgrimage to Non-violence', King shared his personal intellectual journey from his years at the Crozer Seminary in
Pennsylvania and at Boston University. He cited another great
preacher, Harry Emerson Fosdick: 'A religion that ends with the
individual ends. Instead religion must offer a sense of social responsibility that it should never lose.' And it was in Fosdick, who
denounced segregation, not in Rauschenbusch, who had failed to
do so, that King found the inspiration to oppose all racial injustice.

While such intellectual influences gave him the strength of belief
in equality through non-violence, I am in no doubt that his background did as much to make him what he became. It also gave him
his strength of will. Quite simply, while he declined to walk literally
in his father's footsteps and stand in his pulpit, King was his father's
son. His conscience and willpower were formed, in part, by regular
exposure to – and contemplation of – his father's sermons. His
repeated calls for justice came as much from what he heard in his
early years at Ebenezer Church as from his theological study. And

what he heard from his father at Ebenezer had been handed down from a long line of black oral tradition, and from folk preachers who were not only shaping influences on King, but – as we now know – his unacknowledged tutors and authorities. His greatest speeches – with their structure, eloquence and sheer power to move millions – stand firmly within that tradition of the great black preachers; both what he said and how he said it owes much to them.

In this confluence of influences, King was right to acknowledge the debt he owed to Rauschenbusch, but the understanding of the role of the Church as a servant of society was also indelibly the call of Fosdick and other preachers, black and white, in a line that led directly to Martin Luther King Sr. The son was right also to acknowledge Niebuhr's writings on 'the glaring reality of collective evil', but again he had already learned from his father the pervasiveness of sin.

Tillich gave intellectual force to the idea of unconditional love. But for King, the power of *agape* was learned even before it was intellectualised from the familiar traditions of the black Church, and from the closeness of his own family. His insistence in his doctoral thesis that God is personal, and that the closeness of God validates the meaning of life, was nothing more than a further affirmation of the truth he had listened to his father preach every Sunday.

From his father and the ministers who came before, King learned what no theological textbook could ever have taught: that personal growth comes through struggle, progress through sacrifice, and change through pressure from below – and that the black preacher's Bible both depicts and sanctions struggle. Of course, King as a theologian wanted to show that the great thinkers of Protestantism demanded an end to segregation, and that the pursuit of civil rights was the noblest expression of a rigorous mind; but while King wrote eloquently about his pilgrimage of mind, he owed as much or more to Martin Luther King Sr and generations before whose sermons and service had succoured and uplifted the oppressed. They were the wellsprings of his ideas and leadership. Always his father stood before him like a mountain. Yet he went on to face and overcome challenges his father could never have dreamed of.

It was his father's influence that made him stand strong in the face of intimidation and violence, even when he knew that at a crucial moment his courage had nearly failed him. From his father, King believed in the courage to love, and that 'perfect love casteth out fear'. This sustained him amid constant peril and through acute physical dangers. He was grimly realistic about the violent response to his 1966 Chicago march and the routine risks he ran every day – for example in Selma, Alabama, in 1965, when he was punched and kicked by a member of the arch-segregationist States Rights Party after becoming the first black ever to register at a whites-only hotel built using slave labour a century before. After one such incident he remarked, 'If they couldn't protect Kennedy how could they protect me?' He rejected armed security ('I'd feel like a bird in a cage') and in later life told an audience: 'Every now and then I felt discouraged living every day under the threat of death.' In 1967 he asked the Southern Christian Leadership Conference to nominate the Rev. Ralph Abernathy because, as he said, it was time to face up to 'certain realistic actualities'. As he told his friends, you have 'to take risks for what you believe to be right'.

Yet, in the ever-present shadow of violence, with his strength of belief and willpower to withstand the threats of death came the miracle of Martin Luther King's life and leadership. He sought ceaselessly to persuade the black community of the moral and practical value of non-violence, and at the same time worked to persuade the white community of the justice of the civil rights cause.

Persuading his own people was difficult. In urging them to practise non-violence he was asking much of them: he asked them not just to refrain from violence when the injustices inflicted on them seemed to many to merit violence, but also to endure violence themselves and not become violent in response.

In his Nobel Peace Prize speech he explained that non-violence did not mean passivity or resignation. His movement, he said, was 'committed to unrelenting struggle', but he argued that 'civilisation and violence are antithetical concepts':

[N]on-violence is not sterile passivity but a powerful moral force which makes for social transformation . . . If this is to be achieved, man must evolve for all human conflict a method which rejects revenge aggression and retaliation. The foundation of such a method is love . . . I believe that unarmed truth and unconditional love will have the final word.

Publicly, J. Edgar Hoover of the FBI accused King of leading people to violence, but in private he was honest enough to admit that, but for his support of non-violence, King would have been 'a very real contender for the rise of a messiah'. King's supposed obedience to white 'liberal' doctrines (non-violence), Hoover suggested, prevented him from capturing and mobilising the full force of black nationalism.

King would not even support violence as a last resort: 'I don't apologise for non-violence. I have no apology to make,' he said. His defence was to quote the German philosopher Hannah Arendt: 'Violence can destroy power but is utterly incapable of creating it. Violence was the negation of consent . . . the prejudice is the belief that violence by armies . . . is necessary evil towards greater good.'

This was King's guiding star, as he said in 1958:

We had to make it clear that non-violent resistance is not a method of cowardice. It does resist. It is not a method of stagnant passivity and deadening complacency. The non-violent resister is just as opposed to the evil that he is standing against as the violent resister but he resists without violence.

This method is non-aggressive physically but strongly aggressive spiritually . . . The non-violent resister does not seek to humiliate or defeat the opponent but to win his friendship and understanding . . . the aftermath of non-violence is reconciliation . . . the non-violent resister seeks to attack the evil system rather than individuals who happen to be caught in the system, it not only avoids external violence but . . . also internal violence of spirit and so at the centre of our movement stood the philosophy of love. The attitude that the only way to ultimately change humanity and make for the society that we all long for is to keep love at the center of our lives.

Agape was 'overflowing love which seeks nothing in return'. It was 'the love of God working in the minds of men'. It meant that 'you must go on with wise restraint and calm reasonableness but you must keep moving'.

Even as racial tensions mounted in the mid-1960s and militants in his own community derided and isolated him, King continued to preach love against violence. He acknowledged that he and his commitment to non-violence faced growing criticism, particularly from more extreme black groups. He accepted the scorn and the ridicule, but never yielded to it. He responded that 'occasionally in life one develops a conviction so precious and meaningful that he will stand on it till the end . . . This,' he explained, 'is what I have found in non-violence.'

As for King's father and grandfather, non-violent protest was inherent in the Christian gospel, but the genius of King in the struggle against racism was to use his advocacy of non-violence to win white support and to win over the white majority to the cause of civil rights. For him, ends and means were inseparable. To reject non-violence as a means, he said, would be to abandon any hope of achieving the ends he was fighting for. Black violence would provide a further excuse for doing nothing; in other words, only non-violent action would persuade the white community to agree to civil rights.

'Remain committed to non-violence,' he told the people of Montgomery, Alabama. 'Our aim must never be to defeat or humiliate the white man but to win his friendship and understanding. We must come to see that the end we seek is a society at peace with itself . . . If we will go with the faith that non-violence and its power can transform dark yesterdays into bright tomorrows we will be able to change all of these conditions.' King stood for what he called 'organised aggressive and positive goodwill' to 'redeem the soul of America from the triple evils of racism, war and poverty'.

Under constant and almost intolerable pressure from a Black Power movement that disdained King's forbearance, his denunciation of violence and his faith that 'black and white together, we shall overcome', King rejected both the appeal to separatism and the justifications for striking back: civil disobedience yes, civil disorder no. He went even further: 'It is no longer a choice between violence and non-violence. In this world it is non-violence or non-existence. All the sound and fury seems but the posturing of cowards whose bold talk produces no action and signifies nothing.'

Non-violence was not only morally right, he argued, but the truest practical wisdom. In an article for *Ebony* magazine he asserted: 'Our record of achievement through non-violent action is already remarkable. The non-violent strategy has been to dramatise the evils of our society in such a way that pressure is brought to bear against those evils by the forces of good will in the community and change is produced.'

So this was his strategy: to win white support for black rights by disarming his enemy, getting rid of his enemy by getting rid of enmity. Quoting Lincoln, he said, 'Do I not destroy my enemies when I make them my friends?'

It was, he recognised, a perilous balancing act. 'Somewhere there has to be a synthesis,' he said. 'I have to be militant enough to satisfy the militant, yet I have to keep enough discipline in the movement to satisfy white supporters and moderate voters.' He knew the scale of the challenge he faced: 'You just can't communicate with the ghetto dweller and at the same time not frighten any whites to death. There must be somebody to communicate to two worlds.'

Gandhi, another great influence on King and whose life he studied in India, wrote:

One may well ask what is the non-violent resister's justification for this ordeal to which he invites men, for this mass political application of the ancient doctrine of turning the other cheek . . . by suffering the non-violent resister realises his tremendous educational and transforming possibilities.

'Suffering,' Gandhi continued,

is infinitely more powerful than the law of the jungle for converting the opponent and opening his ears which are otherwise shut to the voice of reason . . . To our most bitter opponents we say we shall match your capacity to inflict suffering by our capacity to endure suffering. We shall meet your physical force with soul force. Do to us what you will and we shall continue to love you . . . but be assured that we will wear you down by our capacity to suffer.

So King had to stand up to a Black Power argument which he believed would only serve to heighten tensions between the races and entrench injustice. Black supremacy, he argued, 'would be as evil as white supremacy':

In the final analysis the weakness of Black Power is its failure to see that the black man needs the white man and the white man needs the black man. However much we may try to romanticise the slogan, there is no separate black path to power and fulfil-ment that does not intersect white paths, and there is no separate white path to power and fulfilment, short of social disaster, that does not share that power with black aspirations for freedom and human dignity. We are bound together in a single garment of destiny.

Blacks sought power not to dominate but to participate, King insisted. For King, the real drama of the civil rights movement did not turn on who would be cast as the oppressor and who the oppressed. He was determined to write a new narrative of the American dream in which domination and subjugation had no part at all to play.

The last century, like all others before it, offers up tragic examples across the world of movements for and leaders of noble causes that were undermined and eventually destroyed by the ignoble means through which they set about achieving them. King's motives were honourable, but so too, throughout his strug-gle, were his means. Through his philosophy of non-violence he claimed and held the moral high ground for the civil rights movement, imbuing his followers with the fervour of those certain that their cause is just and their actions beyond reproach. 'We have known the agony of the underdog,' he said. 'We have learned from our have-not status that it profits a nation little to gain the whole world of means and lose the ends, its own soul.'

King understood that the power of non-violence lies in the contrast it presents between the righteousness and a glaring wrong. The innocence and vulnerability of unarmed people, including many children, on a peaceful march confronting angry mobs with faces contorted with hatred, shouting obscenities and throwing stones, touched and moved the conscience of Americans. How could this be happening in their land? Even more shocking were the images of young protesters being attacked and bitten by police dogs and knocked to the ground by the force of police water-hoses. Barbara Holmes described the violent reactions to the civil rights marchers as 'a stunning political drama' which King used 'like an early morning wake-up call' to the nation. And it worked so well in the 1960s because it was televised. Witnessing this violence made it intolerable and brought down with it the constant spiritual violence of legal segregation.

Far from passivity, non-violence demanded mass action and the great courage of participants to suffer the violence their protests would provoke. Thousands of protestors were sent to jail during each campaign. Hundreds were wounded. And inevitably, racist thugs and 'vigilantes' succeeded in murdering a few, safe in the knowledge that their crimes could go unpunished. It was a risky and tortuous path, but King passionately argued that the way of non-violence would not only prove effective in the end, but that it was the only course of action that would.

'The way of acquiescence leads to moral and spiritual suicide,' King explained. 'The way of violence leads to bitterness in the survivors and brutality in the destroyers. But the way of non-violence leads to redemption and the creation of the beloved community.'

So the passion of his principled commitment to non-violence was matched by his strategic judgement that it was also the way to prevail. To those who questioned the efficacy of non-violence, King pointed out that the 'system' they were fighting would always have more might at its disposal than the protestors. Impoverished blacks could never win an outright battle where the test was brute force.

'Now the plain, inexorable fact is that any attempt of the American Negro to overthrow his oppressor with violence will not work,' he insisted. 'We do not need President Johnson to tell us this by reminding Negro rioters that they are outnumbered ten to one.'

Skirmishes, guerrilla warfare, rioting and the looting of businesses – the rioting that broke out in ghettoes and burned in America's great cities from 1964 – would serve only to provide justification for the 'system' to retaliate. The fragile coalition built with moderate whites would, he said, be destroyed if they saw black people smashing the shops they shopped in or bombing police stations they depended upon to protect them. Violence would divide black from white more exactingly than segregation, and give credibility to the white supremacists' claim that it was necessary to keep the black population 'in their place' in order to preserve civilisation.

> The problem with hatred and violence is that they intensify the fears of the white majority, and leave them less ashamed of their prejudices towards Negroes. In the guilt and confusion confronting our society, violence only adds to the chaos. It deepens the brutality of the oppressor and increases the bitterness of the oppressed. Violence is the antithesis of creativity and wholeness. It destroys community and makes brotherhood impossible.

Always King was caught between two polarised and potentially destructive forces: those of black extremism and its antithesis, the white backlash it could so easily evoke. So he needed a strategy which would both isolate the former and curb the latter; he had to be radical enough to keep the black community together – or at least dominated by moderates – and moderate enough to enlist the majority of whites, marginalising and defeating the advocates of racism.

For a time, he succeeded. The great Selma march to Montgomery, in late March 1965, when 25,000 turned out to walk in peace and solidarity, was the high-water mark. Earlier that month, marchers protesting against the denial of voting rights had twice attempted to walk the same route but had been brutally attacked by heavily armed state troopers. 'Bloody Sunday' was televised across America, but King did not yield. The third march came, with whites and blacks from all over America joining together and walking some fifty miles from Selma to the State Capitol in Montgomery. The event raised the consciousness of the whole nation. As one of the organisers described it, 'forces from all faiths and all classes, from businessmen to pacifist radicals,' joined in the pilgrimage to the Deep South. 'Non-violent democratic action was proven by Selma to have even greater power than anyone had fully realised,' he said. 'It was transforming the relationship between government and the governed.' Lyndon Johnson stood before Congress and called for a sweeping Voting Rights act: an American president adopted the slogan of the civil rights movement as his own – and the nation's – saying, 'We shall overcome.'

But while the intellectual defence for non-violence was found in Tillich's idea of love – hate assuaged by unconditional love – the politics became ever more difficult. King might succeed in the short term, and his belief would triumph in the long run. But in 1966, '67 and '68, King was losing ground to the militants. He confessed at that time to having his own 'haunting doubts', and understood the appeal of violence to the most alienated and disadvantaged. But he would not be moved. 'Rioting,' he said 'just doesn't pay off.' This was his pragmatic defence of non-violence.

Now, he decided, blacks and whites together would march on Washington in the summer of 1968, a reprise of the great march of 1963. But this time it would be a Poor People's March for economic justice, and they would stay until progress was made. They would go not to change the Constitution but to uphold it and redeem its promises. If America and its leaders believed in the Constitution then they had to believe in equality and fairness. The Constitution was a promissory note that now had to be honoured.

But King, who would be struck down before the march, knew that his hold on the movement was steadily weakening. Non-violence was labelled by Black Power's Stokely Carmichael as weakness, and King himself acknowledged he was being laughed at for maintaining his faith in its power. But he was willing to risk his position, his place, everything for the sake of a principle that was also, he was certain, the only path to an America that was 'free at last'. He pleaded: 'If I can leave you with any messages,' he said, 'don't lose hope. It may look like we can't get out of this thing. Now it may appear that non-violence has failed and the nation will not respond to it, but don't give it up yet. Wait until the morning.' And from his pulpit came a reaffirmation of the necessity of faith: 'We must still believe that we are going to deal with this problem by enlisting consciences.'

In a wider political context he was vulnerable. King angered the political establishment – and especially President Johnson – by deciding that he had to speak out against America's escalating involvement in Vietnam. He knew the price he would pay: retribution in the form of lessened access for himself and diminished support for equal rights. He was accused of 'hurting' the movement, but he said, quoting a colleague, 'There comes a time when silence is betrayal.' So he reproached 'a nation that brutalises unjustifiably millions of girls and boys, men and women, in Vietnam', and later concluded that if 'America's soul becomes really poisoned, part of the autopsy must read Vietnam.' Eventually, with black soldiers being killed at twice the rate of whites, he admitted that Vietnam had 'broken and eviscerated the movement'.

King was, in historian David Garrow's phrase, 'a reluctant leader', plagued not only by fear and physical danger, but also by profound doubts as to whether his own personal morality was such that he 'deserved' to lead. Only the strength of his belief in his cause explains why, despite the doubts and dangers, he came to appreciate – again, in Garrow's words – that 'his leadership role was not just a matter of accident or chance, but was first and foremost an opportunity for service. It was not one King would have sought, but it was an opportunity he could not forsake.' So, when asked whether he was afraid, King responded:

No, I'm not. My attitude is that this is a great cause. This is a great issue that we are confronted with and the consequences for my personal life are not particularly important. It is the triumph for the cause that I am concerned about, and I have always felt that ultimately along the way of life an individual must stand up and be counted and be willing to face the consequences, whatever they are. If he is filled with fear, he cannot do it. And my great prayer is always that God will save me from the paralysis of crippling fear, because I think when a person lives with the fear of the consequences for his personal life, he can never do anything in terms of lifting the whole community and solving many of the social problems that we confront.

King believed that, while it could succeed without violence, his campaign could not succeed without sacrifice. Indeed, as time passed, he came to realise the scale of the price that might have to be paid. As Peter Ling wrote: 'In many of his sermons in small black churches across the South, he preached a gospel of sacrifice by declaring that any man who has found nothing for which he is prepared to die has not yet found a reason to live . . .'

But while King believed in the power of unconditional love, his 'Letter from Birmingham Jail' – penned in response to an open letter by eight white Alabama clergymen – made clear that this was never a call for patience or aquiescence:

We know through painful experience that freedom is never voluntarily given by the oppressor; it must be demanded by the oppressed. Frankly, I have yet to engage in a direct-action campaign that was 'well-timed' in the view of those who have not suffered unduly from the disease of segregation. For years now I have heard the word 'wait!' It rings in the ears of every Negro with piercing familiarity. This 'wait' has almost always meant 'never' . . .

Perhaps it is easy for those who have never felt the stinging darts of segregation to say, 'wait'. But when you have seen vicious mobs lynch your mothers and fathers at will and drown your sisters and brothers at whim; when you have seen hate-filled policemen curse, kick and even kill your black brothers and sisters; when you see the vast majority of your twenty million Negro brothers smothering in an airtight cage of poverty in the midst of an affluent society; when you suddenly find your tongue

twisted and your speech stammering as you seek to explain to
your six-year-old daughter why she can't go to the public
amusement park that has just been advertised on television,
and see tears well up in her eyes when she is told that Fun Town
is closed to coloured children, and see the ominous clouds of
inferiority beginning to form in her little mental sky, and see her
beginning to distort her personality by developing an uncon-
sciousness bitterness towards white people.

When you have to concoct an answer for a five-year-old son
who is asking, 'Daddy, why do white people treat coloured
people so mean?'; when you take a cross-country drive and find
it necessary to sleep night after night in the uncomfortable
corners of your automobile because no motel will accept you;
when you are humiliated day in and day out by nagging signs
reading 'white' and 'coloured'; when your first name becomes
'nigger' and your middle name becomes 'boy' (however old you
are) and your last name becomes 'John' and your wife and
mother are never given the respected title Mrs; when you are
harried by day and haunted by night by the fact that you are a
Negro, living constantly at tiptoe stance, never quite knowing
what to expect next, and are plagued with inner fears and outer
resentments; when you are forever fighting a degenerating sense
of 'nobodiness' – then you will understand why we find it difficult
to wait.

There comes a time when the cup of endurance runs over, and
men are no longer willing to be plunged into the abyss of
despair . . .

Martin Luther King chose to act rather than to stand aloof, and
he acted out of a sense of moral obligation that, in his view, all
people shared. Action and protest were not just necessities of self-
preservation for those directly under threat; those who were
personally unaffected by injustice had an equal responsibility to
fight injustice in their midst. And his power, his peaceful power,
was such that he convinced America that, in the case of civil rights,
it could not in conscience continue to refuse the legitimate claims of
black citizens.

There would, he knew, be setbacks along the way to 'a promised land', which he sensed that he himself might never reach. The only answer was to strive on and never to yield, even if he had to accept the inevitability of a period of 'conflict'. In the 'Letter from Birmingham Jail', King argued forcefully that every civilising and liberating achievement of humanity has been made through the tireless commitment of countless people throughout history, often at great personal cost:

> We are the beneficiaries of these earlier battles, as well as the guarantors that the progress they won will be passed to next generation. Because we are all both inheritors and guarantors, we all have an inescapable responsibility to preserve what is good in our society and to change what is wrong.
>
> More and more I feel that the people of ill will have used time much more effectively than have the people of good will. We will have to repent in this generation not merely for the hateful words and actions of the bad people, but for the appalling silence of the good people. We must see that human progress never rolls in on wheels of inevitability. It comes through the tireless efforts of men willing to be the co-workers with God, and without this hard work, time itself becomes an ally of the forces of social stagnation. We must use time creatively in the knowledge that the time is always ripe to do right. Now is the time to make real the promise of democracy, and transform our pending national elegy into a creative psalm of brotherhood. Now is the time to lift our national policy from the quicksand of racial injustice to the solid rock of human dignity.

And, he continued:

> I cannot agree with the white moderate, who is more devoted to 'order' than to justice, who prefers a negative peace which is the absence of tension to a positive peace which is the presence of justice . . . I had hoped that the white moderate would under-stand that law and order exist for the purpose of establishing justice, and that when they fail in this purpose they become the

dangerously structured dams that block the flow of social progress . . .

We cannot in all good conscience obey your unjust laws and abide by the unjust system, because non-cooperation with evil is as much a moral obligation as is cooperation with good.

The mass discipline and courage needed to sustain non-violence nationwide were waning in the years preceding King's death. The civil rights movement had succeeded in awakening a passion for equality, and in the new consciousness of race relations many grew increasingly frustrated, disappointed, and angry that too little had changed. Laws might have been written and passed, but life was too much the same. Unemployment among black people was twice as high as among whites, and blacks who did work earned half the income of whites. Seventy-five per cent of all menial jobs in America were filled by blacks, and half the black population lived in substandard housing.

King was dismayed by the increasing appeal of violence and the rising popularity of figures like Malcolm X. Middle America had become alarmed at Black Power. The louder and more determined the shouts, the more difficult it was for King to lead a peaceful revolution of racial and economic equality. The cause was weakened in the country, and King was weaker in his own community. Articles began to appear in which he was referred to as 'Martin Loser King', and editorials asked whether the death knell for the civil rights movement and non-violence had been sounded.

Many people within the movement drifted away from King. He disturbed the powerful in Washington with his broad-ranging 'Poor People's Campaign', which aimed to address issues of poverty amongst all America's poor – black and white. But he stood his ground. And when he spoke in Memphis in early April 1968, the night before he died, he said once again: 'It is no longer a choice between violence and non-violence in this world; it is between non-violence and non-existence.'

A bus boycott in a single city started King on his path. Now, after more than a decade of struggle, King knew that the liberty of blacks would require a great deal more than admission to local beaches and a seat at a lunch counter. It would require a commitment from the whole nation to invest in a programme of action to eliminate the causes of entrenched poverty. Full civil rights demanded investment in decent housing and properly equipped schools, a higher programme to tackle unemployment, a minimum wage, affirmative action, and a willingness to root out systematic and institutional racism wherever it existed. Having defeated the legal segregation of blacks from mainstream society, King set out to defeat segregation by social and economic exclusion.

> The practical cost of change for the nation up to this point has been cheap. The real cost lies ahead. The stiffening of white resistance is a recognition of that fact. The discount education given to Negroes will in the future have to be purchased at full price if quality education is to be realised. Jobs are harder and costlier to create than voting rolls. The eradication of slums housing millions is complex far beyond integrating buses and lunch counters.

King believed the nation could be persuaded to make the commitment, because he believed that poverty was an evil that touched everybody in a community, engulfing not only those trapped in its muddy waters but acting as a polluting force that threatened the clearer waters downstream: 'The time has come for an all-out world war against poverty. The rich nations must use their vast resources of wealth to develop the underdeveloped, school the unschooled and feed the unfed. Ultimately, a great nation is a compassionate nation. No individual or nation can be great if it does not have a concern for the least of these.'

Thus King came to a view on the need for a redistribution of power:

> We are called upon to raise basic questions about the whole society . . . we must recognise that we can't solve our problem until there is a radical redistribution of social and economic power. It is unfair that a small percentage of the population should control all the wealth. . . .

I never intend to accommodate myself to the tragic inequalities of the economic system that denies necessities to the many, in order to finance luxuries to the few.

Remember the march in Washington was for jobs and freedom.

'We are engaged in a social revolution,' he had written from Birmingham Jail, 'to bring about certain basic structural changes in the architecture of American society . . . if we are going to achieve real equality the US will have to adopt a modified form of socialism.' A decade later, the day seemed dark. 'All I have been doing in trying to correct the system in America has been in vain,' he said in December 1967.

Why is equality so assiduously avoided? Why does white America delude itself, and how does it rationalise the evil it retains?

Loose and easy language about equality, resonant resolutions about brotherhood fall pleasantly on the ear, but for the Negro there is a credibility gap he cannot overlook. He remembers that with each modest advance the white population promptly raises the argument that the Negro has come far enough. Each step forward accents an ever-present tendency to backlash . . .

There is not even a common language when the term 'equality' is used. Negro and white have a fundamentally different definition. Negroes have proceeded from a premise that equality means what it says, and they have taken white Americans at their word when they talked of it as an objective. But most whites in America in 1967, including many persons of goodwill, proceed from a premise that equality is a loose expression for improvement . . .

For the vast majority of white Americans, the past decade – the first phase – had been a struggle to treat the Negro with a degree of decency, not of equality. White America was ready to demand that the Negro should be spared the lash of brutality and coarse degradation, but it had never been truly committed to helping him out of the poverty, exploitation or all forms of discrimination.

When Negroes looked for the second phase, the realisation of equality, they found that many of their white allies had quietly disappeared. The Negroes of America had taken the President, the press and the pulpit at their word when they spoke in broad terms of freedom and justice. But the absence of brutality and unregenerate evil is not the presence of justice. To stay murder is not the same thing as to obtain brotherhood.

So King did not seek power for one section of society to the detriment of another; rather, he believed that achieving justice for a downtrodden people would ennoble all races and uplift the entire nation. His 'I Have a Dream' speech is perhaps the most eloquent form of his manifesto, and one of most memorable and moving speeches in living memory. His vision of racial harmony had the nation spellbound – it appealed to all that was good, noble, generous and courageous in his countrymen and women – and his peerless affirmation that justice was attainable inspired others to believe. As the *New York Times* reported in 1963, 'It will be a long time before [Washington] forgets the melodious and melancholy voice of Rev. Dr. Martin Luther King Jr., crying out his dreams to the multitude.'

I have a dream today . . .

I have a dream that one day this nation will rise up and live out the true meeting of its creed – we hold these truths to be self-evident that all men are created equal . . .

I have a dream that my four little children will one day live in a nation where they will not be judged by the colour of their skin but by the content of their character . . .

I have a dream today . . . !

I have a dream that one day, down in Alabama, with its vicious racists, with its governor having his lips dripping with the words of interposition and nullification; one day right there in Alabama little black boys and black girls will be able to join hands with little white boys and white girls as sisters and brothers . . .

This is our hope . . .

With this faith we will be able to hew out of the mountain of despair a stone of hope. With this faith we will be able to transform the jangling discords of our nation into a beautiful symphony of brotherhood. With this faith we will be able to work together, to pray together, to struggle together, to go to jail together, to stand up for freedom together, knowing that we will be free one day . . .

And when this happens, we allow freedom to ring, when we let it ring from every village and every hamlet, from every state and every city, we will be able to speed up the day when all of God's children, black men and white men, Jews and Gentiles, Protestants and Catholics, will be able to join hands and sing in the words of the old Negro spiritual, 'Free at last, free at last. Thank God Almighty, we are free at last.'

Paul Tillich wrote: 'In the act of courage, the most essential part of our being prevails against the less essential.' In the final years of his life, Martin Luther King had to confront not only injustice but his own isolation from many he had led to the frontiers of freedom, and from many whites he had brought to the cause. The Nobel Prize Laureate of 1964 was a prophet beleaguered in 1968. He must have felt that every non-essential part of him had already died a death.

His wife Coretta Scott remembered him falling into a depression and his friends recall his emotional exhaustion. One said that by 1968, the year of his death, 'He found himself working alone, out on a tightrope without a safety net . . . when the tides of history were flowing in a different direction.'

Yet, in his lonely courage, King preached the gospel of non-violence and peace more urgently than ever before:

On some positions, cowardice asks the question, 'Is it safe?' Expediency asks the question, 'Is it politic?' And vanity comes along and asks the question, 'Is it popular?' But conscience asks the question, 'Is it right?'

The ultimate measure of a man is not where he stands in moments of convenience, but where he stands in moments of challenge, moments of great crisis and controversy.

When I first took my position against the war in Vietnam, almost every newspaper in the country criticised me. It was a low period in my life . . .

But when I took up the cross I recognised its meaning. It is not something that you merely put your hands on. It is not something that you wear. The cross is something that you bear and ultimately that you die on.

Martin Luther King was not yet forty years old when he was gunned down by an assassin in Memphis, where he had gone to stand with refuse workers in a bitter strike. Although murdered so young, he had already survived thirteen years of death threats, mob violence, police harassment, smear campaigns and covert investigations by the secret services.

This is the man who demanded for his people a seat on a bus, a place at the table, a ballot paper at election time, and then an end to poverty and a commitment to economic justice. This is the citizen of the world who demanded life, liberty and the pursuit of happiness as an inalienable right for all, not just some, of its citizens. His work is unfinished, but his memory urges it on – in America and around the earth.

The FBI director, his nemesis J. Edgar Hoover, considered him the most dangerous African-American in the United States. To many others, he was the greatest hope for an oppressed people crying out for freedom in a country that proclaimed to be the protectorate of freedom throughout the world. That cry for freedom, that most fundamental of human instincts, found its most eloquent voice in King's 1963 speech in which he described his dream of harmony between the races.

'I have a dream,' he said, 'that one day on the red hills of Georgia the sons of former slaves and the sons of former slave-owners will be able to sit down together at the table of brotherhood.'

As we know now, he has turned the tides of history. America and the world – for all the work still to be done, all the causes still to be won – was transformed by his character, his clarion call to conscience, and his courage even in the hardest hours.

5

Robert Kennedy

We know a great deal about the years of the John F. Kennedy presidency – and perhaps little more that is new can be written about those years. But one unanswered question that continues to fascinate resolves at root into one of personal courage: how, after his older brother's death, did Robert Kennedy – best known for his genius as a political operator – become transformed into a political visionary, and how did he become the leading evangelist for a new politics that took on not just the old right but also the traditional left?

Robert Kennedy may be remembered by many as his brother's follower, the second Kennedy to be assassinated, someone who will always stand in the shadow of what was and what might have been. Yet by 1968 Robert Kennedy's distinctive, not fully formed but genuinely original vision of empowerment had become, for large numbers of people, a defining idea of the times. It was a call not to ask what 'your country can do for you' or just what 'you can do for your country' – John F. Kennedy's classic appeal in his inaugural address – but a summons that went beyond it, the challenge of what, with enabling government, an empowered people can do for themselves. It was a wider and more modern conception of freedom – not just freedom from, but freedom to.

'As our case is new so we must think anew and act anew,' said Kennedy invoking Abraham Lincoln in his book of speeches *To Seek a Newer World*. And he was fully aware of the originality of what he was attempting as he launched his campaign to be President of the United States. 'We will not find answers in old dogmas, by repeating outworn slogans or by fighting on ancient battlegrounds against fading enemies long after the real struggle has moved on,' he insisted. 'We ourselves must change to master change. We must rethink our old ideas and beliefs before they capture and destroy us.'

When he spoke of not looking at the world as it was but dreaming of it as it could be, he dared us, as President Bill Clinton recalled at Kennedy's memorial mass in Arlington Cemetery in June 1993, 'to leave yesterday and embrace tomorrow'. Twenty-five years earlier his brother Edward, quoting Tennyson at Robert Kennedy's funeral, said that his great role was 'to strive, to seek, to find, and not to yield'.

And the shift was much more than just a change of rhetoric. The old, 1950s style of politics he was breaking with pitted big government against a more laissez-faire approach, good intentions – despite results – against the acceptance of inequity and injustice, and social programmes – however ineffective – against inattention and indifference. Roosevelt's New Deal revolution had transformed American society and made it fairer and more prosperous. But the debate now seemed trapped in the amber of that history. The answer, Kennedy sensed and then said, was to widen the terms of choice, to put into the hands of citizenry the power to achieve change through what he called 'numerous, diverse' acts of initiative and daring. Ordinary people on their own, and in their communities, could and should shape their own lives and destinies. It was not an abandonment of social conscience, but a new way to fulfil it. Robert Kennedy never used the phrase 'a third way', but that's the path he was seeking.

What was it about Robert Kennedy that made him an advocate of this new politics before its time had come – a new democrat, as has been written, before the New Democrats had been invented – and made his strongest left-wing critic Michael Harrington acknowledge that 'he was a man who could have changed the course of American history'? Can we explain why Robert Kennedy, who started his political life seen as his brother's hard edge and enforcer

– gaining a reputation as calculating and ruthless – became the hero of a new idealism and passion about the future? What changed the man who was known for years as one of the toughest political operators – to the liberal Adlai Stevenson 'the Black Prince' – into one of the most caring visionaries? What took him beyond politics as the acquisition of power to a conviction that politics only mattered if it had the power to transform lives?

Kennedy's conversion was seen as such a profound and dramatic transformation that even today his detractors doubt whether it was genuine. So was he, indeed, the altruistic, sincere, life-transforming visionary his supporters claim of him – not just in his mission to bring empowerment to the poor but also in his eventual denunciation of the Vietnam war – or was his new message on these matters calculating and contrived to mask a dogmatism and ruthlessness that his critics suggested never left him from his earliest days?

One thing is clear. Unlike his two older brothers, Robert Kennedy was not groomed for greatness. He was ten years younger than his eldest brother Joe, whom his father had thought of as a future president but who died a war hero when his plane, a Liberator modified to become a flying bomb for use against a V-3 cannon installation in northern France, exploded prematurely over the English Channel before reaching its target and before the crew could bail out. And young Bobby grew up very much in the shadow of Jack, his senior by eight years, who served in the US Navy during the war, was celebrated and decorated for his bravery, and who by the mid-1940s had already taken on his older brother's mantle and his father's expectations for the future.

So, Robert Kennedy grew up not just in the shadow of his two older brothers but developed far less commanding a presence, too. There was, also, little paternal pressure for him to become a politician. Quite the opposite: almost all the pressure on him was self-induced, the result of his own desire not to appear weak but to be as strong, courageous and as ambitious as his brothers. 'He was obsessed by his relative inferiority to his older brothers,' said Gore Vidal sarcastically. 'As a result he had to be twice as tough as everyone else, have twice as many children . . . what a tense life it must have been and finally sad.'

Sent off to boarding schools, he had few friends and was seen by contemporaries as awkward and often moralistic. But the Robert Kennedy story is, as one biographer has written, 'the story of an umpromising boy who died as he was becoming a great man'. 'Nothing came easy but he never stopped trying,' said a friend. 'He willed himself into the water to learn to swim and he willed himself on to the ballfield.' Or as another friend put it, 'Bobby felt he was weak. He felt he had to toughen himself up and get rid of the vulnerability everyone had remarked on since he was a boy. This was the way for him to get some place in the family. The drive was incessant, just fierce . . . He got so he could just go through a wall.' And so we read all the stories of teenage and then adult exploits, of Robert Kennedy throwing himself into the icy sea at Cape Cod and hurling himself against opponents at family football matches, risking serious injury, of him white-water rafting in the most dangerous of currents and climbing North America's mountains alongside the great adventurer Jim Whitakker, the first American to conquer Everest. One reason for such bravado might be that, unlike his two older brothers, Robert, only fourteen at the outbreak of World War II, missed all combat. It was only in 1946 that he served in the US Navy as an ordinary seaman aboard a destroyer named in memory of his brother Joseph. It was probably because he did not fight that he was always so in awe of men and women of physical courage – such as General MacArthur, whose First World War citation for bravery he kept in his desk. When asked, says his biographer, Evan Thomas, 'If you could do it all over what would you be?' he replied, 'A paratrooper.'

In the 1950s and early '60s, as the Kennedy brothers emerged as public figures in their own right, not simply as the sons of a prominent father, Jack was widely perceived as urbane, charming and brilliant. Robert's public persona was defined solely by his toughness – an image of which he seemed to approve, or at least to encourage. He aligned himself with the Red-baiting Senator Joseph McCarthy and, though he soon separated himself from the man and his methods, Kennedy exuded a similar brashness. In his twenties he ran a highly successful Senate investigation into corruption in organised labour, berating and even mocking witnesses during televised hearings.

This was Kennedy's role, and he seemed to relish it. Indeed, even as McCarthy was exposed for a gross exaggeration of the Red threat, Kennedy stood by him longer than almost any other, working as a lawyer on his hearings. 'I thought there was an internal security threat to the US,' Kennedy later tried to explain. 'Joe McCarthy was the only one who seemed to be doing anything about it.' He finally left when McCarthy attacked the Eisenhower Pentagon – and served as counsel for the Democrats, who finally stood against McCarthyism.

As his brother's campaign manager, then as attorney-general during the Kennedy administration, Robert played the enforcer while his brother played the conciliator. Few in those days doubted that Robert Kennedy was strong-willed, but it might he said that he was tough rather than bold. He would readily take on the most intimidating enemies, but beyond his frequent impatience with protocol and tradition he was unlikely to challenge political orthodoxies.

Of course he was not entirely, or even mostly, his own man. He was his brother's fixer, keeper and adviser. Robert Kennedy's power flowed in part from his personal sense of discipline, his keen insight and his ability to inspire the men around him, but he was, in a fundamental sense, an extension or instrument of his brother rather than an individual politician in his own right. He could and did display bravery and toughness, but only within these constraints. Although we can talk today about the close partnership between Robert Kennedy and John – Robert as campaign manager in the 1960 presidential race, as attorney-general and principal adviser to Jack in the White House – friends say that in the years before he entered politics, JFK was not nearly so reliant on his brother. It was when John started to think of a serious bid for the presidency that, bound in a mutual cause, they became inseparable. But Robert was always the junior partner – fixing the organisation, criticising opponents, doing behind-the-scenes deals, giving advice, masterminding some of his brother's initiatives – directly involved in advice over civil rights and the Bay of Pigs, and then the showdown with Russia over missiles in Cuba, where he played a central role in talking with the Soviets and resolving the crisis. He was famous, a household name and face, but never so prominent that he was in danger of overshadowing the president.

Then came the devastation of the assassination. He was at home with friends on 22 November 1963 when the head of the FBI, J. Edgar Hoover, rang to inform him of his brother's assassination. Kennedy, it is reported, turned away from his guests, his face and body tortured by agony and disbelief, his own life changed for ever. And while leading his family in public, privately he retreated into himself – 'like a man on the rack' one friend explained – unable to explain his feelings and revealing an almost unreachable sadness.

He was 'kind of floundering' wrote Don Wilson of *Time* magazine. He walked for hours on his own. He felt 'impotent and frustrated', his mother recalled, and he had sunk into 'a state of almost insupportable emotional shock'. 'He literally shrank,' said one of his biographers, Evan Thomas. 'His future and even his identity seemed suddenly an open question and answers were, for a time, not forthcoming.' His bedrock Catholic faith was under severe challenge because of what he saw as the inexplicable waste of his brother's life. He wrote in a notebook, 'The innocent suffer – how can that be possible and God be just?'

According to speechwriter and adviser Richard Goodwin, who served both Kennedy brothers and Lyndon B. Johnson, it was to cope with his grief that Bobby forced himself 'to explore new worlds of thought and poetry and the manifold varieties of human history, almost as if he were equipping himself for a larger role, labouring to become someone worthy of a successor to the romanticised vision of the leader'.

During the spring of 1964, as part of this process, he read *The Greek* Way, by Edith Hamilton, a popular history of ancient Greece which had been given to him by Jackie Kennedy and which he would later always carry with him. 'When the world is storm-driven and the bad that happens and the worse that threatens are so urgent as to shut out everything else from view,' wrote Hamilton, appealing to the idea of courageous lives, 'then we need to know all the strong fortresses of the spirit which men have built through the ages.' For Robert Kennedy, the image at the heart of the works of Aeschylus and Sophocles – of the heroic, fate-driven, wilful hero – appealed both for its sense of destiny and foreboding, and also its awareness of the dignity and moral purpose of life and the anguish on which any mortal success and achievement depended.

It was 'based on the conviction that good grows out of bad, virtue out of hardship, and that wisdom is born in suffering', wrote David Brooks; 'the story of Kennedy's grief is the story of a man stepping out of his time and fetching from the past a sturdier ethic. He developed a bit of that quality, which greater leaders like Churchill possessed in abundance, of seeming to step from another age.'

At a campaign event in Indianapolis in 1968, Robert Kennedy cited Aeschylus when he broke the news of Martin Luther King's death to crowds in an impromptu speech urging calm:

> Ladies and gentlemen, I'm only going to talk to you just for a minute or so this evening because I have some very sad news for all of you . . . for all of our fellow citizens, and people who love peace all over the world, and that is that Martin Luther King was shot and was killed tonight [screams from crowd].
>
> . . . For those of you who are black and are tempted to be filled with hatred and mistrust of the injustice of such an act, against all white people, I would only say that I can also feel in my own heart the same kind of feeling. I had a member of my family killed . . . But we have to make an effort . . . to understand, to get beyond or go beyond these rather difficult times.
>
> My favorite poet was Aeschylus. And he once wrote: 'Even in our sleep, pain which cannot forget falls drop by drop upon the heart until, in our own despair, against our will, comes wisdom through the awful grace of God.'
>
> . . . So I shall ask you tonight to return home, to say a prayer for the family of Martin Luther King, that's true, but more importantly, to say a prayer for our own country, which all of us love – a prayer for understanding and that compassion of which I spoke. Dedicate ourselves to what the Greeks wrote so many years ago: 'to tame the savageness of man and make gentle the

life of this world'. Let us dedicate ourselves to that, and say a prayer for our country and for our people.

But it was not the classical Greek writers but the Frenchman Albert Camus who helped complete Robert Kennedy's education. Camus taught him to come to terms with pain and inevitability. 'This isn't really such a happy existence, is it?' Robert remarked, when, in 1968, he contemplated the possibility of his own assassination. But reading Camus did not make Kennedy an existentialist. When in 1968 he went to South Africa to ally himself with the fight against apartheid he urged his audience to 'resist the danger of futility – the belief there is nothing one man or one woman can do against the enormous army of the world's ills'. Camus made him more realistic but no less determined. 'Perhaps we cannot prevent this world from being a world in which children are tortured,' Kennedy said. 'But we can reduce the number of tortured children and if you believers don't help us who else in the world can help us do this?'

So out of mourning he concluded that destiny summoned him to action, to take a stand, to make some difference, to leave his mark and to engineer some change, however limited, however soon cut short.

Yet, even in 1968, nothing about a presidential bid by Kennedy seemed inevitable or preordained – neither the decision to stand, nor the embrace of a bold strategy. By 1968 there were even more reasons why Robert Kennedy should *not* stand for president. His wife and ten children (and an eleventh on the way) needed him – and so too did his large extended family that now included JFK's children. Not only had his brother been assassinated but his father was crippled and unable to advise or even speak. In one cruel moment Robert Kennedy had gone from being the younger brother of the president to being the effective patriarch of America's most prominent family – and was this not a greater responsibility for now than public service? There was also no reason other than his own determination to push himself forward. He was rich, he was privileged, and since 1964 he had been senator of New York. He was also the subject of numerous death threats. Political calculations weighed against his standing, and at only forty-two he had time on his side. No one had really thought of 1968 as Kennedy's year: Democrat Lyndon Johnson, though increasingly unpopular, was still incumbent president, and taking him on seemed like political suicide. 1972 had already been marked down by Kennedy's friends as the year of his presidential challenge. As he himself said: 'Everyone I respect with the exception of Dick Goodwin and Arthur Schlesinger have been against my running.'

Yet sweeping fear and calculation aside, Kennedy announced his presidential bid – and from then on his whole journey through 1968 was marked by courage: the courage to take on vested interests within his party and among the public – and to question enduring articles of the liberal faith – and the courage to face down very real threats to his life. 'I'm sure,' he said a few years earlier as he talked of what had happened to his brother, 'there will be an attempt on my life sooner or later, not so much for political reasons, plain nuttiness that's all.' On the night of Martin Luther King's murder, two months before his own, he said, 'It makes me wonder what they might do to me too.' But it was a measure of both his bravery and his fatalism that he concluded, 'You've just got to give yourself to the people and trust them and from then on . . . either luck is with you or it isn't.'

Courage is the virtue that both John and Robert Kennedy admired most, acknowledged by Robert himself when he wrote a foreword for his brother's posthumously published *Profiles in Courage*. In his copy of Emerson's *Essays* he underlined words relating to triumphing over fear: 'It was a high counsel that I once heard given to a young person, "Do what you are afraid to do".'

In a eulogy dedicated to Robert Kennedy, the poet Robert Lowell wrote that 'doom was woven in your nerves. He felt he was doomed and you know that he felt that.' But it did not hinder him; perhaps it even propelled him into riskier behaviour. Perhaps Kennedy thought too much of tragedy and destiny, yet throughout he eschewed the safer course and became an even more compulsive risk-taker. 'They lived dangerously,' said Schlesinger of both John and Robert. 'They were rather fatalistic about the prospects of assassination so they didn't go round [in] bulletproof bubbles.' In a way Robert, like John Kennedy, made the most of necessity, not discouraging a cult of courage, celebrating bravery as a virtue, often quoting Churchill that 'courage is the first of human qualities because it is the quality which guarantees all others'.

But if the family tended both to celebrate and exploit stories of personal bravery, this was only the superficial manifestation of a deeper courage that grew in RFK. During the 1960s, the self-conscious displays of strength of a young man matured into a more profound strength of purpose. It was a courage forged out of increasingly strongly held convictions which gave him both will-power and determination and it spurred him to bold action.

We have seen how in the fifties and early sixties Robert Kennedy was most identified with negative campaigns against Communist infiltration and then against corruption in organised labour. And even later in the early 1960s he yielded as attorney-general to FBI director J. Edgar Hoover's demand to wiretap Martin Luther King. But by 1968 a different Kennedy had emerged – still as determined as ever but now equipped with a strong sense not so much of the evil to be pursued but of the good that could be done. And as he challenged the whole political establishment, Kennedy could summon up the strength of his Catholic faith, one sorely tested by the assassination of his brother but which had emerged robust. In the presidential elections of 1960 it was his brother John who had defended his faith as he sought to become the first Roman Catholic President of the United States. But it was Robert who had grown up far more interested than his brother in Catholic teaching, and especially its injunctions on poverty. Unlike John, Robert attended mass and prayed regularly. Robert's daughter Kathleen Kennedy Townsend recalled family life:

> Not only were we quizzed at dinner about history and current events but after dinner we all went upstairs and said the rosary together . . . After we said the rosary we read the Bible. There was a strong sense of religion: you do the moral thing. You do the right thing. I remember this a lot. St Luke's admonition 'from those who have been given much, much will be expected'. He

said that you've been given a lot of privileges, you owe something
to your country; that's a constant theme through our
childhood . . .

Robert's father also continued to weigh heavily on him. He
described the love he received from his father as 'not love as it is
described with such facility in popular magazines, but the kind of love
that is affection and respect, order and encouragement, and support'.

In his youth and well into his thirties, Kennedy was known as
moralistic. He saw the world in black and white, in a perpetual
conflict between good and evil. At first, corruption, greed and
dishonesty were the evils that impelled him to act, but in the years
after his brother's death he was moved to anger and action mostly by
injustice, by wasted lives and opportunity denied, by human suffering. Kennedy, who had mastered the politics of attack, now practised the politics of moral uplift and exhortation. The street fighter
had become a street preacher, the political pragmatist a prophet.

This was not a wholesale reinvention. The strain of moralism was
consistent from his youth to the end of his life. In fact, people wrote of
how from an early age this 'moralistic' young man was always
interested in the excluded and disempowered. Those who knew him
before say that this 'streak of caring' was always there. According to
one friend he never lost that strain of moral commitment. Both as the
political pragmatist of the 1950s and '60s and as the compassionate
idealist vying to change the world in the mid- to late 1960s he
believed in the eventual triumph of good over evil and prized
services to others over personal gain. Both arose from his upbringing
and early influences. They were not created but were brought to the
forefront by the suffering he experienced after his brother's assassination that had given him, in the words of a close friend, 'a
tenderness so rawly exposed, so vulnerable to painful abrasion that
it could only be shielded by angry compassion to human misery or
manifest itself in love and loyalty towards those close to him'.

In *To Seek a Newer World* he was honest enough to describe the two
temptations that in the pursuit of his cause he had to show the
courage to resist: what he called the danger of timidity and the lure

of comfort. On the surface this idea is reminiscent of JFK's study, *Profiles in Courage*, but in fact the meaning is not the same. The essential attributes of courage turn out for Robert to be quite different: moral courage is a rarer commodity than bravery in battle or great intelligence. Yet it is the one essential quality for those who seek to change a world that yields only grudgingly and often reluctantly to change.

> I believe that in this generation those with the courage to enter the moral conflict will find themselves with companions in every corner of the world. For the fortunate among us, the danger is comfort, the temptation to follow the safe and familiar paths of personal ambition and financial success so grandly spread before those who enjoy the privilege of education. But this is not the road history has marked for us, and all of us will ultimately be judged and as the years pass we will surely judge ourselves on the effort we have made to building a new world society and the extent to which our ideals and goals have shaped that effort.

Here was a view of courage different from that at the centre of *Profiles in Courage*. For John, courage was triumphing over vested interests to fashion political compromises and consensus in the national interest. For Robert, courage meant something akin to storming the heavens, and was more about securing the triumph of good over evil than the passage of legislation or the making of a consensus.

But what marked out the Robert Kennedy of the mid-1960s for so many who worked with him – and this perhaps most clearly revealed Robert's deep moral and political convictions – was his passion for children, their fate and their fortune. His interest in practical and bold new policies to alleviate child poverty had started to develop when he was attorney-general from 1961 on-wards. He had become interested in the link between poverty and race and self-worth and crime, and he invited a group of juvenile offenders to his office. 'If I had grown up in these circumstances,' he concluded, 'this could have happened to me.' He met gang members in Harlem. He sponsored legislation aimed at preventing youth crime, travelled to Appalachia and sent President Johnson a memo on racial violence in urban centres.

Wherever Robert Kennedy travelled he was drawn to children: he listened to them, held them, talked to them, got down to their level; these were not staged Kennedy appearances. A friend, columnist Mary McGrory, wrote that she often brought children from the local orphanage for parties at the Kennedy home: 'It was total immersion on both sides. Kennedy needed children as much as they needed him.' He said that aged three or four slum children's faces had 'a certain vitality and beauty' that their well-off middle-class contemporaries did not have, but he speculated that at the age of eight to twelve the faces of these children changed as they sensed the oppressiveness of the world. When he met children in Brazil he begged them to stay on at school but left dejected, saddened because he saw not only the desperate need for proper investment in education, which now had to be fought for, but that they had uttered, at a deeper level, 'a cry for love'. He wanted, as he commented himself, to bind up their wounds.

He 'always saw poverty through the lens of children and young people,' said his adviser Peter Edelman. 'So much of what he did was based on instinct. He was quite different from his cerebral brother in his mode of thought and action.'And in later years Robert Kennedy clung to a scrap of paper left on his brother's desk at the end of the last cabinet meeting they attended together in 1963: an agenda scribbled over repeatedly with the word 'poverty'. For Robert, this became his brother's last will and testament – almost a summons to a lifetime of action.

So when Robert Kennedy returned from the depths that followed his brother's death, he toured the country to see for himself the condition of America, to focus on the poverty that was often forgotten or unseen, and then to speak out on what changes needed to be made. One of his first visits was to meet impoverished black children in the Mississippi Delta in 1967, where he was shocked by what he saw. He was, he said, 'appalled' by the open sores, the stench, the vermin, the lack of nutrition. He was visibly shaken when he rubbed a child's stomach 'and found it distended by starvation'. And he spoke out. What angered him was that this was the America of the 1960s, the richest nation on earth, yet here were 'children with swollen bellies and running sores on their arms and legs that appeared not to be healing'. He reported he had seen 'rat bites on the faces of young children even in the wealthiest city in the world, New York'. It profoundly affected his thinking. After one visit to the Mississippi, Edelman recalled:

> his children say he came home to dinner that night deeply shaken and that he a man of few words so much of the time could not stop talking about what he had seen that day . . . it was one thing to say we needed more jobs or improvements in public education or a better welfare policy. It was something quite different to say we had near starvation in our rich country.

With this first-hand knowledge of the slums he talked openly of the 'obscenity' of poverty. The word 'unacceptable' became a favoured injunction that for him demonstrated moral outrage. As Kennedy said in Kansas in March 1968: 'I have seen these other Americans . . . I have seen children starving, their bodies crippled from hunger.' Theodore Roosevelt's daughter, Alice Roosevelt Longworth, said that with the outrage he showed Robert could 'have been a revolutionary priest'.

But Robert Kennedy did not only expose; he organised and proposed changes in welfare policy that went beyond the offer of food stamps. He had to convince a disbelieving secretary of agriculture that in mid-1960s America there were still children dying of hunger. Robert Coles, a renowned child psychiatrist, recalled Senate hearings where Kennedy organised the medical evidence, working out how it could best be presented to overcome the doubts and even the cynicism of some colleagues. It eventually led to a select committee on hunger and malnutrition.

Another friend, Jack Newfield, wrote of Kennedy's ability to put himself inside other people, 'to see the world with the eyes of its casualties', but it was not just his eloquence, not just his personality or his campaigning style and skill that sums up the new path he took. It was the strength of his belief and the strength of his character that turned what Goodwin called a

'tenderness so rawly exposed' and a vulnerability 'that previously just made him angry' into the 'resolution to achieve
political and social change'.

So Robert Kennedy used his position to organise dissent and
action: it is fascinating to know that it was Kennedy himself who
was the inspiration behind Martin Luther King's Poor People's
Campaign. Marian Wright Edelman was the founder of the
Children's Defense Fund, a lifelong campaigner for children's
rights who invented the slogan 'no child left behind'. And through
her future husband, Peter Edelman, Kennedy urged her to reach
out to King: 'Tell him to bring poor people to Washington, to stay
until Congress is so uncomfortable that it does what they want just
to get them to go home'. It was because of events such as this that
Kennedy's political assistant Adam Walinksy called 1968 the
declaration of 'a people's crusade'.

But what was new was not simply a more energetic and urgent
focus on child poverty, it was to argue that the child poverty, inner-
city, racial and slum problems that scarred 1960s America could
only be solved through a new philosophy of government. Kennedy's originality was that he was the first from the left not only to
express major doubts about big bureaucratic approaches but the
first also to call for a reassertion of personal and social responsibility, an end to welfare dependency, the empowerment of the poor
and partnerships for renewal that brought private as well as public
sectors into urban regeneration. His starting point for empowerment was that work, not benefits, offered the way out of poverty,
and he was the first from the left to put a renewed emphasis on
personal responsibility as the key to civic renewal. 'I'm not for a
guaranteed income, I'm for guaranteed jobs,' he would say.

His was a muscular Democratic philosophy that founded his
ideas of economic and social progress around a new self-reliance
from the powerless and a new engagement from the powerful. He
had come to the view that too much welfare left the poor
dependent. He had seen an alternative to the old welfare in
bottom-up community action during the short-lived War on
Poverty, with communities strengthened by being rebuilt by
the people who lived in them. And he was first to point out

the sheer waste of unemployment and welfare costs to pay for it. New York, he said, spent more on welfare than on education. Putting his faith in the dignity of work and the potential of education, he asked Adam Walinsky to shape a programme founded on these principles for urban reconstruction in all major cities of the USA. But his new philosophy of empowerment was also rooted in his embrace of the goals, the ideas and even the language of the civil rights movement. This embrace had come gradually – and perhaps reluctantly. In the early 1960s – and on the central issue of black rights – Martin Luther King had said of Kennedy that the moral passion was missing, and Robert Kennedy admitted later that he and his brother John were particularly reserved about King during that period of time.

But what Robert Kennedy saw in the ghettoes – the very scale of child poverty – converted him. He now talked of 'the pathology of the ghetto'; and prefiguring a debate about the loss of community amongst the bigness of cities as 'a besetting sin of the twentieth century'; he lamented the decline of civic pride and 'the destruction of thousands of invisible strands of common experience and respect which tie men to their fellows'. 'The whole history of the human race had been the history of community,' he said, 'and it was now disappearing.' He spoke eloquently of the moral imperative of civil rights and of 'the violence that affects the poor, that poisons the relations between men because their skin is different', and urged a radical programme of political, economic and social rights starting with votes and jobs. He concluded that 'the violent youth of the ghetto is not simply protesting his condition but making a destructive and self-defeating attempt to assert his worth and dignity as a human being'.

Of course we must remember that Robert Kennedy said little on women's rights, nothing on gay liberation and that much of what he wrote in 1968 will seem out of date today. However, central to his vision of empowerment was to engage the private sector alongside the public in urban regeneration and to move beyond the old, familiar, self-defeating and sterile battle for territory between private and public endeavour. As senator of New York he encouraged what became the Bedford Stuyvesant Restoration Corporation, a redevelopment project in one of the city's most desolate areas whose distinctive feature was business rather than just government engagement in urban renewal. And just before Kennedy died, the programme he agreed for addressing America's nationwide urban crisis called for private investment, strong law enforcement, participation by citizens, work not welfare and resident-controlled institutions. Ahead of his time, he favoured more experimentation in freeing up school management, new yardsticks for measuring the effectiveness of public action, and neighbourhood health centres that focused not just on cure but on prevention. He promised, if he became president, to call the civic leadership of each city to the White House immediately to encourage this strategy of empowerment.

1968 was the year in which, from the streets of Paris to Prague across Europe, and from the university campuses to the black ghettoes of America, a new politics of change burst through to the surface. Kennedy said he understood the forces at work and that he was 'coming to terms with a world of change [where] we have given our children unrivalled opportunities, yet they seem to grow further apart from us every day'. The answer, he argued, was not the failures of the old democracy but more democracy, where people could be masters of their own fate. This was one of the reasons why he went to South Africa and – speaking near to where Nelson Mandela was held in prison – became one of the first Western politicians to call for an end to apartheid.

Robert Kennedy knew that internationally as well as nationally he had to offer a practical programme that did not just acknowledge these changes but responded to them. His lifelong complaint against the old liberals, such as the 1952 and 1956 Democratic presidential candidate Adlai Stevenson, was that, seeking to remain pure in their ideals and striving to be untarnished by compromise, they finally preferred impotence to power.

For RFK the key to the future was not to surrender his vision but to match his idealism with action. To change power, you had to have power. Even when he made his great speech in South Africa that raised the standard for an end to apartheid he said that:

idealism, high aspirations and deep convictions are not incompatible with the most practical and efficient of programmes, that there is no basic inconsistency between ideals and realistic possibilities, no separation between the deepest desire of heart and of mind and the rational application of human effort to basic problems.

And this was the evolution from President JFK to presidential candidate RFK and to a more aspirational politics. If politics was the art of the possible, Robert saw 'possible' in far broader terms than had Jack only a few years earlier. JFK had done more than any politician since Roosevelt to create a forward-looking vision that could re-imagine what was possible. Robert went further. By 1968 his politics were even more idealistic. Indeed, one could argue that Robert in 1968 was John unbound: politics was not just the art of the possible but making the desirable possible.

The John F. Kennedy who left an indelible impression on the consciousness of the world was also in private a man of irony and self-irony, with a cerebral detachment, 'an idealist without illusions'. The Robert F. Kennedy of 1968 was different, an idealist who saw what others regarded as illusions – the empowerment of the poor, the liberation of the dispossessed – as the only practical outcome for an America true to itself.

If JFK was a man who believed that greatness was defined by great deeds, RFK became a leader who exemplified the greatness of seeing and feeling the hurts and hopes of others. When David Frost asked the 1968 presidential candidates how they wanted their obituaries to read, Robert Kennedy simply replied: 'Something about the fact that I made some contribution to my country or those who are less well-off. Camus wrote about the fact that this is a world in which children suffer' – he paused – 'I'd like to feel that I'd done something to lessen that suffering.'

Both Kennedys left a legacy of poetry as well as power. But in Robert, tempered by the tragedy of his brother's loss, there was vulnerability as well as steel. His appeal beyond leadership was an empathy that did not proclaim itself but was self-evident. To him, the work of change – to redress injustice, to bind up the wounds of violence and indifference, to heal the brokenness of the world – was above all a moral command.

So, the Robert Kennedy who touched the hearts of millions was an inner man on a public stage. You could see the difference between him and his brother in voice and gesture: the older brother's open hand slicing through the air as his words cascaded across an audience; the younger brother's closed hand, thumb extended, reflecting in its uneven movement and then in his staccato delivery the urgency of his insistent call, pointing to a newer world.

But there could be no advance to a new world in 1968 without addressing the question of Vietnam. So was Kennedy's advocacy of a negotiated peace settlement a conversion born of calculation - as contemporaries alleged – to wrest the presidential nomination from Johnson, or was it a brave act of self-sacrifice?

The facts are on Kennedy's side. Firstly, opposing the war in Vietnam was not, even in 1968, a way to win many votes. It was only after the Tet Offensive, in January and February 1968, that a (slight) majority of the American public sentiment went against the war; previously most Americans supported it, and a good number actually thought the US should commit more troops. 1967 was known as 'the year of the hawk'. Thus every time that Kennedy spoke out against the war, as he did forcefully in early 1966 and early 1967, he lost ground in the polls. Part of this was due to perceptions that he was pursuing a vendetta against Johnson. But mostly it reflected the fact that stoking anti-war sentiment was not yet a viable, mainstream political strategy.

For these and other reasons, Kennedy proceeded cautiously on Vietnam. He was for some time reluctant to desert his brother's decisions and those of his former advisers, many of whom made up the chorus urging Johnson to escalate the conflict. But his misgivings came early, and were focused not just on the management of the war but on matters of deep principle and basic strategy. He argued often – privately as early as 1964, and publicly beginning in 1965 – that there would be no military solution in Vietnam without a similarly aggressive commitment to creating political stability and economic opportunity in South Vietnam.

But when in February 1966 he appeared to call for a negotiated settlement, and even a coalition government in Vietnam, he was immediately labelled 'Ho Chi Kennedy' and drew back. He could not afford to break with President Johnson. But what truly hurt him, a friend remarked, was a placard that read 'Kennedy: Hawk, Dove – Chicken?' and another saying, 'You could become President but you don't have the balls.'

Kennedy was caught between his deeply felt moral and strategic qualms about the war and his shrewd understanding of the political game, which suggested acquiescence as the safest approach. It was 'an ordeal' said Arthur Schlesinger of discussions in 1967 and 1968. He had never seen RFK so torn, so obviously divided, about anything. But in the end Kennedy's moral courage prevailed over his political caution. By the start of 1968, after repeatedly rebuffing those who had urged him to lead the movement to 'dump Johnson' and end the war, Kennedy decided that he could simply not live with himself if he abdicated leadership. He took the greatest risk of his political career – the greatest leap into uncertainty – and, as he slid inexorably towards challenging Johnson, he finally spoke his mind about the war.

Kennedy started to allege that Johnson had departed from his brother's policy of self-determination for the Vietnamese and that he had switched from one point of view to another. Johnson, he now believed, had Americanised the war. Once the US had waged war, he claimed, because the South Vietnamese had wanted the war. Now from that standpoint, Kennedy challenged the whole basis of the war, questioning the morality of intervention and the accuracy of the domino theory. He broke from the established view that if Vietnam fell so would the whole of Asia.

But when Kennedy finally broke publicly with Johnson and announced his bid for presidency in March 1968, he had a mountain to climb. He knew that part of his political challenge was to energise newly enfranchised black voters and to win back the young, anti-war Democrats who had abandoned him for Senator Eugene McCarthy – an earlier, passionate and more consistent opponent of Vietnam. But, unlike McCarthy's, Kennedy's was no protest campaign; he intended to win, and to do so he knew he had also to capture the more traditional, conservative, working-class and middle-class Democrats who had been the base of the party since the 1930s. It was an unconventional and unprecedented coalition that he sought – and needed – to create, and whether he could do so was anyone's guess. As he explained himself, 'I think that I really have a chance now – just a chance – to organise a new coalition of negroes and working-class white people against the union and party establishments.' 'Kennedy taught us that you've got to keep the middle class and poor together,' concluded Mario Cuomo, governor of New York State, 'that it is not just a matter of loving your neighbor but that it's good for you to do this as a matter of survival.'

A late arrival to the contest, Robert Kennedy did not achieve as much as he had hoped for in Indiana, where he won the primary with overwhelming black support but failed to win over the white middle and working classes. Then in California he won and became the commander of the anti-war cause. 'On to New York,' he said, the last great primary, and moments later was assassinated. He had privately wanted to offer Eugene McCarthy a deal, that in return for his standing down he would be Kennedy's secretary of state. A family friend, the journalist Joseph Alsop, warned him, 'You must really give more weight to the support of what people call the establishment than I think you do.'

We will, of course, never know whether Robert Kennedy's strategy would have prevailed. But the brilliance of Kennedy's courage was not so much in what he achieved in 1968, but what he foreshadowed for the generation to come. Here was a 42-year-old from a privileged background, his life always under threat. It would have been so much easier to sit things out than to fight. Yet he not only entered the fray but had the courage to think afresh.

No stranger to power, he could so easily have stayed in the comfort zone of his party's establishment but instead he took risks, was prepared to change course, tried to move the whole of the American democratic establishment into new territory and genuinely broke new ground. And in doing so he smashed through conventional orthodoxies, raged against timidity, moved beyond reigning prejudices and tore up traditional party lines. And what's compelling about Kennedy in 1968 is the way he was poised, like no one else in American politics, between past and future, even between left and right, in a state of becoming or evolving, but impossible in the end to pin down – because he was a man in motion.

'A mission of national reconciliation', born of 'a passion for justice, a fierce commitment to make a difference . . . [and] a genuine love of children, all children,' said Peter Edelman of the 1968 campaign. Above all, he praised Kennedy's vision of the empowerment of people – of people themselves in the driving seat, forcing changes that will make them not dependent subjects but active, self-reliant citizens – a vision with so much more to offer. 'Kennedy,' he said, 'was a man who grew every day, he was a work in progress, his journey was truly unfinished.' Perhaps in 1968 an anxious, insecure and divided America needed leaders with heroic qualities to represent the need for change. In Dietrich Bonhoeffer's Germany of the 1930s and '40s it had needed one man of courage to send a signal of conscience.

And the significance of Bonhoeffer's courage is that he carried the burden of a whole nation, arguably allowing post-war Germany to be reborn. Like Bonhoeffer, Kennedy had the physical courage to dismiss the talk of personal danger and the moral courage to think anew about a vision of society in the future. And just as in different circumstances in the 1940s Europe needed the courage of a Bonhoeffer as a reminder of the evil that had to be vanquished, in the 1960s the world needed the courage of a Robert Kennedy as a reminder of what good men and women can achieve. Kennedy had not been born to be courageous – there had been few expectations of the third son – and to some extent with his brothers' deaths, courage was thrust upon him, but what singles Robert Kennedy out from the crowd is that he forged a courage that in life and death came to be timeless and yet very much of its time.

In his eulogy at Robert Kennedy's funeral, Edward Kennedy quoted a speech his brother had made to the young people of South Africa on their Day of Affirmation in 1966. As he said, it 'sums up best what he stood for':

The future does not belong to those who are content with today, apathetic toward common problems and their fellow man alike, timid and fearful in the face of new ideas and bold projects. Rather it will belong to those who can blend vision, reason and courage in a personal commitment to the ideals and great enterprises of American Society.

Kennedy saw how easy it was for politicians to become detached from the real world, to fall out of touch and not to recognise the need for new thinking. But sensing the scale of the dramatic changes taking place in his country and the need for a different kind of leadership, Kennedy was inspired to break with the past – even a successful past in government. He was driven forward by the passion that came from the injustice he saw in the world around him and his belief that practical politics could make a difference. Launching upon a groundbreaking new path he envisaged a new model of democratic engagement that broke with welfare in favour of work and rejected dependency in favour of independence, participation and self-reliance. That intellectual courage, and the courage he demonstrated to bring to life 'the driving power of social conscience' and then to embed the demand for justice in practical politics, is still something from which we can all learn today.

In the end Robert Kennedy did not – in the words of Tennyson, whose poetry he loved – 'sail beyond the sunset', but for his generation, and even more so for the generations that now follow, he pointed the way.

6

Nelson Mandela

Over the last decade I have had the privilege of meeting Nelson Mandela in London on many occasions, but also in Cardiff, New York, more recently at his home in South Africa and then, in April 2006, in Mozambique where he now spends much of his time with his wife Graça Machel, herself a remarkable person. I count it an honour to have been in the presence of and talked with the most courageous man of our times.

Even more so, I am grateful for his advice and friendship. His passion for justice is undimmed by the years and his support in the long struggle for fairness for the developing world spurs me on. His kindness too can reach out in surprising ways. I will never ever forget his phonecall on the day my son John was born: out of the blue, that unmistakable voice brought yet more happiness to an already extraordinarily happy day.

Meeting him for the first time was a joy. His physical presence is impressive. He is a hero of our times, but one with the calm authority of a long life well lived and a modesty and gentleness that belie his huge achievements. Both my growing knowledge over the decades of his achievements and our conversations in recent years convince me that to understand his courageous life one must first understand the strength of his beliefs and the strength of his character.

Mandela's colour would always have marked him out as a target of an apartheid regime and in that sense he had courage thrust upon him. But as a young man whose fate it was to grow up at the height of apartheid repression, the choices Mandela made – and how and why he made them – are key to any understanding of his greatness.

Two stand out for me. The first is his decision, described in detail for me by his trial lawyer, to risk execution in order to send the strongest possible message from the dock in that courtroom in Rivonia in 1964; the second – and arguably the most important and influential choice he made – was his considered decision to work for a multiracial world. The day he was released from prison, with apartheid visibly crumbling and with no thought of 'We are the masters now', he abjured recrimination and revenge. Instead, he called for, and every day worked for – even before he left prison – a peaceful end to apartheid, and then in his five years as president, until he stepped down in 1999, for racial harmony.

So he will be remembered for a courage that was without rancour or bitterness, a courage that shone all the more brightly for the years he spent on the run, severed from his family, and then tortured, humiliated and imprisoned: his freedom taken from him for twenty-seven years, the best years of his life.

But to define Mandela simply as a man of courage who rejected bitterness is to underestimate something that is far greater than a trait of personality: what defines Mandela's courage and his greatness is the sheer towering strength of belief and strength of character that led him from the angry anti-apartheid activist who once favoured black power to the prisoner who after almost three decades of captivity forgave his persecutors – even the prosecutors who called for his execution – and made friends of the warders who sought to deprive him of his dignity.

It would be understandable if Nelson Mandela had become embittered. His liberty was denied him not by accident or misfortune, but by the deliberate and calculated actions of a vengeful regime. His imprisonment came to represent the protracted victimisation of one race by another, and the loss he suffered was permanent. Nothing could ever make up for his absence during his mother's last years, just as nothing could recompense the time lost as his children grew from infants into adults without him ever meeting them or them knowing his face.

He could have been expected to seek revenge against the people who took so much of his life away. People who have been wronged on such a scale often look for retribution for the injustice they have suffered. Mandela's eventual freedom could not buy back the lives of those of his colleagues who had been killed for their actions in the struggle against apartheid, or the years lost as his closest friends whose lives ended behind bars and who never knew that their sacrifice had not been in vain. So he would have been justified in carrying a deep hatred for those who dedicated their lives to crushing the hopes of a nation longing to be free. But Mandela emerged from captivity neither bitter nor burning with angry recrimination. Instead, he radiated warmth and exuded hope.

How is it that Nelson Mandela could bear such loss without seeking to make his enemies suffer as he had suffered? How is it that his heart has not been embittered through so much heartache? It is a question put to him often because it defies every expectation of human behaviour. Yet his greatness of heart is the quality that most endears him to the millions of people who draw inspiration from his example. 'He's good, and people's hearts leap because they say: "this is how we can be",' Desmond Tutu said of Mandela.

Joel Joffe was a young South African barrister when Nelson Mandela and his colleagues were charged with sabotage. At the time, says Joffe, he was planning to emigrate to Australia to escape a climate of fear, a political culture in which brutality and hatred defined the way of life. But just as he was about to leave, he was approached by some of the relatives of the accused who were desperately looking for someone to take on the case. Most of the legal establishment had already turned its back on such a politically charged and risky assignment. Joffe agreed to postpone his emigration, and led Mandela's defence team through one of the most notorious trials in recent history.

Opposite Joffe was Percy Yutar, the leading prosecutor for the state. He left a lasting impression on Joffe for his sheer vindictiveness. 'You'd expect that from the police,' Joffe recalled, 'but not from someone meant to be upholding the law in a dispassionate way. Percy Yutar mocked the accused. He lied. He was calculating.

He did everything that was abhorrent. Yutar tried to get them hanged. I hated him.'

Joffe then described how thirty years later, the newly freed Mandela issued an invitation to the man who had tried so ruthlessly to sentence him to death. It was a well-publicised meeting, and afterwards the press asked Mandela if he had forgiven Yutar. Mandela responded that it wasn't a question of forgiveness, that Yutar had just been doing his job.

Joffe was astonished at Mandela's response. He told Mandela he could not understand how he could have said that Yutar was only doing his job when they all knew he was doing much more than his job; he had been doing the work of politically motivated people determined to keep their power and crush any opposition at any cost. Mandela's response to Joffe was: 'I dedicated my life to the best interests of the country. That is the paramount consideration of everything I do. When you are working for a future in which you act for the best interests of everyone in that society, you cannot afford the luxury of revenge.'

Nelson Mandela's courage in rejecting bitterness and revenge made it possible for a new nation to be born. The whole world knew he had suffered and, by forgiving the people directly responsible for his own suffering, he laid down a path to redemption and gave others the courage to follow him, providing a route for his countrymen and women to follow, and thus liberate themselves from the rage of the wronged. 'He symbolises a much broader forgiveness and understanding and reaching out,' says Graça Machel of her husband. The Truth and Reconciliation hearings were perhaps the ultimate expression of the personal and institutional culture of forgiveness that Mandela fashioned. Desmond Tutu chaired the proceedings. He knew that healing a ravaged country through forgiveness could only be possible because, in Nelson Mandela, South Africa had a leader who would show the way. 'When he says "guys, we've got to forgive", no one could say "you are being facile here, you are talking glibly about forgiveness. What do you know about suffering?"' said Tutu of Mandela. 'Twenty-seven years, you know . . .'

'He is so respected, so admired, so loved because of his courage,' said Joel Joffe. 'People want to be like him. There are a lot of hateful people in this world. But there are a lot of good people. The courage of Nelson Mandela gives them hope and a sense of what is possible.'

Nelson Mandela's achievement could have been to lead a mass protest movement against oppression. It could have been to overthrow apartheid. It could have been to get the African National Congress into power. It could have stopped there, and that in itself would have made him a hero. But Mandela was always more than just a man of his time.

Mandela had the strength of belief and the strength of character to convert the struggle into a moral crusade that sent out a message about the kind of future every society should seek: beyond the mountaintops and towards the promised land. And what emerged was a country where, because of Mandela, a black former ANC activist could, as president, don a Springbok rugby shirt and cheer on the predominantly white national team, and a white general could fly the colours of the new South Africa on the inauguration of a black president, each with equal pride.

So what was the set of beliefs that lay behind this extraordinary life and mission? And what were the circumstances in which Mandela demonstrated the strengths of both his beliefs and his willpower?

In Martin Luther King's America it was the gap between the promises of equal rights and the reality of discrimination that drew many black people into action. Promises made had to become promises redeemed. In the young Nelson Mandela's South Africa discrimination and oppression against the indigenous majority were enshrined in law and custom by a tiny minority. And one of the forces making this possible was the strong sense of tribal identity into which people in South Africa were born, loyalties cynically exploited by the regime to divide the majority against itself. So in apartheid South Africa we saw the anger of blacks denied their rights in their own country; the anger of whites brought up to believe that first their God-given rights and then their safety and prosperity were illegitimately under threat from blacks; the disempowering divisions within the black majority; an explosive cocktail consisting of the perpetuation of racial discrimination; tensions arising from tribal loyalty; and an ever-present, abiding anger.

Migrants had come to South Africa from India and the Far East, but the whites who arrived from Europe in the eighteenth and nineteenth centuries came not as migrants but as conquerors in search of land, wealth, and dominance. Tribal resistance proved futile. The last battle, fought between the Zulu tribe and the whites, took place in the first decade of the twentieth century: the black tribes could not withstand the withering power of the whites' military strength.

Even when Dutch primacy in South Africa gave way to British imperial control after the Boer War, unfettered access to South Africa's riches left the settlers with no compulsion and little inclination to share them with the indigenous population. And the establishment of apartheid in the mid-twentieth century enshrined white supremacy, effectively making it a crime for a black person to get a good education, earn a decent income or live in a nice home.

This was the world into which Nelson Mandela was born in 1918. To be unaware of that history, and to be born into a ruling tribal family in a small village far away from the mines and shanty towns of the city, could provide an illusion of freedom which Mandela had as a child. But to know that history would be a spur to action.

Nelson Mandela was not born angry. 'I was not born with a hunger to be free. I was born free – free in every way that I could know,' he wrote of his idyllic childhood. 'As long as I obeyed my father and abided by the customs of my tribe, I was not troubled by the laws of man or God.'

I came across few whites as a boy at Qunu. The local magistrate, of course, was white, as was the nearest shopkeeper. Occasionally white travellers or policemen passed through our area. These whites appeared as grand as gods to me, and I was aware that they were to be treated with a mixture of fear and respect.

It was only when I began to learn that my boyhood freedom was an illusion, when I discovered as a young man that my freedom had already been taken from me, that I began to hunger for it.

In his autobiography Nelson Mandela charts the road that took him from demanding freedom for himself to demanding freedom for all blacks:

At first, as a student, I wanted freedom only for myself, the transitory freedoms of being able to stay out at night, read what I pleased, and go where I chose. Later, as a young man in Johannesburg, I yearned for the basic and honourable freedoms of achieving my potential, of earning my keep, of marrying and having a family – the freedom not to be obstructed in a lawful life. But then I slowly saw that not only was I not free, but my brothers and sisters were not free. I saw that it was not just my freedom that was curtailed, but the freedom of everyone who looked like I did.

And this was the first stage in Mandela's political education: the realisation that collective rather than individual action was essential for freedom and respect.

That is when I joined the African National Congress, and that is when the hunger for my own freedom became the greater hunger for the freedom of my own people. It was this desire for the freedom of my people to live their lives with dignity and self-respect that animated my life, that transformed a frightened young man into a bold one, that drove a law-abiding attorney to become a criminal, that turned a family-loving husband into a man without a home, that forced a life-loving man to live like a monk.

I am no more virtuous or self-sacrificing than the next man, but I found that I could not even enjoy the poor and limited freedoms I was allowed when I knew my people were not free. Freedom is indivisible; the chains on any one of my people were chains on all of them, the chains on all of my people were the chains on me.

Nelson Mandela was born the first son of the third wife of Gadla Mphakanyiswa, a minor chief. His father gave him the name Rolihlahla, which means – perhaps significantly – 'one who causes trouble for himself'. The name Nelson came later, an English name given to him, as was then the custom in missionary schools, by his teacher Miss Mdingane on his first day at primary school. Though neither of his parents was literate, his father was a highly intelligent man who set great store by education and his mother, a Christian, was a member of the Methodist Church, into which he was baptised in infancy.

Mandela's birth into a ruling tribal lineage gave him far greater opportunities than most other black children in South Africa. Following the death of his father in 1928, when Nelson was nine, he was taken into the care of a much more senior chief, Jonginaba Dalindyebo, the acting regent of the Thembu people. Growing up among the tribal elders at the palace of Mqhekezweni, the Great Place, he attended the debates and meetings at which, under the chairmanship of his guardian, all-important decisions were made. Votes were unknown and the majority did not rule. Instead, decision was by consensus, and if a decision could not be achieved it would be deferred until consensus could be reached. The debates were open and people spoke their minds; young and old could take part, and the chief himself could be openly criticised. Later Mandela wrote: 'As a leader I have always followed the principles I first saw demonstrated by the regent at the Great Place.'

And over the same years, in a society where an oral tradition kept history alive, he heard the stories of South Africa's troubled past, and of the heroic warriors who fought against the invading European forces:

It was at Mqhekezweni that I developed my interest in African history . . . I learned of these men from the chiefs and headmen who came to the Great Place to settle disputes and try cases. Some days they would finish early and sit around telling stories. I

hovered silent and listened. At first they shooed me away and told
me I was too young to listen. But eventually, they permitted me to
stay and I discovered the great African patriots who fought against
Western domination. My imagination was fired by the glory of
these African warriors . . . Chief Joyi railed against the white
man, whom he believed had deliberately sundered the Xhosa
tribe, dividing brother from brother. The white man had told the
Thembus that their true chief was the great white queen across the
ocean and that they were her subjects. But the white queen
brought nothing but misery and perfidy to the black people; if
she was a chief, she was an evil chief. Chief Joyi's war stories and his
indictment of the British made me feel angry and cheated, as
though I had already been robbed of my own birthright.

One of the greatest advantages that Mandela had growing up in a
royal household was the chance to go to school. He was educated at
schools and colleges set up by British missionaries for the betterment of
black children. But the lessons taught in those schools were very
different from the education he received at the knees of his tribal
elders. By omission as much as by anything else, his formal education
imparted the sense that his race had failed to contribute anything
worth preserving and teaching to future generations. Of it he wrote:
'The education I received was a British education, in which British
ideas, British culture, and British institutions were automatically
assumed to be superior. There was no such thing as African culture.'
    One of the passages I found most poignant in Nelson Mandela's
autobiography comes when he leaves South Africa for the first time
in his life. In 1961, in the wake of the Sharpeville massacre,
Umkhonto we Sizwe, the armed wing of the ANC, had been
formed, with Mandela as its commander-in-chief. Soon afterwards
Mandela left the country unlawfully and travelled abroad for
several months. In Ethiopia he addressed the Conference of the
Pan African Freedom Movement of East and Central Africa, and
was warmly received by senior political leaders in several countries.
During this trip Mandela, anticipating an intensification of the
armed struggle, began to arrange guerrilla training for members of
Umkhonto we Sizwe.

If a Hollywood action film were to be made of Nelson Mandela's life at that time, it would probably portray him in a romanticised role as the freedom fighter: attractive, idealistic, courageous and heroic, drilling recruits in makeshift camps deep within the African wilderness. And by all accounts, such a portrayal of this charismatic leader would not be far from the truth. But in his own account of that time, of a visit to Egypt, Mandela wrote instead of spending a day in a Cairo museum – not, he said, out of an 'amateur archaeological interest', but to remind himself that black people do have a culture, a civilised past, a sense of resourcefulness, ingenuity, and creativity. 'It is important for African nationalists to be armed with evidence to refute the fictitious claims of whites that Africans are without a civilized past that compares with that of the West,' he stated perfunctorily, without emotion.

The contrast between Mandela, the great freedom fighter rousing support throughout the African continent, and Mandela, the solitary man standing in a museum, peering silently at precious items in a glass display case – poignantly encapsulates for me the pernicious hold of racism. Here is a black man seeking out the treasures of black civilisations to remind himself that what he had been taught of his race – that it is inferior – is not true. It is the essence of apartheid, a system designed to dehumanise a people, infiltrating every aspect of their existence with such a sense of inadequacy and backwardness that even when the mind overcomes the illogic of its ideology, some remnants of doubt linger on in the creases and folds of bitter experience.

Black South Africans may have been denied recognition of their cultural heritage, but Mandela saw how blacks were readily ascribed certain characteristics by the ruling whites that necessitated their subjugation. Uneducated, they could not be trusted with the right to vote because they would not be able to make rational decisions about what was best for the country. Tribal and territorial, they needed to be corralled into separate areas, divided from both each other and the whites. Caricatured as lazy and untrustworthy, they had to be severely disciplined and threatened with harsh consequences to preserve civic order.

In prison, the distinctions were particularly humiliating. African prisoners were given only short trousers to wear, as though to mark them out as having the capacities of children. They were given different food rations, ostensibly to be more in keeping with their dietary customs, but of poorer nutritional value and of smaller quantity than those given to white prisoners.

The assumption of black inferiority so pervaded ordinary life that Mandela often failed to recognise it. As a student he and his classmates were supposed to accept it as fact, not as anything value-laden or open to debate. Such was its entrenchment that Mandela could recall a school assembly whereby the white principal elicited feelings of gratitude from the black students for condescending to educate them:

> The principal of Healdtown was Dr Arthur Wellington, a stout and stuffy Englishman who boasted of his connection to the Duke of Wellington. At the outset of Assemblies, Dr Wellington would walk on stage and say, in his deep bass voice, 'I am the descendant of the great Duke of Wellington, aristocrat, states-man, and general, who crushed the Frenchman Napoleon at Waterloo and thereby saved civilisation for Europe – and for you, the natives.' At this, we would all enthusiastically applaud, each of us profoundly grateful that a descendant of the great Duke of Wellington would take the trouble to educate natives such as ourselves.

As Mandela grew older he became more acutely aware of the Afrikaner government's caricature of blacks as naturally rural and ethnically segregated, first to justify their attempts to constrict the space in which blacks could inhabit, and more insidiously, to sabotage efforts towards black unity and to encourage racial strife. 'The government, in order to keep Africans in the countryside or working in the mines, maintained that Africans were by nature a rural people, ill suited to city life,' said Mandela. But his arrival in the Johannesburg suburb of Alexandra undermined their claim:

> Alexandra, despite its problems and flaws, gave the lie to that argument. Its population, drawn from all African language

groups, was well adapted to city life and politically conscious. Urban life tended to abrade tribal and ethnic distinctions, and instead of being Xhosas, or Sothos, or Zulus or Shangaans, we were Alexandrans. This created a sense of solidarity which caused great concern among the white authorities. The government had always utilised divide and rule tactics when dealing with Africans and depended on the strength of ethnic divisions between the people.

So long as blacks accepted the place allotted to them, there could appear to be superficial harmony. Polite, well-educated young Mandela had been groomed for success and looked forward to the status and income he could command from his elite education. But even in the days before apartheid became official policy, Mandela would find that race was a more dominant factor in determining opportunity than education, achievement or birth. A black person born into a royal lineage, educated at elite institutions, and professionally accomplished, as Mandela was, would still always be regarded as a lesser being than a white person. 'In those days,' wrote Mandela, 'a black man with a BA was expected to scrape before a white man with a primary school education. No matter how high a black man advanced, he was still considered inferior to the lowest white man.'

At the age of twenty-five, Mandela enrolled in the law school at Witwatersrand University in Johannesburg as preparation to his setting up South Africa's first all-black firm of solicitors. Unlike the other institutions where he had been educated, Witwatersrand was a white-dominated university and he found himself the only black student in the entire law faculty. More sharply here than ever before, he would learn that his race would put him on an unavoidable collision course with the white majority.

Despite the university's liberal values, I never felt entirely comfortable there. Always to be the only African, except for menial workers, to be regarded at best as a curiosity and at worst as an interloper, is not a congenial experience. My manner was always guarded, and I met both generosity and animosity.

Although I was to discover a core of sympathetic whites who became friends and later colleagues, most of the whites at Wits were not liberal or colour-blind. I recall getting to a lecture a few minutes late one day and taking a seat next to Sarel Tighy, a classmate who later became a Member of Parliament for the United Party. Though the lecture had already started and there were only a few empty seats, he ostentatiously collected his things and moved to a seat away from me. This type of behaviour was the rule rather than the exception.

Another story Mandela recalls from his days at 'Wits' is of catching a tram with Indian friends from the university. Indians were allowed to use the tram, but African blacks were not. When the conductor confronted the Indians and told them that their '*kaffir* friend' was not allowed on, the Indian friends protested loudly and the conductor had them all arrested.

Racism was so profoundly embedded in the structures of South African society that a black person could be stopped on the street by a white stranger and sent on an errand or told to perform a chore, and he or she would normally oblige. In his autobiography Mandela related a painful occasion when he was working as a clerk in a white law firm. He was dictating to a white secretary when a white client whom she knew came into the office. 'She was embarrassed, and to demonstrate that she was not taking dictation from an African, she took a sixpence from her purse and said stiffly, "Nelson, please go out and get me some shampoo from the chemist." I left the room and got her shampoo.'

It would have been surprising indeed if indignities such as this did not anger the young Mandela and make him receptive to arguments he heard at university about the roots of racial oppression and its solutions. Political ideas, especially ones that linked race to power and identity, had always stirred Mandela, but had not yet provoked him into changing the course of his life. It was to be in Johannesburg, that great and bustling city of such extremes, where Mandela first became consciously active politically.

'I cannot pinpoint a moment when I became politicised, when I

Edith Cavell

Dietrich Bonhoeffer

Raoul Wallenberg

Robert Kennedy

Martin Luther King

Nelson Mandela

Cicely Saunders

Aung San Suu Kyi

knew that I would spend my life in the liberation struggle,' he
wrote in his autobiography.

To be an African in South Africa means that one is politicised
from the moment of one's birth, whether one acknowledges it or
not. An African child is born in an Africans Only hospital, taken
home in an Africans Only bus, lives in an Africans Only area and
attends Africans Only schools, if he attends school at all. When
he grows up, he can hold Africans Only jobs, rent a house in
Africans Only townships, ride Africans Only trains and be
stopped at any time of the day or night and be ordered to
produce a pass, without which he can be arrested and thrown in
jail. His life is circumscribed by racist laws and regulations that
cripple his growth, dim his potential and stunt his life. This was
the reality, and one could deal with it in a myriad of ways.

I had no epiphany, no singular revelation, no moment of
truth, but a steady accumulation of a thousand slights, a thousand indignities and a thousand unremembered moments produced in me an anger, a rebelliousness, a desire to fight the
system that imprisoned my people. There was no particular day
on which I said, henceforth I will devote myself to the liberation
of my people; instead, I simply found myself doing so, and could
not do otherwise.

The first real challenge to his ideas about identity came when he
was at college. Mandela learned that a popular and well-respected
professor had married a woman from a different tribe. It was an
onslaught to his senses and pitted blind tribal loyalty against logic
and experience. 'Marriages between tribes were then extremely
unusual,' he wrote. 'Until then, I had never known of anyone who
had married outside his tribe. We had been taught that such unions
were taboo.'

His reaction was to let go of the narrow prejudices that had, up
until then, set the boundaries of acceptable behaviour and to be
guided instead by high ideals that transcended tribal custom.
'Seeing [the teacher] and his wife began to undermine my par-
ochialism and loosen the hold of the tribalism that still imprisoned

me. I began to sense my identity as an African, not just a Thembu
or even a Xhosa. But this was still a nascent feeling.'

The alternate widening and constriction of Mandela's emerging
sense of identity underwent another sharp adjustment in his final
year at boarding school, at an event which Mandela likened to a
comet streaking across the night sky. A famous Xhosa poet called
Mqhayi was invited to perform in front of the students. The poet,
much to Mandela's amazement, staged a striking and aggressive
nationalistic performance in front of the impressionable young
audience. Its incongruence excited and troubled him. First of
all, here was a black man drawing direct and explicit attention
to white imperialism in a white-run institution. Then, here was a
fellow Xhosa, proclaiming the pre-eminence of his own tribe in
front of pupils from many different tribes. Shock, pride and delight
mixed with fainter shades of disapproval and disappointment in
Mandela's reaction to the spectacle the poet created:

> Suddenly the door opened and out walked not Dr Wellington,
> but a black man dressed in a leopard skin *kaross* and matching
> hat, who was carrying a spear in either hand. Dr Wellington
> followed a moment later, but the sight of a black man in tribal
> dress coming through that door was electrifying. It is hard to
> explain the impact it had on us. It seemed to turn the universe
> upside down . . .
>
> I could hardly believe my ears. His boldness in speaking of
> such delicate matters in the presence of Dr Wellington and other
> whites seemed utterly astonishing to us. Yet at the same time it
> aroused and motivated us, and began to alter my perception of
> men like Dr Wellington, whom I had automatically considered
> my benefactor.
>
> I was galvanised, but also confused by Mqhayi's performance.
> He had moved from a more nationalistic, all-encompassing
> theme of African unity to a more parochial one addressed to
> the Xhosa people, of whom he was one. As my time at Heald-
> town was coming to an end, I had many new and sometimes
> conflicting ideas floating in my head. I was beginning to see that
> Africans of all tribes had much in common, yet here was the great

Mqhayi praising the Xhosa above all; I saw that an African
might stand his ground with a white man, yet I was still eagerly
seeking benefits from whites, which often required subservience.
In a sense, Mqhayi's shift in focus was a mirror of my own mind
because I went back and forth between pride in myself as a
Xhosa and a feeling of kinship with other Africans. But as I left
Healdtown at the end of the year, I saw myself as a Xhosa first
and an African second.

But events compelled Mandela to see clearly that in apartheid
South Africa his colour was more important than his tribe. Mandela was temporarily suspended from college after a showdown
with the principal during a dispute between the student body and
the college authorities. He returned home to discover that his
guardian had arranged a marriage for him without his consent
to a woman not of his choice. He was shocked and dismayed, and
realised that his exposure to other ideas and cultures had succeeded
in eroding his remaining loyalties to tribal custom. Instead of
marrying, he ran away to Johannesburg.

Here he realised that the comfortable background and status of a
tribal monarchy would not open any of the doors closed to people
because of the colour of their skin. The insistent call drawing him
away from his homeland became the call for justice for the African
people.

'I was beginning to see that my duty was to my people as a
whole, not just to a particular section or branch. I felt that all the
currents in my life were taking me away from the Transkei and
towards what seemed like the centre, a place where regional and
ethnic loyalties gave way to a common purpose,' wrote Mandela of
that era in his life. That common purpose became the cause of
freedom for all.

We can trace the change in Mandela's attitudes. As a very young
child he gained identity from the unquestioned customs of family
and village life where everyone knew his or her place. 'Like all
Xhosa children, I acquired knowledge mainly through
observation . . . My life, and that of most Xhosas at the time,
was shaped by custom, ritual and taboo.' The death of his father,

when Nelson was nine, brought his first crisis of identity. 'I do not remember experiencing great grief so much as feeling cut adrift. Although my mother was the centre of my existence, I defined myself through my father.'

After his father's death and after moving from his mother's village and his uncle's royal palace, Mandela's sense of identity centred on his privileged place within the Xhosa tribe and what would be expected of him from his royal lineage. 'Because of the universal respect the regent enjoyed – from both black and white – and the seemingly untempered power that he wielded, I saw chieftaincy as being the very centre around which life revolved.'

Boarding school broadened his horizons but did not alter his sense of who he was and where his place was in the world:

> Even as I left Clarkebury, I was still, at heart, a Thembu and I was proud to think and act like one. My roots were my destiny, and I believed that I would become a counsellor to the Thembu king, as my guardian wanted. My horizons did not extend beyond Thembuland and I believed that to be a Thembu was the most enviable thing in the world.

Both within himself and with those closest to him, Mandela struggled to find the basis for a single South African identity that included all races. If he had put all his energies at the service of his Xhosa tribe, blind to the problems of the rest of the country; or if he had devoted his life to the promotion of the ANC above all other opposition movements; or if he had dedicated the struggle to the founding a black South Africa where whites did not feel they had a place, as at various times of his life he was poised to do, then history might have taken a very different turn.

But Mandela's first foray into politics was cautious and hesitant. Unfamiliar with the mechanisms of party politics, unsure of his direction, he was also mindful of all the warnings he had been given about the trouble political involvement could bring. He recounts being advised by a well-meaning friend that opposition politics would mean he would probably end up in jail for the rest of his life. 'And that's just what happened,' Mandela said poignantly in the 2003 BBC documentary about his life, *Mandela: The Living Legend*. 'But I was fired up.'

The 'firing up' of Mandela and the strength of will that he developed is the key to the future of South Africa. Privileged within his own community: royal, English speaking, university educated, a legal trainee – Mandela could easily have risen in his own tribal community. But with his eyes now opened to discrimination, inequality and the limitations of tribal politics in an apartheid regime, Mandela's anger at injustice led him to evolve a set of beliefs that were to transform his country. Being, as he said, no longer tentative in his attitudes but 'fired up' with passion against injustice, Mandela, like many young African nationalists who joined the ANC, demanded quick results. An early disciple of Anton Lembede, the first leader of the ANC's Youth League, Mandela started off sharing Lembede's deep suspicion of other opposition groups against white supremacy.

At no point did Mandela go so far as to call for a racially purely black Africa from which whites would be forcibly removed. But he would have been quite happy to see whites fleeing voluntarily. 'Lembede's Africanism was not universally supported,' Mandela writes,

> because his ideas were characterised by a racial exclusivity that disturbed some of the other Youth Leaguers. Some of the members felt that a nationalism that would include sympathetic whites was a more desirable course. Others, including myself, countered that if blacks were offered a multiracial form of a struggle, they would remain enamoured of white culture and prey to a continuing sense of inferiority. At the time, I was firmly opposed to allowing communists or whites to join the struggle.

So, he explains:

> I was sympathetic to the ultra-revolutionary stream of African nationalism. I was angry at the white man, not at racism. While I was not prepared to hurl the white man into the sea, I would have been perfectly happy if he had climbed aboard his steamships and left the continent of his own volition.

Perhaps Mandela's initial rejection of a multiracial struggle in favour of a purely black movement also reflected a lack of confidence at this formative period of his political awakening. He complained of feeling inadequate in the presence of eloquent, seasoned speakers and, perhaps at that stage, the prospect of replicating feelings of black inferiority within the movement seemed more terrible than adopting an inflexible political stance. Mandela admitted that pride, too, clouded his early political judgement. He did not want to share the glory of staging public acts of resistance with other groups or dilute the heady sense of belonging he felt as a founding member of the Youth League.

> I was wary of white influence in the ANC and I opposed joint campaigns with the [communist] party. I was concerned that the communists were intent on taking over our movement under the guise of joint action. I believed that it was an undiluted African nationalism, not Marxism or multi-racialism, that would liberate us. I even went so far as breaking up CP meetings by storming the stage, tearing up signs and capturing the microphone . . . I felt about the Indians the same way I did about the communists: that they would tend to dominate the ANC, in part because of their superior education, experience and training . . . My idea at the time was that the ANC should be involved only in campaigns that the ANC itself led. I was more concerned with who got the credit than whether the campaign would be successful.

Mandela writes candidly about his political shortcomings during that early period of his political activism, but those days were short-lived. Many of us at some stage go through a period where the views we hold are the antithesis of our earliest influences, but foreshadow a richer synthesis to follow. With Mandela's background and with his personality, his conversion to multiracialism was, in my view, always likely, the almost inevitable result of the influences of his earlier life.

From being an advocate of black exclusivity, Mandela became the most inclusive of all politicians, with a vision of unity that would eventually extend even to those who had been his bitterest enemies, but that was because he had a bigger vision than most. From his visits outside South Africa he had already rewritten in his own mind the white colonial view of African history he had been taught. But the very richness of African civilisation he discovered did not make him, in the end, exclusive, but made him see how southern Africa and Africa as a whole could contribute to the progress of all humanity. And most of all his fundamental belief in the potential of human goodness made him see oppression not so much the work of evil men, but of an evil system which had caught weak men in its web. In his first wave of anger Mandela blamed white people for the injustices blacks suffered: now he understood it was an evil system. This made him more ready to be inclusive. Everything he had learned from his background led him to the view that a bad system could be overthrown by good people coming together.

He was no pessimist about the failings of human nature, but an optimist about its goodness. 'I am fundamentally an optimist,' he said. 'Whether that comes from nature or nurture, I cannot say. Part of being optimistic is keeping one's head pointed towards the sun, one's feet moving forward.'

Tragedy also helped consolidate the unity of the opposition groups against apartheid, when a government crackdown on a May Day demonstration in 1950 left eighteen Africans dead. After this Mandela could see others who opposed white supremacy – the Indians, students and Communists – as partners, not competitors, in the struggle for liberation. 'Here, I believed, was a sufficient threat that compelled us to join hands with our Indian and communist colleagues . . . for if our struggle was to succeed, we had to transcend black and white.'

Mandela's strategy of inclusion was also pragmatic. South Africa's best hope for the future was for a campaign as broad as possible, whose supporters could reach as near as possible to a consensus about its aims. The South Africa of his dreams was radically different to anything that South Africa had ever known before. To dismantle the old system and build the new would need a people at ease with themselves and each other.

I think of Mandela's political inclusiveness as an extension of his

courage as well as a farsighted and pragmatic political strategy. It
was the genius of Mandela and his colleagues to formulate the
struggle in the broadest and most inclusive terms, and that in turn
paved the way for the triumph of hope and progress over the dead
weight of anger and bitterness. Mandela's circle could so easily
have fashioned the ANC around policies of conquest, instead they
built it around the politics of principle. At risk of alienating himself
from angry supporters hungry for the spoils of war, Mandela
insisted that the prize of a post-apartheid South Africa belonged
to everyone, even to those who fought against its coming. Justice,
equality, opportunity – these were the goals he aimed for, and they
did not belong to any political group or to any one race. He sought
a victory not just for ANC supporters, not just for blacks, but for all
South Africans.

Nelson Mandela's fate was to come of age as white supremacy
itself came of age. As Mandela's political philosophy matured,
racial oppression intensified; over the next four decades the two
evolved and interacted as though their destinies were inextricably
linked. 1948 was the year that Nelson Mandela turned thirty, and
it was also the year that the Nationalist party swept to power in
South Africa. Led by Daniel Malan, the Nationalists whipped up
fear of a 'black peril' and promised to protect white South Africans
by taking tough action against the blacks. The injustices visited
upon blacks in South Africa by previous white administrations
would turn into an infinitely more overt, determined, and brutal
onslaught.

'The often haphazard segregation of the past three hundred
years was to be consolidated into a monolithic system that was
diabolical in its detail, inescapable in its reach and overwhelming
in its power,' Mandela writes. 'From the moment of the Nationalists' election, we knew that our land would henceforth be a place
of tension and strife.' Mandela's grim prophecy would be fulfilled.

Within months, new legislation made marriage and sexual
contact between mixed races illegal. Education of black children
was to be heavily restricted. Blacks were forced to carry passes
everywhere they went and could be punished severely if they were
found to be without one. Already denied the right to own property,

legislation made it lawful for blacks to be forcibly moved from whole areas of the city and country where they had lived and worked for generations, to make way for whites-only areas founded on the assumption of racial superiority: the creation of rigid geographical, economic, social and cultural barriers between whites, African blacks and other coloured people became apartheid's fullest expression.

So Mandela saw the enemy not as a few white people but as the whole edifice of apartheid, a discredited ideology based on the loathing and fears of a minority whose privileges were dependent upon the continuing subjugation of the majority. And, from that time onwards, by distinguishing between the system of apartheid which he hated and the white South Africans whom he could come to forgive, he was able to overcome the most overwhelming obstacles to unity both during his years as a freedom fighter and during his years as president in post-apartheid South Africa. The strength of these beliefs was the foundation of all that followed. 'Mandela criticised apartheid and not the white community who acted it out. His message of peace, reconciliation and forgiveness caught many supporters off guard but bolstered his moral reputation,' wrote the historian Anthony R. DeLuca. 'His generous spirit, tenacious personality, and passion for tolerance enabled him to transform the racial politics of South Africa and bequeath a rare legacy of political compassion and new hope for racial harmony.'

The collaborative efforts of the ANC and other opposition groups led to the imaginative Congress of the People in 1955, where all South Africans were invited to submit their vision of a land where people enjoyed equal rights. Mandela was the main speaker at the Congress: 'In my speech I called for a national convention in which all South Africans, black and white, Indian and Coloured, would sit down in brotherhood and create a constitution that mirrored the aspirations of the country as a whole. I called for unity, and said we would be invincible if we spoke with one voice.'

From the Congress of the People came the ANC's Freedom Charter, the movement's manifesto and a poetic representation of the hopes of millions of oppressed people. The Charter was personal, in that it reflected the actual experiences of so many people living out their lives as prisoners in their own land. But it also encapsulated the impersonal – or rather, the colour-blind – essence of Mandela's now-entrenched commitment to multiraci-alism. 'Our dream for the Congress of the People', Mandela wrote,

> was that it would be a landmark event in the history of the freedom struggle – a convention uniting all the oppressed and all the progressive forces of South Africa to create a clarion call for change . . . The Freedom Charter is a mixture of practical goals and poetic language. It extols the abolition of racial discrimina-tion and the achievement of equal rights for all. It welcomes all who embrace freedom to participate in the making of a demo-cratic, non-racial South Africa. It captured the hopes and dreams of the people and acted as a blueprint for the liberation struggle and the future of the nation.

So even during the most disheartening years, when the ANC had been all but crushed and the world was looking the other way, Mandela felt assured of their eventual triumph because of his conviction that the human instinct is for freedom and justice. Those who try to oppress the human instinct can never rest easy, Mandela held, because as long as there is human life, there is a seed that will grow towards the light. Mandela saw man's goodness as a flame that can be hidden but burns nevertheless. For the people of South Africa, Mandela provided the flame by which they could find a way out of the blinding bitterness that threatened to condemn the country to darkness.

Once Mandela had railed against the evil of white men. Now he rallied his forces against the evil of the system, not against one race but against racism. But having moved from seeing the root of oppression not in evil men but in an evil system, he also came to see that apartheid, once entrenched, could not be overthrown by non-violent protests alone; reluctantly he concluded it would need violent struggle too. Mandela was the leading proponent of this momentous change in policy, and one of his tasks was to solicit financial and practical help from the international community to build a new, armed wing of the ANC. But even that decision was built on a strength of belief that was in turn, he argued, founded on a basic humanitarianism: the targets of violence would not be white people but only the infrastructure of the state.

As president of the Youth League he had mobilised national campaigns and stay-at-home protests against the government's ever-hardening racism. His strategy had a sharp pragmatic edge. When protests foundered, he called them off. When official reprisals threatened to be more severe than the self-sacrifice of his supporters could bear, he pulled them back. When the government criminalised membership of the South African Communist Party and he feared the ANC would be next, he drew up contingency plans for the movement to operate underground. When all means of protest were made illegal and any show of opposition, no matter how legitimate or peaceful, was crushed with overwhelming force and brutality, he made the momentous decision and called for the ANC to drop its commitment to non-violence.

> I saw non-violence on the Gandhian model not as an inviolable principle but as a tactic to be used as the situation demanded. The principle was not so important that the strategy should be used even when it was self-defeating, as Gandhi himself believed. I called for non-violent protest for as long as it was effective . . . The Nationalist government was making any legal expression of dissent or protest impossible. I saw that it would ruthlessly suppress any legitimate protest on the part of the African majority. A police state did not seem far off . . . Non-violent passive resistance is effective as long as your opposition adheres to the same rules as you do. But if peaceful protest is met with violence, its efficacy is at an end. For me, non-violence was not a moral principle but a strategy; there is no moral goodness in using an ineffective weapon.

As a senior and influential leader in the ANC, Mandela did not take lightly this decision to propose the end of the ANC's policy of non-violence. It was after massive consultation and difficult internal debate that he and his colleagues decided upon the sabotage of important elements of the state infrastructure. They considered that to attack the non-human agents of apartheid was the best means of driving the government to the negotiating table. But even then Mandela was thinking ahead. 'Because it did not involve loss of life, it offered the best hope for reconciliation among the races afterwards,' he wrote later. 'We did not want to start a blood-feud between white and black.'

But to bomb power stations and attack the state's infrastructure were acts of criminality. And it meant that Nelson Mandela would soon became South Africa's most wanted man – hunted, on the run, separated from his wife and young children, living the low and lonely life of an outlaw, planning acts of sabotage and the creation of an armed wing of the ANC.

First arrested in 1956, Mandela, in what became known as the Treason Trial, used the courtroom, shrewdly and bravely, as a platform from which to put the Nationalist government on trial. It was a tactic he would use in subsequent trials to brilliant effect, and in this first instance, the court returned a verdict of not guilty.

When he was arrested again in 1962, this time for inciting strikes and for leaving the country without a passport, the courtroom once more became a public platform for the cause of black rights. This time he arrived in court wearing traditional Xhosa tribal dress – a leopard-skin *kaross* draped across his torso. The almost incongruent image of a South African freedom fighter, resplendent, dignified and defiant in tribal clothing, being interrogated by besuited solicitors in a Western-style courtroom, was designed to show the stark contrast in the lives of blacks and whites within the same country.

I had chosen traditional dress to emphasise the symbolism that I was a black African walking into a white man's court. I was literally carrying on my back the history, culture and heritage of my people. That day, I felt myself to be the embodiment of African nationalism, the inheritor of Africa's difficult but noble past and her uncertain future. The *kaross* was also a sign of contempt for the niceties of white justice. I well knew the authorities would feel threatened by my *kaross* as so many whites feel threatened by the true culture of Africa.

But Mandela's words were as dramatic as his dress. He called no witnesses in his defence and did not deny the actions he had taken, but insisted that he was guilty of no crime and declared he would not desist from his purpose. His bold and moving words were widely reported by the world's media and sealed his international reputation:

Many years ago, when I was a boy brought up in my village in the Transkei, I listened to the elders of the tribe telling stories about the good old days before the arrival of the white man. Then our people lived peacefully, under the democratic rule of their kings, and moved freely and confidently up and down the country without let or hindrance. The country was our own, in name and right. We occupied the land, the forests, the rivers; we extracted the mineral wealth beneath the soil and all the riches of this beautiful country. We set up and operated our own government, we controlled our own arms and we organised our trade and commerce. The elders would tell tales of the wars fought by our ancestors in defence of the Fatherland, as well as the acts of valour by generals and soldiers during these epic days . . .

In such a society are contained the seeds of revolutionary democracy in which none will be held in slavery or servitude, and in which poverty, want and insecurity shall be no more. This is the history which, even today, inspires me and my colleagues in our political struggle . . .

I would say that the whole life of any thinking African in this country drives him continuously to a conflict between his conscience on the one hand and the law on the other. This is not a conflict peculiar to this country. The conflict arises for men of conscience, for men who think and who feel deeply in every country . . . Men, I think, are not capable of doing nothing, of saying nothing, of not reacting to injustice, of not protesting against oppression, of not striving for the good society and the good life in the ways they see it . . .

I was made, by the law, a criminal, not because of what I had done, but because of what I stood for, because of what I thought, because of my conscience. It has not been easy for me during the past period to separate myself from my wife and children, to say goodbye to the good old days when, at the end of a strenuous day at an office, I could look forward to joining my family at the dinner table, and instead to take up the life of a man hunted continuously by the police, living separated from those who are closest to me, in my own country, facing continually the hazards of detection and of arrest.

This has been a life infinitely more difficult than serving a prison sentence. No man in his right senses would voluntarily choose such a life in preference to the one of normal, family, social life which exists in every civilised community.

But there comes a time as it came in my life, when a man is denied the right to live a normal life, when he can only live the life of an outlaw because the government has so decreed to use the law to impose a state of outlawry upon him.

I do not believe, Your Worship, that this court, in inflicting penalties on me for the crimes for which I am convicted, should be moved by the belief that penalties will deter men from the course that they believe is right. History shows that penalties do not deter men when their conscience is aroused, nor will they deter my people or the colleagues with whom I have worked before.

I am prepared to pay the penalty even though I know how bitter and desperate is the situation of an African in the prisons of this country . . . nevertheless these considerations do not sway me from the path that I have taken nor will they sway others like me. For to men, freedom in their own land is the pinnacle of their ambitions, from which nothing can turn men of conviction aside. More powerful than my fear of the dreadful conditions to which I might be subjected in prison is my hatred for the dreadful conditions to which my people are subjected outside prison throughout this country.

Whatever sentence Your Worship sees fit to impose upon me for the crime for which I have been convicted before this court, may it rest assured that when my sentence has been completed I will still be moved, as men are always moved, by their con-science; I will still be moved by my dislike of the race discrimination against my people when I come out from serving my sentence, to take up again, as best I can, the struggle for the removal of those injustices until they are finally abolished once and for all . . .

I have done my duty to my people and to South Africa. I have no doubt that posterity will pronounce that I was innocent and that the criminals that should have been brought before this court are the members of the government.

Mandela was found guilty and sentenced to five years in prison, with no possibility of parole. It was the stiffest sentence yet imposed in South Africa for a political offence, and the sentence would in practice run for twenty-seven years. For Mandela was still serving his five-year sentence when evidence of the ANC's sabotage activities was discovered – evidence that left Mandela in no doubt that in the coming trial he would be sentenced to death. Joel Joffe, his leading defence advocate, also believed that Mandela would be sentenced to the gallows if found guilty. 'The trial was very much about saving lives,' he said.

It is at this point that all Mandela's strength of belief and character came to the fore. Joel Joffe bears witness to the courage of Mandela. Scarcely is it possible to imagine what it must be like to have the spectre of an impending execution clouding every waking moment. 'We lived in the shadows of the gallows,' admitted Mandela. 'The mere possibility of a death sentence changes everything. From the start, we considered it the most likely outcome of the trial.'

The courage that Mandela summoned in the face of probable death is now legendary. 'What was so remarkable is that, as opposed to acting courageously in the heat of battle, Mandela had nine months to think about being hanged,' said Joel Joffe. 'In South Africa they used to execute prisoners about once a week by hanging. The executions would take place at six in the morning. The night before, all the prisoners in jail would start singing, and sing right through the night to give the prisoner courage. Death was a presence in jail. It's not something you could put in the back of your mind.'

In the company of Mandela and his fellow accused throughout the entire trial, Joel Joffe witnessed their darkest days. And his account gives us a picture of the leadership Mandela displayed. For courage itself was on trial. While it would have been much easier to bargain for the least of sentences, Mandela insisted on putting the apartheid system on trial, challenging it directly, utterly indifferent to his own fate.

Joffe recalls the first meeting with all of the accused as they gathered to discuss their defence after being held in solitary confinement for ninety days:

> It was a very emotional experience for everyone . . . The police didn't tell them what they were going to be charged for. They wheeled out the other nine accused first. They were dazed, just coming out of solitary confinement, and they were coming to grips with things . . . Then the doors opened and Nelson Mandela came through. He had lost a lot of weight. His cheeks were sallow and he looked a lot thinner. But everybody was thrilled to see him.

As Joffe says, 'the natural authority in him exuded'.

> There he was in short trousers, while the barristers were all in suits and the other accused in normal clothes. Mandela just quietly assumed leadership. When you meet him, you just feel this is a leader. He just assumed control and laid down the principles for the trial.
>
> Mandela said the trial would be turned into a trial of the government. The whole case was to be prepared for putting them on trial, not for getting off. He and his colleagues accepted responsibility for their actions. Knowing this, that they wouldn't waver, they wouldn't plea for mitigation, they would not apologise.

Mandela's objective was not personal safety but political impact: once again using the high drama of a courtroom appearance to put a whole system on trial. In an ultimate act of courageousness, he defied death and the fear of death. He would make a final stand for the great principles whose ultimate victory he felt was assured. By dying a martyr for the causes of freedom and equality in South Africa, Mandela, as Joffe recalls, believed he would strengthen their cause and inspire his supporters to carry on with the fight.

Mandela refused to plead for his own life and declined to consider any appeal against whatever outcome the court would deliver. He didn't deny carrying out the activities for which he was charged. Instead from the middle of the courtroom he delivered an explosively powerful speech on the moral justification for acting against the discredited and indefensible political ideology of apartheid. Against Joel Joffe's advice, and in the full knowledge that he was personally sealing his own fate, he affirmed his willingness to die for the very principles that make life worth living:

During my lifetime I have dedicated myself to this struggle of the African people. I have fought against white domination, and I have fought against black domination. I have cherished the ideal of a democratic and free society in which all persons live together in harmony and with equal opportunities. It is an ideal which I hope to live for and to achieve. But if needs be, it is an ideal for which I am prepared to die.

The accused were found guilty. Mandela had prepared a speech in the event of a death sentence being handed out, but the judge surprisingly sentenced Mandela to life imprisonment instead.

If Mandela had already mustered the courage to live the harsh and lonely life of a freedom fighter; if he had found the courage to lead his country through the rallies and strikes and the violent retaliation; if he had the courage – as he had done in the early 1950s – to smuggle himself out of South Africa to raise international support for the ANC; and the even greater courage to smuggle himself back in as a fugitive rather than savouring his freedom in the safety of exile; if he had the courage to turn three trials against him into trials against apartheid; and the courage to face his own death with unimaginable bravery; if he had the courage to forge a way for his people through the tumultuousness of extraordinary times, then the summons to a life of courage had just begun. What greater courage would he need to survive for almost three decades in a tiny, suffocating prison cell, locked away completely from the world at the height of his powers, yet incapable of doing anything, leading anything, changing anything?

The hardest courage to sustain is the kind of courage needed to fight despair and to endure when hope is gone: this is the courage that Mandela would have to muster year after year in prison. It demanded the greatest strength of belief and of character upon which the very existence of courage depends. 'We were face to face with the realisation that our life would be unredeemably grim,' wrote Mandela of his first weeks in prison on Robben Island.

In prison he was truly isolated. Communication between prisoners was forbidden. Days were strictly regimented so that prisoners were denied the smallest freedoms of deciding when to get up, when to wash, when to eat, when to sleep. Prisoners were forced to work all day, performing mindless, repetitive tasks with inadequate equipment, serving as a pointed reminder that the work was meant to undermine their willpower – not to extract productive labour from them. 'Prison,' wrote Mandela, 'is designed to break one's spirit and destroy one's resolve. To do this, the authorities attempt to exploit every weakness, demolish every initiative, negate all signs of individuality – all with the idea of stamping out that spark that makes each of us human and each of us who we are.'

We can only imagine how he felt as each door closed on Mandela on Robben Island and eventually he occupied a cell of just eight foot by seven. In his autobiography, Mandela refers frequently to his love of the outdoors and how in troubled times the vast openness of the countryside soothed his heart. Confinement to a small physical space is severe punishment to anyone, but perhaps particularly so to one who drew so much pleasure from the outdoors. The Mandela who wrote of the happiness he felt as a boy growing up in the regent's palace; and of the heady sensation he felt in college being groomed for success, with the world opening up to him and his future assuredly bright; this is the same Mandela who would be forced from his prominent role as an ANC leader to scrounge around the country as an outlaw living underground; and the same Mandela who would eventually be sentenced to life imprisonment in a tiny cell completely cut off from his family and supporters on the outside.

Who is to know what is the hardest part of a lifelong struggle for freedom or the full extent of the price that has to be paid on the road to courage? So much is sacrificed, and so much is lost. But the most haunting sadness that recurs again and again in Mandela's autobiography is his awareness of how his family suffered, too: 'For myself, I have never regretted my commitment to the struggle, and I was always prepared to face the hardships that affected me personally. But my family paid a terrible price, perhaps too dear a price, for my commitment.'

Mandela's mother, living in the remote village of her birth, would never be able to fully understand her son's struggle. She had lived most of her life in poverty and Mandela was tormented by the knowledge that he could have provided for her had he put his personal duties before those of his country. He never reveals what he and his mother said to one another during the infrequent contact they had. But he is explicit about the emotional impact of those visits:

> I wondered – not for the first time – whether one was ever justified in neglecting the welfare of one's own family in order to fight for the welfare of others. Can there be anything more important than looking after one's ageing mother? Is politics merely a pretext for shirking one's responsibilities, an excuse for not being able to provide in the way one wanted?

When Mandela's mother died while he was in prison on Robben Island, he was refused permission to attend her funeral.

> It added to my grief that I was not able to bury my mother, which was my responsibility as her eldest child and only son . . . A mother's death causes a man to look back on and evaluate his own life. Her difficulties, her poverty, made me question once again whether I had taken the right path. That was always the conundrum: Had I made the right choice in putting the people's

welfare even before that of my own family? For a long time, my mother had not understood my commitment to the struggle. My family had not asked for or even wanted to be involved in the struggle, but my involvement penalised them.

Politics had already claimed Mandela's first marriage to Evelyn Mase, with whom he had three children, one of whom died in infancy. The two grew apart as Mandela's political involvement intensified and Evelyn turned increasingly towards religion. They divorced in 1955. Mandela wrote about the painful impact the divorce had on all parties, but he was particularly saddened by the impact it had on his two surviving children, Makaziwe and Thembi:

The break-up of any marriage is traumatic, especially for the children. Our family was no exception, and all the children were wounded by our separation . . . Makaziwe was still very small, and I remember one day, when I was not in prison or in court, I visited her crèche unannounced. She had always been a very affectionate child, but that day when she saw me, she froze. She did not know whether to run to me or retreat, to smile or frown. She had some conflict in her small heart, which she did not know how to resolve. It was very painful . . . Following the break-up, Thembi would frequently wear my clothes, even though they were far too large for him; they gave him some kind of attachment to his too often distant father.

Perhaps the most painful abuse he had to endure during the long years on Robben Island was the deliberate denial of contact with his family. Mandela and Winnie had been married only a few years by the time of his imprisonment and their two daughters were still very young. But visits from children were forbidden and Mandela would not even lay eyes upon them again until they had grown from toddlers into young adults. Any attempts to make legitimate contact with his family via the prison post were sabotaged by the guards, who intercepted the letters and burnt them, leaving only the ashes for him to pick through.

The only news about his family that the prison guards allowed through was information designed to trouble and unsettle him. Scandalous rumours involving Winnie's behaviour were allowed to reach him in prison. He also learned of the persecution that his family was enduring at the hands of the police and security agents: 'This was one of the state's most barbarous techniques of applying pressure: imprisoning the wives and children of freedom fighters. Many men in prison were able to handle anything the authorities did to them, but the thought of the state doing the same thing to their families was almost impossible to bear.'

Shortly after Mandela's mother died, his eldest son, Thembi, was killed in a road accident, aged twenty-five. Again, Mandela was refused permission to attend the funeral and thus denied the chance to grieve properly. 'What can one say about such a tragedy? . . . I do not have words to express the sorrow, or the loss I felt. It left a hole in my heart that can never be filled.'

And that – the torment Mandela suffered and the permanence of his loss – is perhaps the most compelling reason why we would expect him to harbour bitterness towards his persecutors. They went to such lengths to break his spirit, sparing not even the innocence of his children. 'The pettiness, the meanness of prison officials, was stunning. It was very painful,' he told the BBC documentary.

But the source of the courage that makes Nelson Mandela the hero he is could not be suppressed, even on Robben Island, even after twenty-seven years, even after so much of what he had to live for was gone. 'Prison and the authorities conspire to rob each man of his dignity. In and of itself, that assured me that I would survive, for any man or institution that tries to rob me of my dignity will lose because I will not part with it at any price or under any pressure,' Mandela wrote. But he remained an optimist even then – 'head pointed towards the sun . . . feet moving forward', as he put it. 'There were many dark moments when my faith in humanity was tested, but I would not and could not give myself up to despair. That way lay defeat and death.'

The stage may have shrunk considerably, but Mandela was still a freedom fighter in South Africa, and the principles he fought for were as demanding in prison as they were on the outside. 'I was now on the sidelines, but I also knew that I would not give up the fight. I was in a different and smaller arena, an arena for whom the only audience was ourselves and our oppressors. We regarded the struggle in prison as a microcosm of the struggle as a whole. We would fight inside as we had fought outside. The racism and repression were the same; I would simply have to fight on different terms.'

All of the energy that had been directed at organising national strikes and days of mass protest were now channelled into winning the smallest concessions from the prison officials for more humane conditions. The cunning and strategic brilliance that had been directed into building the armed wing of the ANC and coordinating underground activities were redirected into establishing a communication system for prisoners within the compound.

Our survival depended on understanding what the authorities were attempting to do to us, and sharing that understanding with each other. It would be very hard, if not impossible, for one man alone to resist. I do not know that I could have done it had I been alone. But the authorities' greatest mistake was to keep us together, for together our determination was reinforced. We supported each other and gained strength from each other. Whatever we knew, whatever we learned, we shared, and by sharing we multiplied whatever courage we had individually.

When I read the stories of Mandela's battles with the prison authorities and the small victories he and his fellow political prisoners won, I was struck by his perseverance when progress was so painfully slow and the achievements so soul-destroyingly small. The thought of a great leader reduced to fighting for the right to wear trousers instead of schoolboy shorts could be lamented as a ludicrous waste of a talent and an outrageous humiliation to the cause; and in many ways it was. But those prison battles were also battles for the moral high ground, and they provided the grit against which Mandela and his compatriots could keep their ideals sharp. 'There are victories whose glory lies only in the fact that they are known to those who win them. This is particularly true of prison, where you must find consolation in being true to your ideals, even if no one else knows of it.'

But people did come to know of it. In prison Nelson Mandela continued to cultivate his politics of inclusiveness, drawing once-hostile people into the freedom struggle – non-political prisoners serving time for criminal offences, other political prisoners of different loyalties and persuasions, and in time the young fire-brands who arrived at Robben Island almost a generation later. Even some prison warders were won over to the cause after spending time in conversation with Mandela, as he preached the importance of respect and tolerance, and became both the messenger – and the message.

That for a full twenty-seven years in prison he continued to fight for the cause of freedom without wearying and without losing the sharpness of focus he had when the public eye was upon him is incredible enough. But what is harder to fully comprehend is that the strength of his belief and his willpower – the essence of his courage – actually grew in prison. And in these years he cultivated that part of the human spirit from which springs the ability to create a space through which, free from hate, your enemies might one day freely walk.

It was his courage to hold out a hand to his seemingly intractable enemies that made possible the rebirth of South Africa as a multiracial, democratic country. Take the Pan Africanist Congress, a political organisation which Mandela often accused of perpetuating misguided policies against the ANC. In a manner that would come to typify Mandela, he set aside his deep irritation with them in an attempt to build bridges. 'I thought that once the heated polemics had cooled, the essential commonality of the struggle would bring us together. Animated by this belief, I paid particular attention to their policy statements and activities, with the idea of finding affinities rather than differences.'

He used the same big-heartedness to reach out to the young firebrands who were thrown alongside him in prison some fifteen years after he had first arrived.

They were almost as sceptical of us as they were of the authorities. They chose to ignore our calls for discipline and thought
our advice feeble and unassertive. It was obvious that they
regarded us, the Rivonia Trialists, as moderates. After so many
years of being branded a radical revolutionary, to be perceived as
a moderate was a novel and not altogether pleasant feeling. I
knew that I could react in one of two ways: I could scold them for
their impertinence or I could listen to what they were saying. I
chose the latter.

This inclusiveness, or openness, came to be a defining element
of Mandela's political persona, and of his greatness as a leader
and as a human being. To gain the title of leader is often a matter
of time and chance, the coming together of time, place and
circumstance. But a truly great leader has the vision and courage
to use power to transform high-minded aspirations into concrete
change. No one who watched it will ever forget where they were
when the first pictures came through of Mandela walking free
from prison, when what he called his long walk to freedom
became a reality. No one will ever forget either the message of
reconciliation he sent out. 'Mandela brought the policy and
philosophy of the ANC on reconciliation and nation building
down to ground level,' wrote Ahmed Kathrada, one of Mandela's
closest friends and colleagues. 'Everyone talks of reconciliation.
He gave it content.' Or as Anthony R. DeLuca writes: 'As a
leader in our time, Mandela has truly been without peer, because
no contemporary political figure possessed the distinctive character trait that made Mandela truly exceptional, namely his
moral authority.'
But the critical decisions that ensured peace and reconciliation
were made the night Mandela, and his fellow freedom fighters,
were released from Robben Island. A fellow prisoner recounts in his
autobiography the importance of what Mandela did. Calling all
the freedom fighters together for one last time Mandela said they
could create a blood bath and that they would be justified in doing
so; or they could eschew bitterness and work for peace and
reconciliation. This was the courage that came from both strong

beliefs and the strongest of character. As his wife Graça Machel states: 'If he had come out of prison and sent a different message, I can tell you this country could now be in flames.'

And this was the third and ultimate test of the courage of Mandela, aged seventy-one, after 10,000 days of imprisonment. He said to the people of Cape Town that he came as a 'humble servant of you the people. Your tireless and heroic sacrifices have made it possible for me to be here today. I therefore place the remaining years of my life in your hands.' And when he arrived back in Soweto he told the crowds 'no man or woman who has abandoned apartheid will be excluded from our movement towards a non-racial united and democratic South Africa'.

To say simply that Nelson Mandela appeals to the best in people misses the intensity of his personal force. In the BBC documentary of his life, his friends, relatives and associates speak of that sense of power he has to connect to people across the barriers that divide us. 'I admire him personally because of what kind of person he turned out to be after what they did to him for twenty-seven years,' said Bill Clinton. 'He has a huge impact on people who are sixty or more years younger than him. A lot of people feel like he's their father or grandfather. It's a beautiful thing.'

'It's almost as if he doesn't realise how big he's become,' Zelda Le Grange, Mandela's personal assistant, says. 'He doesn't realise the excitement that he creates. I don't think it's that he doesn't appreciate his own abilities. I really just think it's because of his humility. It doesn't matter who you are . . . he makes you feel like you're the only one in that room.'

In February 1990 Nelson Mandela came out of prison after almost three decades and showed the world how to forgive. His magnanimity verges on the saintly, yet he himself would firmly resist any such label. 'I wanted to be regarded as an ordinary human being, with virtues and vices,' he said. Rejecting greatness himself, he is ready to ascribe it to his comrades, whose bravery and courage sustained the movement during its bleakest period, and to the people in South Africa who carry their own stories of stoicism and heroism but whose stories will never be known. For Mandela, they are the truest heroes of South Africa.

The policy of apartheid created a deep and lasting wound in my country and my people. All of us will spend many years, if not generations, recovering from that profound hurt. But the decades of oppression and brutality had another, unintended effect, and that was that it produced the Oliver Tambos, the Walter Sisulus, the Chief Luthulis, the Yusuf Dadoos, the Bram Fischers, the Robert Sobukwes of our time – men of such extraordinary courage, wisdom and generosity that their like may never be known again. Perhaps it requires such depths of oppression to create such heights of character. My country is rich in the minerals and gems that lie beneath its soil, but I have always known that its greatest wealth is its people, finer and truer than the purest diamonds.

It is from these comrades in the struggle that I learned the meaning of courage. Time and time again, I have seen men and women risk and give their lives for an idea. I have seen men stand up to attacks and torture without breaking, showing a strength and resilience that defies the imagination. I learned that courage was not the absence of fear, but the triumph over it. I felt fear myself more times than I can remember, but I hid it behind a mask of boldness. The brave man is not he who does not feel afraid, but he who conquers that fear.

I never lost hope that this great transformation would occur. Not only because of the great heroes I have already cited, but because of the courage of the ordinary men and women of my country. I always knew that deep down in every human heart, there was mercy and generosity.

But for thousands, perhaps millions of people worldwide, it is Nelson Mandela who has come to personify the almost inhuman courage to overcome hatred and bitterness and reach out to forgive his enemies. 'More than any other individual, Mandela set the example of the great reconciler, amazing the world with his lack of rancour or bitterness against his former oppressors despite a twenty-seven-year imprisonment,' wrote Lyn S. Graybill in her book on the Truth and Reconciliation hearings. Mandela did not deny the injustices done to him or try to understate the evil of the apartheid regime. But he refused to allow the injustices of the past deny him the pleasure of the present or the hope of the future. And that, Mandela insists, is liberating: 'If we don't forgive them, then that feeling of bitterness and revenge will be there. And we are saying let us forget the past. Let's concern ourselves with the present and future – but to say the atrocities of the past will never be allowed to happen again.' And he adds: 'If I had to live again I'd do exactly the same thing. As long as our people are oppressed and deprived of everything that makes human beings happy, it was my duty to be involved and I would do it over and over again.'

By itself, his leadership of a mass movement of protest against oppression would have secured Mandela's place in history. In any century, his role in overthrowing apartheid would have been a monumental event. Leading the ANC into power, in peace and partnership with the former racist parties, was unprecedented. It could have stopped there – all that would have made Mandela more than a hero of our age. But he has not stopped. For Mandela was always more than just a man of his own time. Having climbed one mountain – overcoming apartheid – he is now, as he himself says, still climbing, even approaching his ninetieth year, yet another: this time, campaigning against the shackles of global poverty. As we have seen with his work on HIV/AIDS, and as I found when he came out of retirement recently to launch the crusade to give education to every child in the world, the cause always dearest to him is that of the poorest children, whose future is most insecure and most in need of champions. Why? Because Mandela's mission is freedom for all from discrimination, poverty and injustice.

Persecuted, denounced as a traitor, narrowly escaping execution, confined for so long in prison – but never giving up hope, his courage never failing – Nelson Mandela embodies one of the greatest triumphs of the human spirit. No prisoner's cell could diminish Mandela; time has not withered his spirit but has made him the greatest beacon of hope for men and women in every continent of the world. Demonstrating an optimism that is bold, infectious and will travel down the centuries, he tells us that 'man's goodness is a flame that can be hidden but never extinguished'. With Mandela, and because of Mandela, no noble cause seems unachievable.

7

Cicely Saunders

The suffering of the dying has been eased for unknown thousands of people because of the courage of Cicely Saunders. In the words of her biographer, Shirley du Boulay, 'Through her, dying has lost some of its sting.'

It is said that societies should be judged by how they treat their very young, their very old, their sick, their poor, and dying. 'A society which shuns the dying must have an incomplete philosophy,' she once said.

Because of Cicely Saunders, societies around the world are now beginning to treat their dying in the way in which we would wish to be treated ourselves. 'A dignified death proclaims the significance of man,' wrote Dr Robert Fulton, whose book on dying Cicely Saunders read in the formative stages of her career. A colleague of hers, remarking on her life's work, said: 'It is dignifying the least of us. It dignifies the leper in Calcutta, the elderly person. It is a countervailing force to the disregard that we generally express towards the elderly.'

Cicely's life spanned the twentieth century and she is one of its greatest humanitarians. In a century where war in the first half was replaced by disease in the second as the biggest killer in the Western world, she has bequeathed a promise to the twenty-first century that death by disease would be kept within the limits of our endurance and that we need never face it alone. 'Suffering is only intolerable when nobody cares,' she often said. Her work has made it possible for people with progressive illnesses to live – fully and purposefully – until the last. Because of her, the final years, months, days of mortally ill people have been transformed from what was often excruciating, painful, fearsome, isolating, humiliating and meaningless, to a period in which they can discover intense creativity, reconciliation, intellectual and spiritual development, and peace. As Cicely Saunders wrote:

> To talk of accepting death when its approach has become inevitable is not mere resignation or feeble submission on the part of the patient, nor is it defeatism or neglect on the part of the doctor. For both of them it is the very opposite of doing nothing. Our work then is to alter the character of this inevitable process so that it is not seen as a defeat of living but as a positive achievement in dying; an intensely individual achievement for the patient.

This, then, was her work, and her vision: to reverse the prevailing medical practice so that instead of abandoning the incurable, it provided them with the best medical attention, together with the most compassionate human regard.

The courage of Cicely Saunders is the courage of a visionary. She saw beyond the limited vista of the medical establishment to pioneer a movement that has revolutionised the way terminally ill people are cared for. Because of this, she has become known as 'the woman who changed the face of death'.

There is another, more personal, aspect to Cicely Saunders's courage – her courage to love what she must lose. Twice she fell in love with men diagnosed with incurable cancer. These profound relationships exposed her to such joy and grief as to push her to the boundaries of emotional endurance. 'Fools rush in where angels fear to tread. I think love is so important that it doesn't matter that it's vulnerable. When you fall in love you feel you have no choice, but in a sense it's the freest thing you ever do.' From their deaths she emerged with the reserves of compassion and conviction needed to lead a revolution.

Her courage led her to battle against the age and gender expectations of her time to enter medical school in her mid-thirties and qualify as a doctor before her fortieth birthday, and to found St Christopher's Hospice – the first modern hospice – with nothing more than vision, determination and a gift of £500. As a result, she positioned palliative care for the terminally ill within the spectrum of mainstream medical enquiry and, at its centre, the irreducible dignity of the human being.

'She stayed her ground and took on the medical system in Britain and in the States. Those who understood just what this involved admired her for having the courage of her convictions, for persisting in the face of tribulations and vicissitudes, for being a fighter,' wrote Shirley du Boulay, her biographer.

Her tribulations and vicissitudes were many indeed. She had an unhappy, though materially comfortable, childhood. Her parents' marriage was unsuccessful and she and her two brothers grew up in a tense household bereft of parental affection. Sent to boarding school – Roedean – against her will, she was a shy child who would rather miss morning cocoa than face the humiliation of having no friends with whom to sit. Years later she would recall those school days as a good grounding for identifying with society's abandoned. 'In a sense, I was an outsider there, which was good for me in that being unpopular when you are young gives you a feeling for others who feel like they don't quite belong.'

When war broke out in 1939, Cicely was studying politics, philosophy and economics at St Anne's College, Oxford. But she did not feel 'right' being closeted away at university when so many other young lives were being uprooted and torn apart, so, against the advice of her parents, she abandoned Oxford and turned instead to nursing training at St Thomas's Hospital, London. Its stark demands released her from herself, redirecting the redundant energy of self-consciousness into hard but purposeful work.

Nursing the wounded and dying with no penicillin or modern drugs deepened her sensitivity towards the suffering. 'Young patients dying of tuberculosis and septicaemia from war wounds begged us to save them somehow,' she said, but 'we didn't have all the drugs, and we didn't really have anything to offer but ourselves, and a personal relationship.' By the end of the war, she was a fully qualified state registered nurse.

Having embarked upon a career she found meaningful and for which she was well suited, she was told by her doctor that a spinal deformity was causing her severe back problems and that she must give up nursing because of its heavy physical demands. The news was devastating. But Cicely decided to retrain as a medical social worker – or lady almoner – so she could stay within the medical profession and continue to have direct contact with patients.

In 1947 Cicely Saunders's life collided with that of David Tasma. She was twenty-nine, had been back to Oxford to qualify as a medical social worker, and was working again at St Thomas's Hospital. He was forty, a Polish Jew who had fled the Warsaw ghetto at the start of the war, and was alone in Britain with no family and no friends. He was a patient; and he was dying. Cicely met him first on her ward as a social worker at St Thomas's but continued to visit him frequently when he was moved to another hospital, until his death two months later.

I knew then the truth that he [David] was dying, which he did not. So I followed him up and I waited . . . it was in fact I who finally told him . . .

He needed skills which were not then available, but still more he needed a sense of belonging, and somehow to find meaning. He felt that he had done nothing in his life for the world to remember. One day he said, 'Can't you say something to comfort me?' So I said the 23rd Psalm, The Lord is My Shepherd. Then I said, 'shall I read to you?' And he said, 'No. I only want what is in your mind and in your heart.'

We talked together about somewhere that would be more suitable for him than the very busy surgical ward where he was. We wanted a place not just for better symptom control, but for trying to find out, in a way, who he was. I told him I was going to try to found a home, a place where people who were dying would have the space and openness so hard to come by in a busy surgical ward.

The encounter was to be the inspiration for Cicely's life's work and her greatest achievements over the next forty-five years. It was the source of her belief, or at least its manifestation, that people can continue to live deeply meaningful lives even when they are dying and that the death of someone loved can inspire the survivors to dedicate themselves to something worthy of their memory. She would refer to her relationship with David Tasma in nearly every speech, book and article she wrote on care for the dying.

> David's influence on my life was enormous. He was very poetic and when he died he left me £500 in his will and said, 'I will be a window in your home', meaning the Hospice. It took me 19 years to build a home around the window, but the core principles of our approach were born out of my conversations with him as he was dying. His use of the word 'window' led me to understand that we should be open to the world, to all who would come – patients, families and those who wanted to learn.
>
> After his quiet death, I finally felt assured that he had made his own journey, looking to the faith of his fathers after many years of agnosticism. He had made this journey in a complete freedom of the spirit. Hospice has therefore adopted these principles: openness, mind together with heart, and deep concern for the freedom of each individual to make his or her own journey toward their goals.

Dame Cicely referred to the symbolism of the window being the first part of the hospice, 'offering light to the journey our patients must take'. It is a story which illustrates the importance of individual action, each doing what we can with what we've got, as Tasma did. Gandhi expressed this well: 'It is the action, not the fruit of the action, that is important. It may not be in your power, may not be in your time, that there will be any fruit, but that doesn't mean that you stop doing the right thing. You may never know what results from your action, but if you do nothing there will be no result.'

I think of Cicely Saunders at the bedside of David Tasma and of the conversations they had together, each knowing that he would soon die. I think of her courage in befriending someone so utterly alone and of her courage to stay with him and bear witness to his physical pain, emotional anguish and death. The dying and the bereaved are, in her own words, 'almost like social outcasts'. Yet she stayed firmly by the side of a stranger who felt like his life had been without value and that his death would be without meaning. It was because of her courage that they were able to imagine together a better way that the dying might live out their final days, and it was her courage that inspired David Tasma to leave her all he possessed so that she could begin to build their dream.

'David Tasma was and remains St Christopher's founding patient, the inspiration for what was to follow: a man who felt he had achieved so little in life and yet for whom the manner of his dying resulted in so much,' wrote David Clark, an academic who has chronicled Saunders's life and vast collection of writing. Immediately after David Tasma's death in February 1948, Cicely Saunders enrolled as a volunteer nurse at St Luke's Hospital, Bayswater – one of the established homes for terminal care. Her philosophy was that grief can be creative, and that 'love is certainly as strong as death if not stronger . . .'. 'There can be something very creative about bereavement,' she once said in an interview; 'think of all the people who lose a child and then start a charity, as if there's something in that much loved person's life that you're fulfilling.'

The answer to her grief was to use its terrible energy to give to others what she had been able to give to David Tasma: all that was in her mind and in her heart. Unhappy, lonely, and, worst of all, consumed by a feeling of meaninglessness, David Tasma's life changed when he met Cicely Saunders. Her mind – her professional concern as a nurse and medical social worker about his physical symptoms, together with her heart – her friendship, her honesty, her willingness to expose herself to the vulnerability that comes with emotional intimacy, these were the gifts she discovered she possessed through her relationship with a dying man, and the gifts she felt bound by her memory of him to share.

It was at St Luke's Hospital, as a volunteer nurse, that Cicely first came across the practice of the 'regular giving' of pain-killing drugs to terminally ill patients to manage pain. It was a radical departure from the widespread practice of making patients 'earn' their relief by enduring agonising pain until they could no longer bear it, by which time the dosage would often have to be so big as to make the patient drowsy or even unconscious.

Unlike the 'productive' pain from injury or illness that tells a body it is damaged in order that it might be healed, Cicely saw how the futility of terminal pain drained life and a sense of meaning out of its sufferers. Chronic pain held patients captive. Dying patients living in pain could do nothing other than fear it and curse it as it demanded all of their energy and deprived them of their humanity.

For Cicely the practice of 'regular giving' was revolutionary. She saw that strong pain-killing drugs could be given in small, regular doses, without the patients becoming dependent, allowing them to remain alert and more fully themselves as regular giving suppressed the pain before it had a chance to take grip of the patient. 'For the first time I saw the constant pain of terminal cancer getting constant relief,' she said. 'With effective pain control you are giving the patient space to be themselves. Pain control allows the patient to complete their journey in the search for meaning.' With pain under control, Cicely saw that cancer patients could be freed from actual pain, freed from the anxiety and terror of anticipated pain, and therefore free to live life even as they were dying.

Cicely became evangelical about the practice of 'regular giving'. She could see the potential it had to turn the experience of terminal illness on its head. The prospect of a slow and painful demise – most commonly from cancer – was amongst the most dreaded but increasingly likely causes of death. To be able to release people from the fear of pain from terminal cancer – to be able to promise a virtually pain-free death – seemed a miracle within reach.

The hours she had spent with David Tasma exploring ideas about how to care for patients for whom the hospital bed was a deathbed now had its most concrete expression in the practice of pain control through this method. To have been able to relieve David Tasma's suffering in this way would have been a mercy. But Cicely knew that there was much more to his suffering than physical pain. She intuitively rejected the artificial division between care of the body and care of the soul that straitjacketed medical convention in the West. For Cicely Saunders, caring for people as a professional necessarily included helping them find a way through their distress from non-physical pain too.

She had learned pain management from St Luke's, and care for the wellbeing of the person in their entirety from David Tasma. These discoveries were coming together in Cicely Saunders's thinking and would lead her to develop a comprehensive new approach to the care of terminally ill patients that would change the course of modern medicine. The direction her life would take was beginning to be marked out.

Now in her early thirties, working as a medical social worker by day and volunteer at St Luke's Hospital by night, a recent convert (from agnosticism) to evangelical Christianity, restless, energetic, imbued with a sense of vocation, and still grieving for David Tasma, Cicely was at a crossroad in her life. Most women her age were busy bringing up families. Still single, she considered other options open to her. The ideas she had discussed with David Tasma, and her exposure to pain control at St Luke's, beset her, but she had no clear means of exploring them further. She had neither the clout nor the opportunity in her work as a medical social worker to decide the course of her patients' care.

Cicely often complained to friends and colleagues of the poor treatment that terminally ill patients received from doctors and spoke enthusiastically of the ideas she had been formulating for a new approach. 'It appears to me that many patients feel deserted by their doctors at the end. Ideally the doctor should remain the centre of a team who work together to relieve where they cannot heal, to keep the patient's own struggle within his compass and to bring hope and consolation to the end,' she wrote in one of many essays. It was, as David Clark puts it, 'an ambition of singular proportions which would require a monumental transformation in professional knowledge, attitudes and behaviour for its realisation'.

During one such conversation with a renowned surgeon for whom she worked, she said to him, 'I've got to go back and nurse the dying somehow.' And it was he who said, 'Go and read medicine. It's the doctors who desert the dying, and there's so much more to be learned about pain. You'll only be frustrated if you don't do it properly, and they won't listen to you.' He convinced her that she would never be listened to with any seriousness unless she became part of the profession she accused of deserting the dying. So, at the age of thirty-three, she entered medical school. 'It was quite a thing to start off in medicine at thirty-three. But I went into medicine entirely to do something about end-of-life pain. I knew what I had to do it for.'

Cicely studied medicine at a time when advances in medical knowledge and the rising status of the physician were developing spectacularly quickly.

> There was a revolution in medicine. There were all the new pills, and all the new techniques, and so much we could do and cure that the people who weren't being cured were more and more second-class citizens. And people don't like looking at their failures. If you feel you've failed to help a patient, you walk past the bed, because you don't want to look them in the eye.

In Shirley du Boulay's biography of Cicely Saunders, Sir Douglas Black, a former president of the Royal College of Physicians, recalled the prevailing attitude of the medical profession in the middle of the twentieth century:

> . . . the very high mortality which was accepted in earlier times had begun to yield to improved social conditions; and what has been described as the therapeutic revolution was under way. The excitement of new treatments, and the challenge of new technologies were paramount in the outlook of both doctors and nurses. Concentration on acute, and particularly on curable illness, was tending to divert attention from the problems of chronic illness, and especially of illness which was shortly going to prove fatal.

The increasing detachment of medical inquiry from anything that was not directly treatable by observable cause and effect had created a professional atmosphere in which its own terminology – the word 'clinical' for example – could be used to describe something bleakly absent of emotional engagement.

Even more telling was an essay published in 1959, the very time that Cicely qualified as a doctor. It appeared in one of the only books available at the time on care for the dying, and Cicely read its pages eagerly, striking up a correspondence with the doctor who edited it. The essay was by August Kasper, a doctor, and in it he described with remarkable candour and insight the attitudes that the medical establishment held towards death and the dying:

> The dying are thus not neglected, but they are very rarely approached with hope or even interest, because, I suppose, they simply will not feed the doctor's narcissism by responding and getting well. Their care is demanding, frustrating, and far from helpful to the medical magician's self-esteem . . .
>
> It is often unfortunately true that the serious or hopelessly ill patient senses the doctor's emotions clearly. The doctor's disillusionment, depending upon his maturity, will show as sympathy, anger, disgust, indifference, interest, disappointment, or embarrassment. Though not exhaustive, this list suggests the many ways a patient may perceive how his doom affects his physician. The hardest to bear is indifference because it is so defensive, so weak, that the patient cannot believe that which such a man tells him. Those feelings at the opposite pole – true grief, sympathy – are most supportive for the dying one, not only because he feels loved, but because then he sees that the living need his help. He feels called upon to soothe the physician's hurt, to comfort those who will mourn, to assure men of their dignity. Such a man will live his life to the end, as well and as productively as he ever was able.
>
> And the doctor will help to this end if he can know his own fear and weakness and hope. Realising the human condition, he will not be too disturbed by his failure and disillusionment. He can function as comforter, and, while not promising life, can offer hope.

In the same collection of essays, Gerald Aronson, also a doctor, wrote movingly of a patient's often futile struggle to hold on to dignity and a sense of value in the face of a terminal illness. The

quote at the start is from the French novelist Marguerite Yourcenar:

'It is difficult to remain an emperor in the presence of a
physician and difficult even to keep one's essential quality as a
man. The professional eye saw in me only a mass of humours, a
sorry mixture of blood and lymph.'

How to help the patient be an individual being even though
gravely ill and dying? We know how dehumanising illness is,
even where death is not a probable outcome . . .

We know from our experiences in helping at the bedsides of
the dying or in prowling our ghoulish vigil in hospital corri-
dors trying to get autopsy permissions, how often the patient
murmurs even toward the end, 'I don't want to make a fuss.'
He wants to be a human, to play a role consistent with his
identity, his individuality.

Hope must never die too far ahead of the patient; either
hope of getting better, or hope of enjoyment of conversations
tomorrow, etc. More good deaths are spoiled because the
physician tries to jolly the patient or neglect him as a sentient
being. Terrible as it is to die, it doesn't have to be ignominious.

In brief, the physician should try to bring about a situation
where he gives, unsolicited and anticipating the patient's need
before the patient himself may recognise it, a gift – a piece of
tender interest and affection exacting no counter-service
from the patient. We may view the gift from the physician
as an evidence of sublimated love, reinforcing the waning
testimony of the internal good object against the isolating
agony of death.

But these were lone voices, fighting the medical profession for
more compassionate care for the dying, and heeding the nine-
teenth-century surgeon John Hinton's admonition: 'We emerge
deserving of little credit: we who are capable of ignoring the
conditions which make muted people suffer. The dissatisfied dead
cannot noise abroad the negligence they have experienced.'

Cicely Saunders qualified as a doctor in 1957 aged thirty-nine.

She won a research grant to pursue her seminal work on the control of pain and carried out her clinical research at St Joseph's Hospice. St Joseph's was run by philanthropically minded nuns whose kindness and devotion were faultless, but who had no medical knowledge. She introduced a sophisticated and individualised method of 'regular giving' based on detailed records of each patient's needs and responses. The effect she had on patients seemed miraculous. 'Introducing the regular giving of oral opiates was like waving a wand over the house,' she said.

Her research into pain control was ground-breaking. More complex than the mere search for the relief of physical pain, her simple but transforming calling – to *care* for the dying – led her to develop the concept of 'total pain', an understanding of pain as the complex interaction between physical pain caused by disease, and pain caused by mental, emotional, and spiritual malaise. This in turn would have huge consequences for the medical profession: it implied an acknowledgement on the part of the physician of the patient as a full person and not just a body, and required a collaboration between physicians and a range of other professionals whose combined skills could come to bear on the individual in their joint efforts to treat 'total pain'.

'There can be little doubt that when Cicely Saunders first used the term "total pain" in the early 1960s, she was in the process of bequeathing to medicine and health care a concept of enduring clinical and conceptual interest,' David Clark commented.

It also reflected her willingness to acknowledge the spiritual suffering of the patient and to see this in relation to physical problems. Crucially, total pain was tied to a sense of narrative and biography, emphasizing the importance of listening to the patient's story and of understanding the experience of suffering in a multifaceted way. This was an approach that saw pain as a key to unlocking other problems and as requiring multiple interventions for its resolution.

In 1958 Cicely Saunders's article, 'Dying of Cancer', was published in the St Thomas's *Hospital Gazette*. It was her first occasion to report the findings of her clinical research and disseminate her ideas to a wider audience in print.

The next year, the *Nursing Times* published a series of six articles where Cicely reported the astonishing transformation she had achieved in patients at St Joseph's. Straightforward clinical evidence would sit side by side with photographs and transcriptions of conversations she had with patients where the patients' own words and experiences were allowed to speak for themselves. It was her philosophy, and it would become her trademark, to keep the human face at the centre of her studies and care for the dying.

As she described it: 'I started lecturing with slides and personal stories – I'd just turn the lights out and let the patients speak. This gave a voice to the patients, and I've always said the patients are the real founders of the hospice movement.' Where before they were voiceless, the dying now had in Cicely Saunders a tribune through whom others could hear their anguished cries. 'I learned to listen and that enabled me to be a voice for the voiceless. It was that which stirred me into seeing so much of what needed to be done.'

At first, Cicely seemed to make little headway in changing attitudes within the medical establishment. 'I experienced a lot of indifference and a certain amount of hostility. The hostility came from doctors who felt that I was making a fuss about something that wasn't a problem.' In one letter she described an impenetrable wall that seemed to protect the profession from anything that threatened its equilibrium:

> I have tucked in a copy of my own review [of an article about the care of the terminally ill] which I did for the *Nursing Times*. It was well written up in *The Times*, the *Telegraph* and *Manchester Guardian*, but so far the medical journals have treated it with lofty unconcern. At least I have not been able to find anything about it in them and I think this is rather indicative of the medical profession's attitude to this problem and why it remains such a problem.

Cicely's articles did, however, provoke a good deal of response from the readership of the journals and newspapers in which they were published and she began to receive the first of many letters from professionals interested in her research, along with invitations, particularly from institutions in the United States, to speak as a visiting lecturer. Interest in her work and ideas on terminal care had started to gather pace.

Now qualified as a doctor with a body of published research on pain control, Cicely was prepared to take the next step in realising the dream she created with David Tasma more than a decade earlier. She wrote a detailed proposal for a purposefully designed home, the ideal setting in which to provide care for the dying. It was the blueprint for what would become St Christopher's Hospice, the most famous hospice in the world, and the physical manifestation of Cicely Saunders's medical revolution.

Cicely's life at this time seemed to have kept at a frantic pace. But she made sure that that pace included time within it to linger with her patients at St Joseph's, listen to them talk about their illness and the effect it was having on their lives and wait with them silently when they could not find the words to express the tumult they felt inside. 'Time isn't a question of length, it is a question of depth, isn't it?' she often said.

During these times of great depth spent at bedsides, one patient, Antoni Michniewicz, fell in love with her – and she with him.

Like David Tasma, Antoni Michniewicz was a Pole who had fled to England in the chaos of the Second World War. And like David Tasma, he was dying. His wife had already passed away and his only daughter was comforting him in his illness. Antoni spent six months as a patient at St Joseph's under Cicely's care, and it was she who had to explain to him that he was dying: 'When I told him, he said, "Was it hard for you to tell me that?" And when I said, "Well, yes, it was," he said, "Thank you. It's hard to be told, but it's hard to tell, too." '

For many years only Cicely's closest friends knew the true extent of her relationship with Antoni Michniewicz. But she allowed her biographer, Shirley du Boulay, access to her diaries. Extracts from these, published in 1984, reveal the emotional and spiritual depth of their relationship:

There are so many things I would like to say and hear about [Antoni] . . . I wish I had given him more, I wish I had known sooner, I wish I could help him through the every last but I know it is in Thy hands O Lord and I leave it there – or try to do so. Please comfort and help him and his daughter as they part.

He was weaker and could hardly speak. He said good nights and hardly had any pain at all. And he ate a little supper with me feeding him. And I said that I had come back to make sure he was all right. And that it wasn't pity, it was admiration. And that I would be in in the morning. He said 'Monday – a good day – Monday, Wednesday and Friday are good days!' And he said, and repeated when I didn't catch it, 'For me, the day is easier when you come.' And he looked and smiled.

The details of their courtship, recorded in Cicely's diary, are almost unbearably poignant. They could never be alone together and their relationship could never be made public because of Cicely's position in the hospice. They both knew he was dying and that it was futile to imagine a future together as is the right and instinct of every couple once love has been declared.

Went over [to see Antoni] in the morning – and curtains round as I came in and my heart turned over but he was all right. Though poor and tried to say something I couldn't understand. So he said sadly, 'We don't understand each other,' and then had a fit of coughing and I left him to get some linctus with a sword in my heart. But at 1.30 he was more alert and held my hand and said, 'I cannot tell you how much it means to be visited by you,' and kissed and kissed my hand and I held it to his cheek but I couldn't stay – we were in the ward.

. . . I did tell him that I loved him – rather – but that the Lord loved him much more and that was what mattered, not me. He made me repeat it to be sure. And just smiled. And then I said good night and kissed him swiftly – hoping that the Lord had put up a screen . . .

Agony to wait till midday – and then I had an excuse to ring and so did just about know when I drove in – but it gets worse and worse. Short sessions and left photographs and books. I cannot tell him anything now, I think I have perhaps had my last long session – and this once again is how the world ends or rather, how my world ends – by screwing myself up to be controlled when by nature I am the reverse. O Holy Spirit, direct and hold me.

Equally fervent in their religious beliefs, they often expressed their passion through words of religious devotion and imagery. Cicely would later describe her relationship with Antoni Michniewicz as 'the hardest, the most peaceful, the most inhibited and the most liberating experience I have ever had'.

He said, 'I am waiting till you come.' I said, I had a quiet heart. That if I could have a long time it was lovely and if I could only have a short time – it was enough. And he said, 'I want you beside me all day long,' and I agreed. He said, 'I can only hurt you. I can give you nothing but sorrow' and I said, 'The only way you could hurt me would be if you didn't love me anymore' . . .

And he brought out his fear of 'a very hard death-bed'. And I promised and I promised that I would somehow be there . . . And I finally had to go, but still my heart is quiet – and I think his is too – and we could not touch at all but only look in love and caress with our eyes. And said good night and God bless and lighten your darkness. And he could wave.

Rather poor when I came [back] in – bronchospasm. Settled with ephedrine and reassurance – and slept all morning until 3pm. I did listen to his chest which meant that we held hands briefly. Then at five he had a lot of bronchospasm and looked very ill and frightened. 'Do please help me.' . . . He went to prepare a place for us – by the Cross. He comes to fetch my dear love – by the Cross. And I watch him and wait – by the Cross. We are together in Him, by Him, through Him . . .

He was so incredibly emaciated, I had not realised. Quieter, indeed almost semi-conscious till 2pm . . . I was in and out (as I had been all morning), but now I lifted him up several times to see the crucifix (the only time I have ever held him in my arms) . . . and once could just rest my head against his for a second . . . There was no need for words any more and there weren't really any thoughts in my mind either. He could see the crucifix I think – once he tried to make the sign of the Cross. And then, suddenly, he gave me a really heavenly smile. And as I think of it I am not certain of all that was in it. Not sorry at all. It looked so happy and there was certainly a gleam of amusement and strength somehow. And then that look of pure love, I have so often had from him. Then his eyes went down my face and wandered in weariness – but it was peaceful – and my feelings were quiet. I was just there to keep him as comfortable as I could. No time to think, no thoughts to come.

Antoni Michniewicz died shortly afterwards. It was August 1960, one of the busiest periods of Cicely Saunders's life. Fundraising efforts for St Christopher's Hospice were demanding every free moment she had. On top of her clinical work, she had to constantly update patients' notes and review treatments. Letters kept pouring in with queries about her research. And there were lectures to prepare. Few people who knew her in her professional capacity realised that she was, in fact, close to emotional breakdown. Her biographer wrote: 'Cicely was so happy with Antoni that she did not anticipate her grief while he was alive – but once he had died she was absolutely broken. She could hardly bear to go into the ward that had been their only home, the pain was so great . . . It was a long, she now feels a pathological, grieving.'

Conviction is faith unless it is sprung from experience. Cicely Saunders's belief in an eternity was founded on her religious faith. But her conviction in the absolute value of temporal life, even at the onset of death, could not have had firmer groundings in experience. 'In the midst of death she had been in life; at the bedside of a dying man, surrounded by the dying, she had lived more intensely than ever before; in the face of eternity, she had loved for three weeks, never sure which day, which hour, would be their last. She had found human love and she had lost it,' wrote Du Boulay.

She learnt that it is possible to live a lifetime in a few weeks: that time is a matter of depth, not length; that in the right atmosphere and with pain controlled so that that patient is free to be himself, the last days can be the richest; that they can be a time of reconciliation that makes the dying peaceful and the mourning bearable.

She learnt, with her whole being, that in work with people the giving is two-way, the caring mutual. The patient gives to the relative as much as the relative to the patient; he gives as much to those who care for him as he receives from them.

If, in the months immediately following Antoni's death, she was nearly incapacitated by her grief, Cicely ultimately emerged stronger by once again converting her anguish into the energy she needed to fight a revolution. In an entirely human way she had experienced a type of birth in Antoni's love, death in his death, and then resurrection. 'I missed him quite dreadfully afterwards,' she recalled in an interview recorded in the last years of her life, 'but it gave me a terrific head of steam to do the work, as I understood very deeply what it was like to be losing someone. I felt I had the right to say to families that I understood how they were feeling . . . to be alongside terminally ill patients and their families. I'd been in their position myself and that gave me a new confidence.'

Here was proof in the most personal form that with the right care and in the right environment, people on their deathbeds could experience happiness and give as much to other people.

David Clark's collection of letters chronicle Cicely's ensuing struggle to turn the written proposal (or as she termed it 'the Scheme') for St Christopher's Hospice into the world's leading centre for the teaching, research and practice of the best palliative care. The 'head of steam' and confidence she built up from her relationship with Antoni, together with a clear sense that she was doing God's bidding, combined to make her a force to be reckoned with. Doggedly determined, sometimes fierce, often exacting, occasionally intolerant: these qualities would lead her to make St Christopher's worthy of David Tasma and Antoni Michniewicz's memory.

There were difficulties and dilemmas, of course. The Hospice was, from its inception, to have a religious dimension to it. One of the hardest decisions Cicely Saunders faced was what form the religious aspect should take. Cicely's letters at this point in her life are filled with deliberation as she searched for answers from religious mentors and friends. In the end, the religious aspect of the Hospice would take its most overt form in the chapel and daily prayers. Otherwise, St Christopher's was, and remains, in Cicely Saunders's words, 'a community of the unlike', where people of all faiths and none are cared for together and where the manifestations of grace appear in the tenderness and compassion of the care-givers.

St Christopher's was also, from the start, to be a pioneering centre, independent of the National Health Service but tied to it contractually and philosophically. The NHS would buy a certain number of beds and refer patients, and treatment would be based on need and not the ability to pay. Beyond the beds bought by the NHS, however, running costs would have to be met by other sources of income, and its initial construction costs were met purely by charitable donations.

Cicely corresponded widely and maintained professional friendships with people in the United States, Canada, and throughout Europe. She tapped every conceivable source of financial support, and would often write letters to possible donors before making formal applications to charities and trusts – letters that reveal an infectious enthusiasm for her mission, together with a clear sense of purpose; they also suggest an indomitable and gracious spirit, confidence, and a dry sense of humour.

'I think that you know that I have been interested in the problems of the dying for a number of years and qualified with that work in mind,' began one such letter in 1959.

For the past year I have been working in two of the Homes which only take in patients who are actually dying of cancer. It has been infinitely interesting and rewarding both from the medical and the spiritual point of view. Now I am being impelled to get down to some practical planning of a new foundation for such patients and I enclose a scheme with which I am trying to get interest and eventually money. I am afraid that at the moment the 'we' throughout is editorial (or even royal!) but I am gradually meeting people who would be prepared to be either Trustees or be on a Board of Reference . . . I am convinced that this is a great need, and that many people would help once we are really organised, and once it is not just an individualistic affair.

Those who know Cicely Saunders personally write of her reluctance to be hailed as a revolutionary who forged a new path in medicine. 'I didn't set out to change the world,' she once said. 'My role has been to reshape, not to innovate.' But they also acknowledge that her charisma and courage excited other people as much as her theories and ideas. 'There are many reasons for people working at St Christopher's, but one which crops up time and time again is Cicely herself,' writes Du Boulay. 'They were drawn in the first place to what she was trying to do, but they wanted to do it with her, feeling she had the drive and vision to make it happen. She has a quality which pulls people to her and inspires them.'

Cicely Saunders's letters also show the extent to which the change she effected in palliative care was her own achievement, made possible by her own determination. Having single-handedly written the proposals for the building, running and guiding philosophy of St Christopher's Hospice, she was also the one to assemble core supporters and raise the hundreds of thousands of pounds that she would need beyond David Tasma's founding £500.

Halfway through the construction of the building, money ran out and the sources of income Saunders had expected to help turned her away. It was an uncertain and bleak period but her letters show that her courage and humour never wavered.

Somehow we will get it [need £150,000 within six months], and those who have helped us will not let it sink . . . At the moment I feel rather like that small and diligent wader, the turnstone, who bustles up the beach turning over every single stone it meets to find what lies underneath . . . There is nothing like a crisis to mobilise things . . . we have to do something rather smartly . . . it is the idea, not one individual, that will get us the means to go on . . . the contractor and the sub-contractors have all agreed to go on building knowing that the money may come in rather more slowly than their bills will reach us. This is very good indeed of them and we are most grateful and all the more impelled to raise the rest of the money so that they do not have to wait. I believe it will come.

The best thing about having any kind of trouble is the discovery of how much other people care and how nice they are. This, perhaps, is one of the reasons why a hospital which specialises in our kind of care also specialises in goodness . . .

Cicely Saunders persevered and the money did come in: 'I kept the faith day by day. There is a place for sheer bloody-mindedness; it does give you strength.' St Christopher's Hospice opened in 1967 – the culmination of twenty-five years of academic, spiritual and practical and emotional preparation. From the start, St Christopher's was a movement. It was a prototype, a physical manifestation of a spiritual longing to relieve suffering, and the realisation of a professional quest to conquer pain. 'We [St Christopher's] are a reaction against the impersonal medical city,' she wrote.

Teaching and research were central to St Christopher's from the start but its ultimate aim was to change the way the dying many were looked after, so it would never be the dying few within reach of a single doctor. As David Clark comments: 'There was a sense that the whole endeavour amounted to an elaborate pilot scheme which could have extremely far-reaching implications.'

Every detail of St Christopher's was purposefully planned with the patient and family in mind. Cicely Saunders did not want it to be known as a place where people came to die, a ghoulish centre where sick people arrived and were never seen alive again. The Hospice was not to be set in remote grounds away from the bustle of the world but to be located instead on a main road with a garden to the rear. Beds were to be placed 'so that the patients can see the life of the world outside'. Her design for St Christopher's included a residential wing for retired members of staff or volunteers and their relatives, a playgroup for the children of staff, and a wing for elderly patients so that old and young, sick and healthy mixed together. Terminally ill patients who were able to go home for weekend visits or longer spells were encouraged to do so and assisted in every way by outreach workers. Parties and merriment were encouraged to mark every special occasion, and there were no restrictions on visiting hours. Cicely's philosophy was that the Hospice should be like someone's home. Visitors should feel free to drop by any time according to the limits of courtesy and consideration, not bureaucracy. The only exception was to be Mondays. The Hospice should be closed to visitors one day a week to give the friends and relatives a break from their responsibilities without being made to feel guilty.

Patients at St Christopher's were given the space and encouragement in their search for meaning. Perhaps for the first time in their lives, patients would find themselves the absolute centre of attention, where the world revolved around them, surrounded by people whose job and whose mission seemed to be to help them make the most of their remaining life. An emphasis on self-discovery brought with it professionals trained to locate sources of creativity and tap into rich emotional depths in patients faced with their own imminent mortality.

The effort and attention and solicitude put into looking after the wellbeing of patients would be on a scale never experienced before. 'Looking after the dying is a corporate act, everyone is involved: the nurses who make him comfortable, the doctors who prescribe him drugs and answer his questions, the priest who visits him, the physiotherapist who eases his movement, the occupational therapist who interests his mind, the kitchen who tempt his appetite, the study centre who teach others of his needs,' she wrote. It is the way she would have liked David Tasma to have lived out his final months, rather than alone and spiritually defeated in a busy hospital ward.

In 1993 Cicely Saunders published the third edition of a book on the management of terminal disease. In her introduction she provided a perspective on what St Christopher's was, and had been about, a generation on from when its doors first opened. Her words are both a description of what happens at St Christopher's, and a tract on what it means to bear witness to the divine element inherent in every human being:

The realisation that life is likely to end soon may well stimulate a desire to put first things first and to reach out to what is seen as true and valuable – and give rise to feelings of being unable or unworthy to do so. There may be bitter and most understandable anger at the unfairness of what is happening, and at much of what has gone on before, and above all a desolating feeling of meaninglessness. Here lies, I believe, the essence of spiritual pain and the greatest challenge to our patients and to members of the team committed to care for them.

So how do we help others in their struggle to find a way out of the pain of meaninglessness? We start in concern for the body, with the freedom and space we can give by skills in symptom control and care for role and appearance; we welcome the whole family group and help in their search for their own resources – but what else should hospice or palliative care have to offer? Hospitality to our patients must surely include the readiness to help them as they look at what is most important of all, their inner griefs, guilts, and longings.

It is a question of time – and timing – a readiness on the part of all staff to stop and listen at the moment this particular area of pain is expressed and to stay with it. We are not there to take away, or explain, or even to understand, but simply to 'Watch with me' as Jesus asked of his disciples in the Garden of Gethsemane. As we have worked so hard and so successfully to relieve physical pain and other symptoms, we may have been tempted to believe that spiritual pain should be tackled and solved in a similar way . . .

If we can manage the progress of inexorable disease, even when pressed for time, in such a way that the patient feels affirmed at every step, there is often a surprising amount that he can do, not only in physical ability but in relationships and in a final discovery of worth and meaning.

To tell the story of Cicely Saunders's life work, it is necessary to borrow from the traditions that honour great humanitarians to describe her accomplishments – relief of suffering, comfort to the dying, helping people find meaning in a world of despair and pain, tapping into reserves of strength and endurance; opening up latent creativity; creating space for broken relationships to heal. But it is equally necessary to draw on the traditions that celebrate the great inventors and pioneers – the genius of the visionary who has the tenacity to pursue a dream; the willpower and determination to forge a new path in an unyielding field; the marvellous capacity of the mind to discover nature's secrets and unlock the mysteries of the natural world.

Was she a doctor who put the heart back into medicine? Was she a pastor who brought science to bear on the affairs of the spirit? Or is her accomplishment the fusion of the material body with all its immaterial elements, advancing medicine to new heights as it corrects its historical neglect of the body's immaterial aspects, and reasserting the essential value that is the claim of every human being?

Cicely Saunders's conversion to Christianity at the start of her career helped direct her in her own search for meaning. Her faith, and her life's work, cannot be divided, as one is an expression of the other and its very lifeblood: 'I think that God will pick up any old tool. Well, God tapped me on the shoulder and said, "You get on with it. As a vocation." ' St Christopher's Hospice might be seen as the culmination of the forces working inside her at the time: a restless spirituality looking for an outward means of expression; the place where her intellectual and professional capabilities could be freed from bureaucratic and institutional intransigence; the means by which to remember and grieve for the love she lost. But if the period leading up to the establishment of St Christopher's was characterised by a sense of longing, loss and yearning – creative in its hunger – the period that followed seems to have been marked by fulfilment.

In 1966 a third Polish man, the artist Marian Bohusz-Szyszko, entered Cicely Saunders's personal life. It would be with Marian that Cicely was finally able to share the happiness of falling in love beyond the shadow of death. But his arrival in Cicely's life was quite by chance. Driving by a London art gallery Cicely was particularly taken by a painting on display and she stopped her car to look at it more closely. The painting spoke to her of the agonies of death and the promise of resurrection. She bought the work and wrote to the artist thanking him for painting such a marvel, telling him how it now hung in the chapel of a hospice she was building. Moved by her letter, Marian Bohusz-Szyszko asked if they might meet. They did, and fell in love. She was forty-five years old; he was sixty-two.

Marian Bohusz-Szyszko was a Polish war refugee who had moved to England. Unlike David Tasma and Antoni Michniewicz, he was in good health, vibrant and full of life. 'He was a wild, mad artist, bless his heart,' Cicely once said of him. He had been separated from his Polish wife for many years but they had never divorced. He and Cicely bought a house together with two of his friends in a happy, if unconventional arrangement. Marian became the artist-in-residence of St Christopher's Hospice and the Hospice became his permanent gallery. His paintings and sculptures still decorate its hallways, chapel and garden. Shortly after the death of his wife, he and Cicely Saunders married: she in her early sixties; he in his late seventies. They had already been together for seventeen years, and would enjoy fifteen more together before Marian's death at St Christopher's Hospice in 1995.

Marian brought fulfilment and peace to the longing and rest-lessness that had beset Cicely Saunders since childhood. As she found herself spending less time in work and prayer than before she married, she commented: 'I know when Marian dies I'll be on my knees again, but I can't screw myself down there.' He referred to her as his 'complementary colour', 'which is a lovely thing to hear from an artist', she said fondly.

Marian was in his nineties when he died and was still drawing days before his death. He had told his wife that he thought of death as an adventure, had been completely happy in life, and was ready to die.

This great love of Cicely Saunders's life died in circumstances she would have wished for David Tasma and Antoni Michniewicz. She had been able to do little for David Tasma's physical suffering but she was able to offer him love and honesty in an otherwise hostile environment. For Antoni Michniewicz she had been able to give more: relief from physical pain, as she applied her new expert skill

on pain management, and a reciprocated love in a caring environment. But for Marian, she could assure him a pain-free death in a
peaceful and happy setting geared to meet his every need, as
comfortable to him as his own home, surrounded by people who
knew and loved him. It was the fulfilment of her life's ambition: to
defeat the isolation of death so that no one need die alone and in
agony.

The circumstances of Marian's death spared her from the
anxiety she would have felt had he died in the painful, isolating
circumstances she witnessed as a young nurse, almoner, and newly
qualified doctor. Her faith spared her from a descent into despair
wrought by unfathomable grief. But it could not spare her from
missing the man she loved and lived with for the second half of her
life. 'Loving inevitably means loss,' she wrote in a deeply personal
introduction to a book on coping with bereavement:

> Death and other devastating misfortunes cut short relationships
> that are more important to us than life itself. Sooner or later we
> all suffer wounds to make us cry out, 'Why should this happen to
> me?' or more poignantly '. . . to the one I love?' Life is above all
> about learning to love and most of us have merely begun when
> we die. That is the main reason why many of us long for and
> expect another life.

Cicely Saunders did not set out to defeat death. But she rescued
the dying from death by repositioning the dying process within the
embrace of life. Since the opening of St Christopher's Hospice,
hundreds more hospices have sprung up, inspired by what St
Christopher's has achieved. More important has been the paradigm shift that has taken place in mainstream medical practice as
was Cicely Saunders's greatest hope and most satisfying accomplishment. 'The movement for palliative care has risen around the
world as a protest against the pain, isolation and neglect of dying
people,' she said.

David Clark wrote too of the revolution she brought about in
palliative care:

Within a very few years of St Christopher's opening, the movement began to evolve in just the kind of organic way in which Cicely had hoped it might. The principles having been defined, they were now being interpreted – on both sides of the Atlantic and eventually all over the world – in different ways to suit different needs.

We also see an increasing recognition that palliative care is something which can be developed in many modes and settings. It can be extended beyond its initial success with cancer patients to include those with non-malignant conditions, initially motor neurone disease, and in due course the challenge of caring for people with AIDS.

Above all, its major purpose comes to be seen as the improvement of care within the mainstream setting [. . .] through education and training and the broader diffusion of appropriate knowledge, skills and attitudes.

Cicely Saunders has been hailed as one of the greatest doctors and humanitarians of our time. She as a person, and St Christopher's as an institution, have won countless awards. In 1989 the Queen awarded her the Order of Merit. She has also won the Conrad Hilton Humanitarian Prize and the Onassis Prize for Services to Humanity. She holds twenty-five honorary degrees from prestigious universities in Britain and the United States. In April 2003, a survey of doctors named Cicely Saunders the third greatest doctor of all time. At the age of eighty-five, two years before her death, she still visited St Christopher's patients nearly every day. To the end she was still in great demand as the pioneering expert in palliative care.

Balfour Mount, a Canadian colleague and friend of Saunders, rated her amongst the giants of medicine. 'The twentieth century saw several physicians who qualify as giants based on their contributions to the relief of human suffering: Fleming, Banting, Salk, and Saunders. The first three are remembered for their discoveries. Dame Cicely's contribution differs in kind. She has been the catalyst for a paradigm shift in global health care.'

Mount enumerates the numbers of people whose lives are

touched by St Christopher's each year: the patients living in the hospice; the hundreds more who drop in for day programmes; the patients cared for at home by outreach workers; the families of them all; the thousands of visitors and researchers who come to conferences and workshops; the thousands more around the world whose own doctors and nurses have adopted the palliative care approach forged by Cicely Saunders. Countless people – it is not impossible to know how many and how far spread – have been touched by her. But as he says, the numbers alone do not do her justice: 'As impressive as the statistics are, numbers do not convey the significance of Dame Cicely's work. Compassion cannot be tabulated in columns, nor are we yet able to assign a value to the significance of diminished suffering.'

Sir Douglas Black said of her: 'The requirement is that those responsible should be infected by the attitude that the dying patient needs and deserves not only compassion and consultation, but also the full deployment of medical and nursing skills which, Christopher-like, can ease their journey. Cicely Saunders has been foremost in forming, proclaiming and confirming this attitude.'

In his foreword to Shirley du Boulay's biography of Cicely Saunders, John Taylor, the former Bishop of Winchester, praised her thus:

Some biographies are an indispensable duty required by the status of the subject. But this is a story that simply had to be told. For here is someone who, almost single-handed (though she would fiercely deny this), has tackled and overcome one of the greatest unspoken fears that haunt human beings today, the fear of a painful and humiliating death from an incurable disease. The dread that this might befall some beloved relative is often greater than the fear for oneself. Hence the despair that lends such force to the case for euthanasia. And it is this despair that Cicely Saunders has dispelled with the light of a new hope.

These accolades were written by the living and the well. But perhaps those most qualified to tell of her achievement are her patients themselves. Many, many patients have had their

experiences recorded by the thousands of medical students con-
ducting research at St Christopher's and by Saunders herself. They
are maybe simpler and more poignant, written, as they were, by
men and women about to die.

> Death and I are only nodding acquaintances,
> We have not been formally introduced,
> But many times I have noticed,
> The final encounter,
> Here in this hospice,
> I can truly say,
> That death has been met with dignity,
> Who can divine the thoughts,
> Of a man in close confrontation:
> I can only remember,
> One particular passing,
> When a man,
> With a sustained smile,
> Pointed out what was for him,
> Evidently a great light,
> Who knows what final revelations,
> Are received in the last hours?
> Lord, grant me a star in the East,
> As well as a smouldering sunset.

Written by Sidney Reeman,
a patient at St Christopher's, a few weeks
before his death on 28 January 1975.

8

Aung San Suu Kyi

In the early 1990s I wished to invite Aung San Suu Kyi to address the Labour Party conference. Of course, I knew that she would be unable to attend so I approached her husband, Michael Aris, and arranged to meet him, wondering if he might take her place, but he felt it was not the right time for him to make any public statements. It was only as I prepared to meet him and began reading about the couple in more detail that I discovered the story of their lives together and the sheer scale of their struggle.

Indeed, the more I read, the more I wondered at Aung San Suu Kyi's great courage; lonely and sustained, it had shaped her life and resulted in her becoming the world's most renowned female prisoner of conscience. Facing one of the most tyrannous regimes in the world, she had demonstrated that courage by living under house arrest for most of the last two decades, far apart from the husband she loved, and from her beloved children, missing all their years of growing up.

It was a few years later, in 1997, that the strength of Aung San Suu Kyi's character and beliefs was tested even further. As her husband lay dying of cancer in London, she learned that she would be granted her wish to visit him only at the price of never being allowed to return to Burma, her homeland. In the years since, that courage has further enhanced her standing as a world-renowned champion of non-violent protest for freedom.

Since I was not able to interview Aung San Suu Kyi, as I wished to do, I read all that had been written about her and talked to her husband and to people connected with her struggle. What emerges is a unique and still unfolding story of courage of the highest order.

To understand Aung San Suu Kyi's courage we need to understand firstly her devotion to duty – and in particular, the influence of her father, Aung San, who secured Burmese independence from the British in 1948 but who did not live to see that independence come into force – and secondly, and most important of all, the strength of Aung San Suu Kyi's underlying belief in democracy and human rights. Her courage has shown itself not in the fearlessness of impetuous confrontation, but in a strength of character rooted in passionately held beliefs – beliefs that have sustained her through years of oppression and deprivation and cruel separation from her loved ones.

For Aung San Suu Kyi the turning point in this process occurred in the spring of 1988. 'It was a quiet evening in Oxford like many others – the last day of March 1988,' her husband, Michael Aris, recalled. 'Our sons were already in bed and we were reading when the telephone rang. Suu picked up the phone to learn that her mother had suffered a severe stroke. She put the phone down and at once started to pack. I had a premonition that our lives would change for ever.'

Until that day Aung San Suu Kyi had been an academic and housewife, married to a professor, and bringing up two young sons in the tranquillity of Oxfordshire. The next day she left England for a Rangoon in the grip of demonstrations and protests. As she tended her critically ill mother, she bore silent witness to the growing restlessness of the country's youth. Within a few weeks of her arriving in the city, General Ne Win's twenty-six-year-long dictatorial rule came to an end as he announced plans to allow the country to decide its fate in a referendum.

As pro-democracy fervour swept from Rangoon across the country, 'She, like the whole country, was electrified,' Michael Aris recalled. 'The people at last had a chance to take control of their own destinies. I think it was at this moment more than any other that Suu made up her mind to step forward.'

But with mass demonstrations drawing millions of people on to the streets, General Ne Win orchestrated not the democratic transition people hoped for but a human rights crackdown which culminated on 8 August in what Desmond Tutu and Václav Havel have subsequently exposed in a report to the UN Security Council as a massacre of the innocents: thousands of unarmed demonstrators – mostly students – gunned down in the streets.

Aung San Suu Kyi had arrived in Rangoon at the end of March 1998. She had no weapons, troops or band of followers, but she saw at first hand the brutality of the military and she knew the fate awaiting the countless demonstrators rounded up on the streets. Yet it was precisely because she wanted for others in her own country the freedoms she enjoyed in the United Kingdom that at this point, the point of greatest danger, she stepped forward.

Standing in front of half a million protestors on 26 August, speaking under a poster of her father by the Shwedagon Pagoda, Aung San Suu Kyi told the crowd: 'I could not, as my father's daughter, remain indifferent to all that was going on.'

Within weeks, Aung San Suu Kyi and colleagues had established the National League for Democracy, and she became its general secretary. When her mother, Daw Khin Kyi, died in December of that year, the funeral procession turned into a peaceful protest, and Aung San Suu Kyi's life changed irrevocably as she embarked on an exhaustive tour of the country, demanding democracy and human rights.

While Aung San Suu Kyi's decision to lead the protest was made in the days of turmoil following the repression of August 1988, it was a decision that had been twenty years in the making – though she would have been surprised to become not only a focus for a nation's hopes but also a symbol of unbeatable courage around the world.

For me Aung San Suu Kyi defines the meaning of courage. Once courage was seen chiefly as a battlefield virtue. In most accounts the emphasis is on the physical – physical risk, physical vulnerability, or physical triumph. It has been seen as an almost exclusively male, physical attribute: courage as daring and bravado, even recklessness; indeed in many languages the word for courage is derived from the word for 'man'. But Aung San Suu Kyi represents the power not of the powerful but of the powerless: a woman, a prisoner of conscience up against a state with one of the worst human rights violation records in the world: a country of 52 million people with 1,000 political prisoners, 500,000 political refugees, poets and journalists tortured just for speaking out.

In the collection of her writings, *Freedom from Fear*, Aung San Suu Kyi describes the courage that she admires the most. It is not fearlessness but conviction – a courage of the mind; not so much a momentous act of daring as a constant condition of the mind defined by strength of belief and strength of will.

> Fearlessness may be a gift but perhaps more precious is the courage acquired through endeavour, courage that comes from cultivating the habit of refusing to let fear dictate one's actions, courage that could be described as 'grace under pressure' – grace which is renewed repeatedly in the face of harsh, unremitting pressure.
>
> Within a system which denies the existence of basic human rights, fear tends to be the order of the day. Fear of imprisonment, fear of torture, fear of death, fear of losing friends, family, property or means of livelihood, fear of poverty, fear of isolation, fear of failure . . . It is not easy for a people conditioned by fear under the iron rule of the principle that might is right to free themselves from the enervating miasma of fear. Yet even under the most crushing state machinery courage rises up again and again, for fear is not the natural state of civilised man.

The wellspring for courage and enduring in the face of unbridled power is generally a firm belief in the sanctity of ethical principles combined with a historical sense that despite all setbacks the condition of man is set on an ultimate course for both spiritual and material advancement. So courage is founded not on acts of daring but a state of mind, principled beliefs, driven forward by an optimism about human nature, supported by hard endeavour, repeatedly refusing to let fear undermine your actions even under the greatest pressure.

So, what lay behind Aung San Suu Kyi's actions? What had taken her from the comfort of her life in England to the violence, and then loss of liberty, in Rangoon, and depriving her of her husband and children? And what later would make it impossible for her to agree to visit her husband, even on his deathbed? What had brought husband and wife to decide that, in the interests of the cause they both believed in, they might never meet again? And from where did the strength of character come from that made her not only stand up for her principles but triumph over risks and fear to act upon them?

For this we have to look further back to Aung San Suu Kyi's birth, education and background. She was not only the daughter of the deeply revered Burmese nationalist hero, Aung San; she herself had grown up revering him. As the dedication in *Freedom from Fear* bears witness, she sees him as the exemplar of an integrity that is at the heart of her beliefs. It reads: 'In honour of Bogyoke [General] Aung San. When I honour my father, I honour all those who stand for political integrity in Burma.'

Aung San Suu Kyi's life seems, in many respects, a continuous dedication to her father's memory. Like him, she took on the weight of her country's unfulfilled hope for freedom. Both bent their lives to the call of duty to their country. And both paid a heavy price – the father with his life; the daughter with her liberty.

Aung San, one of many student agitators at Rangoon University in the 1930s, emerged as a national leader when Burma was still under British rule. During the Second World War he and his civilian supporters joined the Japanese in a calculated bid to secure Burmese independence, but finding the Japanese to be more oppressive than the British, Aung San and his newly trained civilian army switched allegiance to join the British against the Japanese. During 1947, Aung San negotiated Burma's complete independence, became leader of the first Burmese government, but tragically only a few months later, at the age of thirty-two, he was assassinated. His daughter Aung San Suu Kyi was then only two years old.

It is illuminating to recall what Aung San Suu Kyi admired in her father – his courage – and how she defined it:

Always one to practise what he preached, Aung San himself
constantly demonstrated courage – not just the physical sort but
the kind that enabled him to speak the truth, to stand by his
word, to accept criticism, to admit his faults, to correct his
mistakes, to respect the opposition, to parley with the enemy
and to let people be the judge of his worthiness as a leader. It is
for such moral courage that he will always be loved and
respected in Burma – not merely as a warrior hero but as the
inspiration and conscience of the nation.

It is this courage she identifies in her father, a moral courage,
which was why he was loved. Mahatma Gandhi and her father, she
wrote, were very different personalities, but 'as there is an inevitable sameness about the challenges of authoritarian rule anywhere
at any time, so there is a similarity in the intrinsic qualities of those
who rise up to meet the challenge'. According to Nehru, Gandhi
had instilled courage in India. 'The greatest gift for an individual
or a nation was fearlessness,' Nehru said, 'not merely bodily
courage but absence of fear from the mind.'

In a sense, Aung San Suu Kyi's rebellion has been that of a
daughter fulfilling her duty to the father she loved. By her own
admission the legacy of Aung San the father both haunted and
inspired Aung San Suu Kyi the daughter – and fired her with a
sense of civic duty. Her country was her father's unfinished work.
'When I first decided to take part in the movement for democracy,
it was more out of a sense of duty than anything else,' she said in an
interview with the founder of the Burma Project in California, Alan
Clements, in 1997. So duty was the starting point; but, she went on
to explain, 'On the other hand, my sense of duty was very closely
linked to my love for my father. I could not separate it from the love
for my country, and therefore, from the sense of responsibility
towards my people.'

After Aung San's murder, Aung San Suu Kyi remained with her
mother and brothers in Rangoon until she was fifteen. In 1960, her
mother, Daw Khin Kyi, was appointed Burma's ambassador to
India and Nepal and Aung San Suu Kyi moved to Delhi with her,
learning much about Indian history and the life and philosophy of

Gandhi. She would later search the life and teachings of Gandhi for wisdom and inspiration in her own struggle to wage non-violent protest.

From India she travelled to Britain – and to study philosophy, politics and economics at Oxford University. It was then she first met Michael Aris, a scholar of Eastern politics, with whom she fell in love. After graduating she moved to New York and worked for the United Nations Secretariat. It was during this period of separation from Michael that she wrote many of her letters to him, including the ones he published in his foreword to *Freedom from Fear*. In those letters she wrote of her love for Burma, of her sense that her fate and that of Burma were inextricably linked, and of the duty she felt called to honour as her father's daughter.

'She always used to say to me that if her people ever needed her, she would not fail them,' Michael Aris once explained; 'she constantly reminded me that one day she would have to return to Burma, that she counted on my support at that time, not as her due, but as a favour.'

So the road Aung San Suu Kyi was to travel was marked out not in 1988 when she returned to Burma, but in the early 1970s when she and her husband agreed what she would have to do if the need arose. Her decision to fight for democracy in Burma was not a spur of the moment act of indignation: it was a long-term commitment made in the early years of her life, and one she consistently held to and honoured.

In 1972 Michael Aris and Aung San Suu Kyi married and settled in Oxford. Michael had by then earned a doctorate and was teaching at Oxford University. Their first son, Alexander, was born in 1973 and their second son, Kim, was born four years later. For the next ten years, Aung San Suu Kyi's life revolved around home, family, and her own academic interests. Studying widely, but in particular Asian and Indian political history, she travelled and researched in detail her father's life – and the political and ethical ideals that guided his leadership through such a turbulent and momentous period of Burmese history.

Her scholarship and research into her country's past and her own political inheritance were preparation for the leadership she would eventually take. That she would do something for Burma was not the question. The only question was what form her work would take.

But during this period living in Oxford she led the life not of a political activist or campaigner but that of a scholar, wife and mother, far from the darkening political clouds gathering over Burma. She travelled regularly to visit her mother in Rangoon and, to advance education and to honour her father's memory, she planned for Burma a system of public libraries and scholarships for Burmese students.

Duty to her father's memory was important. In an interview Alan Clements asked her if she thought of her father every day. 'Not every day, no,' she replied,

> I'm not obsessed by him, as some people think I am. I hope that my attitude towards him is one of healthy respect and admiration, not obsession . . . [But] when I started doing research into my father's life, I was struck by our similarities. I was surprised that we thought so much alike. At one time there were some thoughts and feelings that I thought were my own, and then I discovered that he had them already.

What bound them together, she asserts, is more their shared beliefs than their shared background. She understood what her father wanted to achieve on an intellectual and moral level as well as on a patriotic and political level. In the following passages she explains that her struggle in Burma is for a 'revolution of the spirit' and boldly uses the term *metta*, which means 'loving-kindness'. And that for her father, politics was about establishing a trust and respect between a nation and its leaders, the only secure guarantee for a democracy.

So for Aung San Suu Kyi, like her father,

> the quintessential revolution is that of the spirit, born of an intellectual conviction of the need for change in those mental attitudes and values which shape the course of a nation's development. A revolution which aims merely at changing official policies and institutions with a view to an improvement in

material conditions has little chance of genuine success. Without a revolution of the spirit, the force which produced the iniquities of the old order would continue to be operative, posing a constant threat to the process of reform and regeneration.

And she defends herself against the charge that this is too other-worldly.

Some have questioned the appropriateness of talking about such matters as *metta* (loving kindness) and *thissa* (truth) in the political context. But politics is about people and what we had seen in Thamanya proved that love and truth can move people more strongly than any form of coercion.

Democracy is about your job and your children's education; it's about the house you live in and the food you eat; it's about whether or not you have to get permission from somebody before you visit your relatives in the next village; it's about whether or not you can reap your own harvest and sell it to the person you want to sell it to. The struggle is about their everyday life. It's no use saying to a farmer that democracy is about better investment rules: that makes no difference to him at all. But democracy is about securing him the right to sow what he wants to, and to reap at the time he thinks the harvest is ready, and then to sell it to whomsoever he thinks will give him the best price. That's democracy.

For a businessman, democracy is a system where there are sound commercial laws which are upheld by the institutions of the state, so he knows his rights and what he is allowed to do or not. He knows how to protect himself if anybody infringes those rights. For a student, democracy is the right to be able to study in good schools and in peace, and not to be dragged away to prison because you happen to be laughing with your friends over some funny characteristic of a minister. Democracy is the right to discuss your political views with your friends and to have the right to sit down at the tea shop on the campus and talk about whatever you want to, without wondering whether the MI are listening. When Uncle U Kyi Maung was under detention, one of the Military Intelligence officers interrogating him asked, 'Why did you decide to become a member of the National League for Democracy?' And he answered, 'For your sake.' That's what our struggle is about: everybody's everyday lives.

So it was strength of belief that drove Aung San Suu Kyi – even when she considered herself and her father less than typical politicians. Her father, she wrote in a biographical essay on his life, had few of the political graces, was uncomfortable with the trappings of power and was indeed prone to passionate and angry outbursts. 'The total picture is one of a young man of great integrity and strong character who led his country to independence with single-mindedness and a high sense of purpose.'

Accusations of ruthless ambition, unreasonableness and dupli-city have been made by some political opponents and by those who saw Aung San's fight against the foreign rulers of his country as 'treachery'. Such charges have been evaluated against a considera-tion of the record of his actions and achievements. As long as he believed that another was better able to provide the leadership, he had accepted subordinate positions readily, assuming the central role only when it became clear that he was the one man who could unite the country and lead it to freedom.

Aung San's appeal, she believed, was not so much to extremists as to the great majority of ordinary citizens who wished to pursue their own lives in peace and prosperity under a leader they could trust and respect. In him they saw that leader, a man who put the interests of the country before his own needs, who remained poor and unassuming at the height of his power, who accepted the responsibilities of leadership without hankering after the privileges, and who, for all his political acumen and powers of statecraft, retained at the core of his being a deep simplicity. For the people of Burma, Aung San was the man who had come in their hour of need to restore their national pride and honour.

Yet even more unlikely than her father's rise to power was the extraordinarily swift emergence of Aung San Suu Kyi as the voice for modern Burmese democracy. But for Michael Aris there was 'a certain inevitability in the way she, like [her father], has now become an icon of popular hope and longing. In the daughter as in the father there seems an extraordinary coincidence of legend and reality, of word and deed.' But, importantly, he added:

> what binds the father and daughter is an inheritance of conviction, a shared commitment to ideals that transcend both themselves and their country. Suu, like her father, is a servant. But she is not a servant to the memory of a heroic parent, nor simply to the hopes of a beloved country. She, like her father, is a servant to the ideals of democracy and liberty as the conditions in which human dignity is assured.

Like all great leaders, Aung San Suu Kyi's achievements reverberate far wider than the boundaries of one country. All liberty-loving people can claim her for their own. She is a champion of human dignity. As Václav Havel put it:

> By dedicating her life to the fight for human rights and Democracy in Burma, Aung San Suu Kyi is not only speaking out for justice in her own country, but also for all those who want to be free to choose their own destiny. As long as the struggle for freedom needs to be fought throughout the world, voices such as Aung San Suu Kyi's will summon others to the cause. Whether the cry for freedom comes from central Europe, Russia, Africa, or Asia, it has a common sound: all people must be treated with dignity; all people need to hope.

However, until the fateful events of August 1988 unfolded, it had never been Aung San Suu Kyi's intention to strive for anything quite so momentous. As Michael Aris recalled: 'She knew she would contribute something but time, place and circumstance catapulted her into a life she could never have imagined for herself.'

Within a few weeks of returning to Burma she had led a mass demonstration, formed a new political party, and planned to win a referendum. And she had set out and preached a gospel of non-violent protests. She had no army behind her, no weapons at her disposal, no protection against the savagery that was meted out with devastating frequency to her supporters by the military. Certainly there were those who urged armed struggle. She did not criticise those who adopted violence and she recognised that her father had used armed struggle to achieve independence.

However, borrowing from Gandhi, she held that the strength of her people's claim to democracy lay in their inviolable right to freedom. Its legitimacy was self-evident, and could not be won through violence.

Military coups, which have happened enough in Burma, are violent ways of changing situations and I do not want to encourage and to perpetuate this tradition of bringing about change through violence. Because I am afraid that if we achieve democracy in this way we will never be able to get rid of the idea that you bring about necessary changes through violence. The very method would be threatening us all the time.

As Michael Aris said: 'All that Suu had to draw on were her very finely cultivated sense of commitment and her powers of reason.'

But it all became even more difficult, as the military formed the State Law and Order Restoration Council – or SLORC – in September 1988 and turned the entire machinery of the state against her in an attempt to silence her by intimidation. On 5 April 1989, Aung San Suu Kyi and her colleagues confronted an army unit whose rifles were raised and aimed at them. She motioned for her colleagues to step aside while she walked on alone towards the soldiers, offering herself as an easy target. An army major finally intervened and the rifles were lowered. This poignant scene, of an unarmed solitary figure advancing towards the aimed weapons of a paranoid military dictatorship, can be seen as an allegory of her struggle for freedom in her land. In those few minutes, Aung San Suu Kyi showed extraordinary physical courage in the face of an acute mortal threat, adding still farther to her stature as the leader of democracy in the face of tyranny.

But I am even more fascinated to think of her courage to withstand the isolation of house arrest and separation from her family that would follow – even when she knew she could walk away.

Unwilling to allow her to continue to stoke the flames of democracy, but unwilling to risk the disapprobation of her assassination, SLORC had Aung San Suu Kyi and other NLD leaders arrested in July 1989 without charge, and she was placed under house arrest. She was now at the mercy of the military.

However, unlike most other demonstrators, Aung San Suu Kyi's high public profile afforded her some protection. She understood the greater vulnerability of her supporters who had been arrested and put in prison, so she immediately went on a hunger strike until the authorities could give her assurance that her supporters would be treated humanely.

Throughout her tumultuous entry into Burmese politics, Aung San Suu Kyi's family had been her steadfast support. Michael and her young sons had travelled to Burma and stayed with her during the school holidays. They had accompanied her on some of her campaigning rallies. Both sons were with her, in fact, when she was placed under house arrest and began her hunger strike. But SLORC then sought to harness all the bargaining power they could by preventing her family from visiting her.

As soon as the boys had returned to England, SLORC stepped between Aung San Suu Kyi and her family. Her access to them was no longer a private matter to be negotiated around school holidays and half terms. Her love for her family would become a weapon that SLORC could turn and use on her. From then on, her children were denied visas, though the authorities allowed Michael further visits at Christmas – with the expectation that he would persuade her to give up the struggle and quit Burma. He wrote of their Christmas as a bittersweet occasion:

> The days I spent alone with her that last time, completely isolated from the world, are among my happiest memories of our many years of marriage. It was wonderfully peaceful. Suu had established a strict regime of exercise, study and piano which

I managed to disrupt. She was memorizing a number of Buddhist sutras. I produced Christmas presents I had brought one by one to spread them out over several days. We had all the time in the world to talk about many things. I did not suspect this would be the last time we would be together for the foreseeable future.

When SLORC realised that her husband would not persuade her to abandon Burma and return to her family in England, he too was denied further entry. All phone lines to Aung San Suu Kyi were cut and letters from home and supporters, which had initially sustained her, no longer reached her. She would accept nothing from SLORC, not even their offer to be a channel for communication with her family. For Aung San Suu Kyi, accepting the help of SLORC, even for survival, would corrupt the clarity of her resolve and dilute the significance of her resistance. These were desperate, lonely days.

Sometimes I didn't even have enough money to eat. I became so weak from malnourishment that my hair fell out . . . I couldn't get out of bed. I was afraid that I had damaged my heart. Every time I moved, my heart went thump-thump-thump, and it was hard to breathe. I fell to nearly 90 pounds from my normal 106. I thought to myself that I'd die of heart failure, not starvation at all. Then my eyes started to go bad. I developed spondylitis, which is a degeneration of the spinal column.

Despite Aung San Suu Kyi's imprisonment, the NLD went on to win the elections held in May 1990 by an incredible landslide – taking 81 per cent of the seats. SLORC refused to recognise the results of the election, and she remained under house arrest.

So the first uncertain weeks of house arrest turned into months, then years. Aung San Suu Kyi was almost completely cut off from the outside world and her family. She discovered that SLORC might be willing to grant her the right to leave Burma to visit her family in England; but she knew that if she left she would never be allowed to return and her work for Burma would be over. To see her family again, she would have to abandon her country in its

darkest hour. Yet Aung San Suu Kyi knew it was a false choice: the
decision was not whether to choose family over country, but
whether to abandon the very ideals upon which her love for both
her family and country were grounded.

Her husband knew her well, and knew she would never cave in.
He wrote shortly after visiting her at Christmas, 1989:

> Very obviously the plan was to break Suu's spirit by separating
> her from her children in the hope she would accept permanent
> exile. I myself was allowed to return once more to be with her for
> a fortnight the following Christmas. It seems the authorities had
> hoped I would try to persuade her to leave with me. In fact,
> knowing the strength of Suu's determination, I had never even
> thought of doing this . . . The promise to support her decision
> which I had given in advance so many years ago now had to be
> fulfilled . . . I know Suu well enough to be sure she will not do
> this: she is firmly committed to her chosen path, whatever the
> sacrifice it entails.

And each month away from her family was a month missed in
the lives of her growing children. Each month in isolation marked a
severance from the husband who was, in every regard, her life's
companion. What resources of strength did she have that enabled
her to endure the loss of those she most loved? Her oppressors tried
to equate her refusal to leave Burma with neglect of her children,
claiming she sought personal glory in Burma over and above family
duty.

But on the few occasions she has spoken of her separation from
her family we gain glimpses of the scale of her sacrifice. In one essay
she wrote of seeing her son, Kim, for the first time after years of
separation:

> Two years is a long time in the life of a child. It is long enough for
> a baby to forget a parent who has vanished from sight. It is long
> enough for boys and girls to grow into young adolescents. It is
> long enough to turn a carefree youngster into a troubled human
> being . . . When I saw my younger son again for the first time

after a separation of two years and seven months he had changed
from a round-faced not-quite-twelve-year-old into a rather sty-
lish 'cool' teenager. If I had met him on the street I would not
have known him for my little son.

In one of her interviews she wrote that people identified with Nelson
Mandela because they knew him as a father and husband as well as a
leader and political prisoner. The same may be said of Aung San Suu
Kyi. In one conversation, she spoke with ease and familiarity of
parental concerns for her teenage son – and its very ordinariness puts
into sharp relief the extraordinariness of her own loss:

> With my sons, I was always running around with them, playing
> together. Also, I would have long discussions with them. Some-
> times I would argue with them – tremendously passionate
> arguments, because my sons can be quite argumentative, and
> I am argumentative, too . . . [Kim] is very musical and I've
> learned a lot about the kind of music that he likes. I have no
> problems with him . . . it's his father who has arguments with
> him about the kind of music he likes. Michael objects to Kim
> playing his music so loudly. Whereas that never troubles me. I
> can tolerate it. I never stop him because I don't like him listening
> to this music on his earphones. I think that damages his ears. I'd
> rather put up with all that noise than have him damage his ears.

Long before she was held under house arrest, she wrote prophe-
tically to Michael of her fears of an impending separation from him:

> Sometimes I am beset by fears that circumstances and national
> considerations might tear us apart just when we are so happy in
> each other that separation would be a torment. And yet such
> fears are so futile and inconsequential: if we love and cherish each
> other as much as we can while we can, I am sure love and
> compassion will triumph in the end.

But neither Aung San Suu Kyi nor anyone else could have
known for how long or how relentlessly her endurance would be

tested. The outside world had no way of contacting her, and apart from a radio, she had no news of the outside world. Her isolation was complete.

In 1991 Aung San Suu Kyi was awarded the Nobel Peace Prize. She learned of this after hearing it on the BBC World Service while under house arrest. Her fourteen-year-old son Kim accepted the prize on her behalf. For a brief moment, her family hoped that as a result of the award, world attention might prompt an improvement in her circumstances. This too was the motivation for Michael having the series of essays *Freedom from Fear* published. The anguish of their separation is apparent in Michael's introductory words:

> I was informed today that my dear wife Suu has been awarded the Nobel Peace Prize . . . She is a prisoner of conscience in her country, totally isolated from the world . . . We, her family, are denied any contact whatsoever with her and know nothing of her condition except that she is quite alone . . . The joy and pride which I and our children feel at this moment is matched by sadness and continuing apprehension . . . It is my earnest hope and prayer that the Peace Prize will somehow lead to what she has always strived for . . . Selfishly, I also hope our family's situation will be eased as a result of this supreme gesture of recognition for her moral and physical courage, and that we may at last be allowed to pay her visits again. We miss her very much.

Four more years would pass before Michael or her children would see her again. Aung San Suu Kyi was released from house arrest on 10 July 1995 and immediately resumed her pro-democracy work. Her family enjoyed a reunion in 1995. But through the joy, the precariousness of her freedom was never far from anybody's minds. Aung San Suu Kyi's children and husband could not stay in Burma. At any time, the authorities could reject their next visa application, and the torment of separation would resume just as she had become reintegrated in their lives. Indeed, soon after her release, the military began to restrict her movement and prevent her from meeting with supporters or addressing rallies. The harassment and intimidation escalated to such an extent that she was unable to travel beyond Rangoon, and often not beyond her front door. The increasingly anxious military resorted to unofficial imprisonment. And once more, the authorities refused visa applications from her children and husband.

In 1998 Michael Aris was diagnosed with advanced prostate cancer and told he had not long to live. This devastating news brought about energetic efforts to allow him a final visit to his wife. Appeals from embassies throughout the world failed to move the Burmese military authorities. Instead they stepped up the propaganda war and offered to assist with arrangements for Aung San Suu Kyi to leave the country so that she could be with her terminally ill husband. Once again they hoped that she would finally be persuaded to quit Burma, this time in order to see her husband alive one final time. It is scarcely possible to imagine the torment the couple must have endured in those months before Michael's death. She was never able to say goodbye to him. He died on 27 March 1999.

What determined Aung San Suu Kyi to resist the temptation to turn her back on Burma and return to the family she loved? What strength did she draw upon, knowing as she did that freedom and the comfort of her family's love was within her grasp? An interview conducted by Alan Clements shines a light on the firmness of her resolve:

AC: Did the authorities ever make it perfectly clear that you could be free if you left the country and did any SLORC members ever come to you directly to negotiate a settlement?

ASSK: No, but at one time they did make a suggestion that it might be a good idea. But they never put it to me in quite the way in which they put it to other people: 'If she leaves the country . . . she can be free'. But they knew that I knew because it was publicised on the BBC.

AC: You were never tempted by their offer of freedom?

ASSK: No. My main reaction was surprise that they ever thought that I could take up such an offer. And to a certain extent it indicated that they did not know me at all. I don't think this applies only to me. They do not

really get to know people in general. I think it's very
difficult for those who work by intimidating and using
their power to repress others to ever have the opportunity to get to know people really well.

Had her presence in Burma been merely a personal gesture of
defiance with no consequence or importance, then her continued
imprisonment might have seemed more of a stubborn act of
brinkmanship. But Aung San Suu Kyi's captivity was far more
than a personal confinement. The military government did not
realise just how much her detention had become a persistent,
growing symbol of resistance to the tyranny they had imposed
on the country. Like her father, she was no longer just one person
persecuted but the voice of a nation's hope. Her presence in Burma
– as a prisoner of conscience – kept the flame of democracy alive.

Her own words best attest to the reason she stayed behind in
Rangoon while her children grew up on the other side of the world
and her husband died slowly from his advancing cancer.

Throughout the years of my house arrest my family was living in
a free society and I could rest assured that they were economically secure and safe from any kind of persecution. The vast
majority of my colleagues who were imprisoned did not have the
comfort of such an assurance. They knew that their families were
in an extremely vulnerable position, in constant danger of
interrogation, house searches, general harassment and interfer-
ence with their means of livelihood . . .

   Political prisoners have to speak to their families through a
double barrier of iron grating and wire netting so that no
physical contact is possible. The children of one political prisoner
would make small holes in the netting and push their fingers
through to touch their father. When the holes got visibly bigger
the jail authorities had them patched up with thin sheets of tin.
The children would start all over again trying to bore a hole
through to their father: it is not the kind of activity one would
wish for any child . . .

   When the parents are released from prison it is still not the end of the story. The children suffer from a gnawing anxiety that their fathers or mothers might once again be taken away and placed out of their reach behind barriers of brick and iron. They have known what it is like to be young birds fluttering helplessly outside the cages that shut their parents away from them. They know that there will be no security for their families as freedom of thought and freedom of political action are not guaranteed by the law of the land.

Aung San Suu Kyi realised that her responsibility extended beyond her private life, and that she could not depend on a demarcation convenient to her, between her struggle for democracy and the consequences that struggle would have on her personal life. 'I do not think I'm leading a life which is completely different from the kind of life I would like to live,' she told Alan Clements. 'Of course, I would have liked to have had my family around me – especially I would have liked to have brought up my sons – seen them grow up. But that's only part of my life, my country is also part of my life . . . I also know that you have to make choices in life and give up some things.'

So, as her country's best-known prisoner of conscience, she fully recognised the wider consequences of imprisonment endured by all the far less well-known prisoners of conscience. Only by fully sharing their privations for herself and her family could she draw international attention to their plight. Were she to exercise a privilege, life would be easier for her, but there would be little hope for the other prisoners and future protestors, to whom anything could happen if there was no pressure of public exposure. She was their shield; her imprisonment was their best protection. It was only by bravely sacrificing her own family life that she could do anything to safeguard them.

But courage is about the strength of belief as well as the strength of willpower.

People who think that anybody can be bought, that human minds and hearts are mere commodities subject to the laws of supply and demand, such people would not be able to under-

stand other human beings who work for a cause and are prepared to sacrifice themselves for that cause.

But strength of character mattered. It was not enough to believe
in a cause; you had to do everything in your power to advance that
cause. Alan Clements asked her: 'When you reflect upon your
people's suffering, what is it that first comes to mind and stirs your
heart?' Her response is illuminating and defining:

That we ought to do something about it, whenever we can. That
is always my reaction when I see something that should not be.
It's no use standing there wringing your hands and saying, 'My
goodness, my goodness, this is terrible.' You must try to do what
you can. I believe in action.

So Aung San Suu Kyi's courage is the courage to sacrifice her
own happiness and a comfortable life so that through her struggle
she might win the right of an entire nation to seek happy and
comfortable lives. It is the absolute expression of selflessness.
Paradoxically, in sacrificing her own liberty she strengthens its
cry and bolsters its claim for the people she represents.

Her sacrifice is made even more poignant because she seems to be
very much in love with liberty and life. She writes movingly and
with great joy of ordinary things – the changing seasons, the rituals
of traditional Burmese festivals, the arrival of a new baby in
someone's family, the spirit of cooperation and friendship that
turns ordinary working days into small celebrations of the human
spirit. She is alive to the wonder and mystery of the world and
rejoices in its pleasures. That other people are denied the cup does
not diminish her joyfulness but strengthens her resolve to secure
their place at the table.

In one essay she writes:

This is the eighth winter that I have got out of bed in the
morning and looked out at the clean freshness of the world and
wondered how many prisoners are able to savour the beauties of
Hemanta of which our poets have written so nostalgically. It

would be interesting to read poems of winter behind the unyielding walls of prisons which shut out silvery dew and gossamer
sunshine, the smell of pale winter blossoms and the taste of rich
warming foods.

The passage is typical. She is as alert to joy as she is to the injustice
in the world around her.

Perhaps her strength and resolve to continue the struggle come
from the hope she perceives in the people around her and in her
country's national resources. Her hope is restless and demanding.
With hope comes the responsibility to nurture its potential. The
joyful birth of a baby to a family friend spurs her on in her work to
secure a future fit for the new life:

A couple of weeks ago some friends of mine became grandparents
for the first time when their daughter gave birth to a little girl.
Babies, I have read somewhere, are specially constructed to
present an appealingly vulnerable appearance aimed at arousing
tender, protective instincts: only then can tough adults be
induced to act as willing slaves to demanding little beings utterly
incapable of doing anything for themselves. It is claimed that
there is something about the natural smell of a baby's skin that
invites cuddles and kisses. Certainly I like both the shape and
smell of babies, but I wonder whether their attraction does not lie
in something more than merely physical attributes. Is it not the
thought of a life stretching out like a shining clean slate on which
might one day be written the most beautiful prose and poetry of
existence that engenders such joy in the hearts of the parents and
grandparents of a newly born child? The birth of a baby is an
occasion for weaving hopeful dreams about the future. Some of
the best indicators of a country developing along the right lines
are healthy mothers giving birth to healthy children who are
assured of good care and a sound education that will enable them
to face the challenges of a changing world. Our dreams for the
future of the children of Burma have to be woven firmly around a
commitment to better health care and better education.

Aung San Suu Kyi does not see herself engaged in a battle of the titans but in a struggle for the freedom to an 'ordinary' life. The grandest and noblest ideals – freedom and liberty – are but a means to enjoy the simplest and basic pleasures in life. Yet she knows that the foundation for such an ordinary life is truly radical because it requires a system based on trust, respect, and freedom.

> How many can be said to be leading normal lives in a country where there are such deep divisions of heart and mind, where there is neither freedom nor security? When we ask for democracy, all we are asking is that our people should be allowed to live tranquilly under the rule of law, protected by institutions which will guarantee our rights, the rights that will enable us to maintain our human dignity, to heal long-festering wounds and to allow love and courage to flourish. Is that such a very unreasonable demand?

After five years of unofficial harassment and confinement, the mirage of freedom was dropped on 23 September 2000 and once again Aung San Suu Kyi was placed under house arrest. Becoming re-familiarised with the routine of house arrest must have been bleakly easy. Asked by one journalist what she missed most during this second period of arrest, she commented: 'Actually, I didn't miss anything. It wasn't a new experience for me.'

She knew the routine of confinement well: the presence of guards around the house day and night, turning away the supporters, colleagues, and journalists who made a pilgrimage to her home every day; her every movement watched, curtailed, restricted. But most of all, adjusting from the frenetic, all-consuming work of readying her country for democracy to the slow quietude of isolation.

Aung San Suu Kyi's re-arrest was a blow. The outside world had seen her first 'release' in 1995 as a sign that a new age was dawning and fed hopes that the transition to democracy might finally be achieved in her lifetime. Comparisons to Mandela were irresistible. British journalist Fergal Keane, who has interviewed both Nelson Mandela and Aung San Suu Kyi on a number of occasions, wrote

of the strong similarities between their personalities as well as in
their struggle for their country's political freedom:

> Both have a stoic capacity to endure, both are believers in
> negotiation and both consistently refused to draw any distinction
> between their own liberty and that of their people. As Mandela
> once wrote from his prison: 'My freedom and yours are insepar-
> able.' But the most important similarity can only be described in
> blunt terms: they are both as tough as nails.

Like Mandela, many hoped that Aung San Suu Kyi would lead
Burma's rehabilitation to democracy and open up its economic
potential to the rest of the world. But the old guard was not ready to
give up and could not let go of the power they had seized by force.
The new dawn was a false dawn.

The reversal of fortune could have been devastating, if not a
cause of despair for an economically ruined country, weary of
oppression. Aung San Suu Kyi and the Burmese people had held
the faith for so long and sacrificed so much. Already, she had
endured house arrest for six years and lost her husband while her
children grew into adults in her absence. She had watched helplessly while her vision for a free Burma unravelled as branch after
branch of NDC offices were closed and Party workers were arrested
or killed. Meanwhile the military rule embedded itself further in
the psyche of her country, bringing out the worst instincts in
people. Rivalries between ethnic groups intensified. Fear undermined everything. Corruption flourished.

The sequence of events that led from her jubilant release in
1995 to five years of increasing intimidation and harassment
under a false freedom, then to a second period of house arrest in
the first year of the new millennium, might have plunged Aung
San Suu Kyi into depression as hope disintegrated once more.
How much longer could this go on? Will anything ever change?
Can anything ever change? What has my life been worth? What
has the suffering brought? These are the questions her captors
may have hoped would torment her mind in the solitude of her
confinement.

But Aung San Suu Kyi's spirit did not break. Instead, it now appears, she used her house arrest to lay the ground for a new strategy for bringing about change. From the start of this second period, she engaged in secret talks with the military authorities, brokered, until 2004, by the United Nations envoy Razali Ismail, to try to find a way through the impasse. She refers to the period as a phase of confidence-building. With the Burmese economy on its knees, the military generals needed her help in attracting foreign aid, and in their desperation, they were prepared to make concessions that her years of 'freedom' had failed to win.

Aung San Suu Kyi was officially released from house arrest on 6 May 2002, along with several hundred political prisoners. No restrictions were put on her movement. And she was able to reopen some of the NDC offices that the military had closed down. Like Mandela, she may have purposefully delayed her release until these concessions were won. Fergal Keane surmised that

> when the Burmese regime prevented Suu Kyi from campaigning and locked her up again, she didn't simper and try to make a backdoor deal. Just as Mandela could have done a deal which would have seen him go free years earlier (but at the expense of broader change), Aung San Suu Kyi will not be tempted by any deal which makes her a pliant partner of the junta. She was profoundly influenced by the South African example. When I met her she described how she had listened intently to the BBC radio reports of the transition and she bombarded me with questions about how Mandela and his comrades had persuaded De Klerk to hold multiracial elections.

Her re-release in May 2002 brought scenes of jubilation to the streets of Rangoon reminiscent of 1995. World leaders hailed her release as a very positive development and watched intently to see whether this time things would be different. Some commentators observed that the power had shifted, that the military regime was running out of money, opening up the possibility of compromise. Meanwhile Aung San Suu Kyi once again travelled across Burma to help rebuild the structures that would make democracy possible. Also, crucially, she sought to mobilise rebel ethnic groups into the political process by demanding that eventually, they too must be offered a chair at the power-sharing table as an equal member.

Journalists and commentators talked of a shift in Aung San Suu Kyi's demeanour after her 2002 release; that she was less combative towards the military regime and that a wariness that comes from disappointment and experience could be detected in her carefully chosen words. As her release was again hailed as 'a new dawn', she said: 'We only hope that the dawn will move very quickly to the full morning.' When pressed for details about the negotiations she had, and about the prospects for real change, she replied: 'I've always said I'm a cautious optimist and I've never had any reason to change my mind about this.'

Hailed as national leader and a symbol of the country's best self, Aung San Suu Kyi eschewed the heroic status heaped upon her by her fervent followers. Upon her release she insisted: 'I don't think my release should be looked upon as a major triumph for democracy. After all that is not the object of the struggle. It was never to assure my freedom. It was to assure that all the people of Burma enjoy the democratic freedoms to which they should be entitled.' Her battle cry was for freedom and democracy, not for the toppling of a regime or electoral victory for her own party. After years of intense work, after so much personal loss, and with an overwhelming democratic mandate, Aung San Suu Kyi might have insisted upon her right to take up her position at the helm of the nation. Instead, she said simply:

> The NLD has always said that we want to be flexible and we are ready to negotiate an outcome which will be favourable to the people of Burma. Negotiations should not be aimed at the betterment of the situation of the NLD or the betterment of the situation of the authorities. Negotiations should be aimed at the betterment of the people of Burma.

This kind of pragmatic flexibility underlines Aung San Suu Kyi's disinterest in securing power for herself. Her willingness to compromise, and to give the military a chance to prove that they believe in their own rhetoric, flies in the face of detractors who would portray her as someone driven by personal ambition. She seems willing to give her oppressors the chance to orchestrate the transition to democracy rather than be overthrown and kicked out. She is prepared to believe in their capacity to redeem themselves. She is not being naïve. She is simply giving them no excuses for lack of progress. Her rhetoric is a match to their own. They say they are prepared to open up the political process to the whole of the country. She calls their bluff and says she will work with them. But she, too, is anxious to see words matched with deed. In a video distributed to neighbouring countries on the twelfth anniversary of the pro-democracy uprising, for example, she summoned the international community, 'everybody who cares for the future of Burma', to support her calls for concrete change: 'the demand for the release of all political prisoners, speedily and unconditionally. Unless political organisations are free to go about their work unhindered and unintimidated by the authorities, we can never say that we have started the process toward changed democracy.'

But there was little noticeable progress since her release from house arrest in May 2002. If hopes were raised by her release, the impatience with the lack of change since was evident. An editorial in Thailand's the *Nation* newspaper expressed the country's frustration with the regime's intransigence to change.

> When Aung San Suu Kyi was released from house arrest in early May, there was much hope that the situation in Burma would improve. The Burmese people would be given more freedom to cope with day-to-day life while the process of reconciliation, marked by dialogue between Suu Kyi and the military leaders, would begin in earnest. But that has not yet happened.

As one journalist wrote, progress in Burma is measured by millimetres.

A year after her release, the Burmese nightmare took a familiar turn when Aung San Suu Kyi and her followers were attacked by government forces. More than eighty people were beaten to death; more than a hundred were arrested. This time Aung San Suu Kyi was thrown in prison, where she remained for some months. She was allowed home following hospital treatment for ill health, but remains once again under house arrest.

Still, the Burmese people put their hopes for a better life in Aung San Suu Kyi. She is still their inspiration, and still represents their greatest chance for a life free from fear. In August 2002, the Asian equivalent of the Nobel Peace Prize, the Ramon Magsaysay Award, was won by Cynthia Maung, a Karen doctor fighting to improve the health of Burma's displaced people. On hearing she had won the award, she said: 'I attribute the award to all Burmese people. My message to them is they must be strong as our lady, Aung San Suu Kyi.'

Has she been too idealistic? Could there be a way forwards even after all these years? Twice in 2006 the UN's representative Ibrahim Gambari met her, in May and then in November, the later meeting being well publicised as an hour-long encounter away from her home. Is there a chance that she could lead the way to a new future for Burma, as a unifying figure whom the newer, younger generation of future Burmese leaders could work with and accept as a leader or even figurehead? The former UN representative Razali Ismail says that the last time he saw Aung San Suu Kyi, in May 2004, 'she reiterated her readiness to meet the generals for the sake of the people. Suu Kyi had come a long way to realise that democracy can only be done through the generals, with the latter still in the driving seat. This realisation of hers is in stark contrast to the imperious, principled and unbending Suu Kyi I encountered over twenty meetings ago. I was unable to the very end to make the generals realise and acknowledge the changes in Suu Kyi.'

Yet three years later, in 2007, she is still under house arrest. Her helpers have been reduced from seven to three. Letters could be sent in until eighteen months ago, but not now. All she has for communication with the outside world is a short-wave radio. And her only regular contact is with her doctor, whom she meets only once a month. Conditions in her home were described to me by Charles Petrie, the UN's special representative in the country who met her regularly until 2004, as 'rudimentary'. He told me, 'When I met her the first time the sense that overwhelmed me was one of profound sadness – listening to how much she was willing to put up with. As an individual she is very focused, at first sight a stern and distinguished lady – and she is utterly selfless, always in conversation more concerned about others under arrest than herself. When Mr Gambari offered to work to reduce the severity of the conditions she is under, she refused, saying others had to receive the same treatment too.'

As I write, in March 2007, another period of raised expectations for Aung San Suu Kyi's release has come to yet another frustrating end – with hopes of freedom once again crushed. Once more Burma's military junta has made it clear that she will not be a free woman; their only concession – that a doctor will continue to be allowed to visit her, but only periodically – *may* do a little to reverse her declining health. So, seventeen years after an election landslide in her favour, in the fourth year of her third period of house arrest, Aung San Suu Kyi remains the world's most prominent prisoner of conscience.

The telephone call she received one night in March 1988 led her far away from the home she loved and the family she cherished. She can never go back and can never reclaim the years she lost from the lives of those she loves. Her husband has died and her children have grown up. Yet detention and imprisonment have not made her less desirous of returning to the ordinary joys of life – a mother spending time with her family – and personal tragedy does not seem to have made her less optimistic about the good that human beings can do. Even amid personal loss and suffering the iron has never entered her soul. And hers is an enduring courage, much more than a single act of daring; it is a deep, lasting commitment to a cause that sends a message to the world that no confinement or prison cell, no intimidation or brutality, no personal loss or even the threat to life itself can destroy the spirit of a true leader nor her faith in human nature – and it can never extinguish her determination that one day her people will be free.

Conclusion

In this book I have made no secret of who I admire, and what it is I admire in them. Each of the people I write about showed or shows high courage, and in the best of causes: Mandela in the ending of apartheid; Martin Luther King in the pursuit of civil rights; Bonhoeffer in his stance for Christian values in a barbarous state; Wallenberg in his campaign to save Hungarian Jews from the Holocaust; Edith Cavell working in great danger to save escaping prisoners of war; Cicely Saunders in her long struggle for better care of the dying; Robert Kennedy – while fully aware of the risks he ran – in pioneering a new and empowering concept of democracy in the USA; and Aung San Suu Kyi for the sacrifices she has made every day for nearly twenty years to keep the idea of democracy alive in her native country. Even today Burma's elected leader is a hostage in her own home, defiantly refusing to yield to her captors, continuing to insist that every human being has the right to live in freedom and in a democracy. Her fortitude sends a message that reverberates across the world.

Taken together, these eight people have done more than almost any other men or women I can think of to advance the great causes of our times. Each of them stood firm, and often they stood alone. They refused to give in, instead showing an endurance that the world has come to admire. What their lives and abiding influences – their struggles and their sacrifices – demonstrate is that courage is, indeed, the greatest of all virtues. All of us value duty, honesty, kindness, humility, responsibility, integrity, but none of these can exist without courage. As Winston Churchill said, 'Courage is the first of human qualities because it is the quality which guarantees all others.'

People of courage will always be loved, because they ennoble the human race to which we all belong. We are drawn to them and revere them because through their actions they open up the possibility of hope in times of cynicism, dignity in times of degradation, and purpose in times of despair. They give us glimpses of the nobility of which humanity is capable. They raise our sights and challenge us to be all that we are capable of being. They answer the human hunger for meaning and invest in our human condition a value so great as to assure its pricelessness.

I thought about such influences and determinants of courage as I read about these eight very different people, and also as I read more widely about courage as a concept. Of course scholarship can add to our understanding of courage as an abstract phenomenon, and dictionaries of quotations sometimes encapsulate insights into it in memorable ways. But again and again I was struck by how much more I learned from the details of the lives, reasoning and actions of the eight people whose courage I celebrate in this book.

I hope the reader will come to share my admiration for them, and learn from them as much about courage – as shown in all its complexity and particularity in their lives – as I did. But I hope too that they will bear with me as I try to summarise briefly some of the thinking around the subject.

We claim to love courage no matter where it springs, and admire its every manifestation, even amongst our enemies. Courage, said Samuel Johnson, is a quality so necessary for maintaining virtue that it is always respected, even when it is associated with vice. John F. Kennedy, too, afforded courage a great breadth, asking doubtfully in *Profiles of Courage* whether it is necessary to agree with a man's motives in order to admire his courage. We know roughly what it is, said William Miller in *The Mystery of Courage*, because we so desperately seek it and admire it and love to hear it told about. And yet we are not content to allow courage to be used to describe behaviour we don't approve of. In our discourse on courage, we continually seek to draw distinction between acts of courage and acts of fanaticism, mindless recklessness, fury-driven malevolence and other extreme behaviour that may masquerade as courage.

Nearly every enquiry into the nature of courage has included a litany of much that it is not. Philosophical discussion of courage is as old as philosophy itself. In Socrates' conversation with Laches, as recorded by Plato, courage is progressively stripped down to its elements and absorbed into broader, overarching notions such as goodness and wisdom, pitted against evil and ignorance. In this and subsequent philosophical enquiries, the fundamental question – what is courage? – broadens to a consideration of divergent views on the nature of humankind: that we are innately good, courage is good, and so we are logically drawn to it; or, that we are innately selfish and appear to act courageously when in fact we are merely acting to reward ourselves, even if in doing so we perish.

For amid the depths of suffering caused by our own inhumanity and the recklessness of nature and accident, we have also witnessed its relief by the generosity, compassion and heroism of courageous people. We embrace courage as a virtue we value, and therefore try to understand it so that we can cultivate and nurture it. We ask what we can learn from the lives of men and women whose courage has already asserted itself in the world. And we seek out others who have been courageous, those whom history has either failed or declined to honour. We ask how they learned right from wrong and thus try to understand something of their moral make-up. In our own time, from a very different perspective and using distinctly more modern methodologies, social scientists have asked what courageous people have in common, where they grew up, what their childhoods were like, how their cultures influenced them, what education they had, what society expected of them; and so have sought to determine whether the courageous are thus pre-disposed to be courageous – their courage rooted in influences that build up to its eventual manifestation.

Different classifications of courage have of course been attempted. One of particular interest to me is that of the American writer Frank Farley, who has researched heroic behaviour and divided coura-geous people into three different types: first, career heroes – emer-gency workers, police, paramedics, firefighters, members of the armed forces and others who train for what they do and whose work exposes them to risk as a matter of course, and who on occasions may make sacrifices – as we saw with Major Hugh Seagrim's work for the SOE in Burma – far beyond the call of duty; second, situational heroes, who 'sprint into action' and courageously rise to the occasion as demands, like the passengers on United Airlines Flight 93 on 9/11.

Theirs was the first and most dramatic of the responses to the terrorist outrages of that day. In shocking and unprecedented circumstances, the nature of which was still unfolding, they deliberated as captives, then acted as free men. They could have pleaded, prayed or simply done nothing; instead – in the most hopeless of circumstances – they chose to storm the cockpit. 'Let's roll' are the now immortalised words of Todd Beamer as he led the charge, but I will never forget reading his words that preceded the charge – 'We're going to do something. I'm going to have to go out on faith' – showing that the decision to act reflected the values he had learned during a lifetime.

Their actions did not save the aircraft, or their lives and those of their fellow-passengers, but their captors – who had not planned to crash into a field in Pennsylvania – had, by the determined actions of Todd Beamer and his colleagues, been diverted from their far more lethal purpose: most probably an attack on the White House, or on the Capitol and the Congress of the United States of America.

After 'career' and 'situational' courage, Frank Farley identifies a third type of courage, that of the 'sustained altruists' who devote long periods, sometimes their entire lives, to principled causes. Of course such classifications are not mutually exclusive. But in these essays I have concentrated mainly on people who might be described as sustained altruists, those who have put themselves at risk over a prolonged period of time because doing otherwise would have been to betray deeply held principles. All overcame formidable challenges, most faced extreme physical danger, and some died as martyrs to their cause. And, from Edith Cavell to Aung San Suu Kyi, there is in each case moving evidence not only of 'grace under pressure' in the most testing of circumstances, but of the strength of belief and strength of character that inspired their sacrifices and made them possible.

Down the ages, investigative approaches such as Farley's have addressed the question of courage in ways and with outcomes that admit of at least one immediately obvious and incontrovertible conclusion: that courage is a matter of lasting importance to us as human beings. So we strive endlessly to determine the conditions that must be present for courage to be recognised; we seek out the common threads that run through courageous acts and courageous people, and scan the external circumstances and the act itself – the presence of danger, the risk of harm, the bold action, the uniqueness of the courageous act set against a norm. And then we scrutinise the courageous person and look for common internal elements – the overcoming of fear, a guiding set of principles, evidence of morality, or a pervading ethic – and so seek to determine whether the courageous are thus predisposed to courage. And then we can learn from the lives of men and women whose courage has already asserted itself in the world and we try to understand it so that we can cultivate and nurture it.

Another way of thinking – however tentatively – about courage is to ask of ourselves what we might have done in the most difficult of situations. Would we have been able to summon up the strength of purpose to do courageous things? One of the themes of this book is that there was nothing inevitable or pre-ordained about the triumphs and tragedies of the heroes I studied. All of them faced difficult decisions. All of them had turning points in their lives, moments of doubt and moments of choice. And as I read I discovered that for those I wrote about courage was not the absence of fear. It was as though something else became more important than fear; they are heroes not because they are fearless, but because their beliefs and willpower were strong enough to overcome their fears. Fear may have threatened to drive them back, but moral purpose drove them forwards, converting good intentions into great acts.

This helps us begin to answer a truly important question: can courage be learned, nurtured and encouraged? Or are there simply men and women – a predestined elite, as it were – who are so wholly exceptional and set apart from us that they are uniquely capable of courage while others are not? Does the study of courage and its qualities tell us something only about them, or can it also tell us something about ourselves? In other words, is there simply a class of people whom we can admire and follow but never aspire to resemble or imitate?

One thing is true: the exercise of courage is not something found only in the actions of celebrated people in the context of great historic events. It is an everyday requirement in our society, an essential weapon in the struggle against prejudice, racism, violence, discrimination and injustice, and in the creation of a good society. Without men and women of courage we cannot meet and master evil and nor can good triumph.

And when we ask, 'Can willpower and endurance in service of a greater cause be learned? Can the strength of purpose that is vital to the exercise of courage be nurtured? Can ordinary men and women be helped to summon up the willingness to struggle and endure for worthy ideals?' the answer is surely in the affirmative. And if more of us have the capacity for courage, then how can we do more to encourage the exercise of that courage?

I believe that we can be inspired – if not always transformed – by reading about courage, learning more about it, and about the people whose lives have personified it. Without the telling of stories of courage, too many of our heroes will in any case suffer what the historian A.J.P. Taylor called 'the condescension of posterity'. But to look at the records and achievements of people of courage is important not just in the interests of historical accuracy. It matters because stories of courage tell us about what affects us deeply, what we retain and value in our collective memory and what messages we want to pass on to future generations. In their discourse on the nature of courage, Socrates tells Laches they should set about trying to discover how the young might attain courage 'with the help of study and pursuits'. And the reading and study of stories of courage can indeed tell us how a single life lived for a purpose can make a difference. They help us understand how, challenged by difficult situations, ordinary men and women can summon up the strength of purpose to do extraordinary things. They tell us how courage can so often turn goodness into greatness. And I believe that if we can understand the elements of courage better, we can consciously cultivate them. And I also believe that, just as the heroes I have studied found reserves of strength and resilience they did not know they had, so can we all.

So there are good reasons why we continue to read about the courageous, and to write about them and erect monuments and statues to them. There are good reasons why we continue to immortalise them in films, songs and poetry, to commemorate them on stamps, coins, and T-shirts, and to name our streets, public buildings and mountains after them. I believe we continue to do so because we believe that the concept of courage says something about us and the best in us, and about what we are capable of at our very finest. It reminds us of the consequences of our connectedness to one another and how, although that same connectedness can sometimes be the source of our greatest miseries, it is the wellspring of some of the most exalted of human achievements.

While this brief attempt to examine courage in philosophical, sociological and cultural terms has at least served to show that every age and society has addressed the mysteries of courage according to its own prejudices and preoccupations, courage itself continues to thrive in our collective consciousness, retaining its age-old fascination and withstanding all claims to exclusive ownership by any nation, race, gender or creed.

As the lives I write about have shown, courageous people can push back a tide of darkness that can sometimes seem to overwhelm an era. So it is not surprising that many of the metaphors we use to commemorate courageous deeds are about light: how they shine and illuminate, how their brightness brings clarity, how they cut through the darkness, and how they lead and guide us. Whereas evil is accepted as fact, its presence self-evident in daily acts of malice, goodness is less obvious, and perhaps more easily portrayed as something that must be summoned up to be pitted against the heavy presence of evil. Evil has on its side the fear of death, the dread of pain, the anguish of affliction or separation – an endless supply of ammunition with which to further its wrongs – whereas goodness offers only states of being – peace, happiness, cooperation, harmony – and thus seems feeble in comparison. But against the very worst the good has a mighty weapon, and that is courage.

Courage does not abolish fear and dread, but it can determine that they shall not prevail, and so liberate us from the power of evil. Courage is what gives goodness its force, and so gives us hope – often our greatest, sometimes our only hope.

But if such an important virtue ultimately resists neat definition, are we really any the worse off? We should note that others have been there before us, right from the start of philosophical enquiry. During their conversation about courage, Laches complained to Socrates, 'I am truly vexed at finding myself unable to express offhand what I think. For I feel that I conceive in thought what courage is, but somehow or other it has given me the slip.' It still does, as much for us today as it did for Laches nearly two and a half millennia ago. However, having worked – for some years now – on this book I am convinced that courage, and perhaps especially the kind described above as sustained altruism, is both a legitimate continuing object of our fascination and a force for immense good in our world.

Reading and writing about courage has been for me a voyage of discovery, a humbling and illuminating revelation of human greatness. People whose lives and deeds I already admired emerged as far more complex and – perhaps surprisingly – sometimes much more hesitant than first impressions had indicated. And the great scale of their lives and deeds came across most vividly in the unexpected details – the consolation Aung San Suu Kyi found in flowers, weather and the passing of the seasons; the powerful influences of fathers on her and on Martin Luther King; Bonhoeffer's developing ideas in theology even as he faced death; and Nelson Mandela's shrewd, complex and ultimately life-enhancing dealings with his captors – each detail serving to amplify and enhance the larger picture.

Of course we cannot all be courageous in the way these eight people whose lives I describe have been, but I firmly believe there is no one who cannot learn from how they lived and what they achieved.

I first thought of writing this book at a time of personal tragedy. Our beloved first child, Jennifer, had lived only briefly, filled our lives with love, and all too soon left us to aching sorrow. In her memory a charity to support vital research into the causes and consequences of prematurity was set up, and the idea of a book of biographical essays, with any proceeds going to that charity, came to me very early.

In those dark days, and over the years since, I often reflected that when tragedy seems to overwhelm us those things that are precious and true in life can become clearer. Courage, I believe, is among the most precious and truest of them, and as I worked on this book I discovered much that enlightened and sustained me. Now, as it goes to press, my hope is that others will share my sense of wonder at the greatness of the human spirit at its best: a greatness we can all recognise and which ultimately enriches us all, challenging and inspiring us to make the most of ourselves, and be the best that we can be.

Notes

Introduction

3 **I realise that** Edith Cavell's ('EC') last interview with Rev. H.S.T. Gahan, Gahan Memorandum, issued by Press Bureau and reprinted in *Manchester Guardian*, 23 October 1915, Cavell Papers, Imperial War Museum, London ('IWM/Cavell').

4 **The end we seek** Martin Luther King ('MLK'), speech to people in Selma, Alabama, quoted in MLK and Clayborne Carson (ed.), *The Autobiography of Martin Luther King Jr* (London, 2000), p. 281.

1. Edith Cavell

10 **I would love** EC letter to cousin, cited by Rev. Phillip McFadyen and Rev. David Chamberlain, 'Edith Cavell, 1865–1915 – A Norfolk Heroine', at www.edithcavell.org.uk.

10 **I have seen death** Gahan Memorandum, IWM/Cavell.

10 **Being a governess** EC letter to cousin, quoted in Rowland Ryder, *Edith Cavell* (London, 1975).

12 **It was an intelligent way** Madame Hélène François quoted in A. E. Clark-Kennedy, *Edith Cavell: Pioneer and Patriot* (London, 1965), p. 25.

12 **helpless, hurt and unhappy** EC to her cousin Eddy Cavell, first quoted in ibid., as recalled by Eddy (Edmund) Cavell in conversation with the author.

12 **something useful** EC to Eddy Cavell, quoted in ibid.

12 **I have had no** EC in her application form to become an assistant nurse class II at the Fountains Fever Hospital in Tooting, London.

13 **You will, I think** EC letter to Eva Lückes, 5.11.1903, quoted in ibid., p. 56.

13 **I am beginning** EC letter to her sister, 7.11.1904, quoted in ibid., p. 57.

14 **I have been trying** EC letter to Eva Lückes, 12.1.1906, quoted in ibid., p. 59.

14 **I have told you** EC letter from prison, 11.10.1915, IWM/Cavell.

15 **My dear Matron** EC letter to Eva Lückes, June 1907, quoted in Helen Judson, *Edith Cavell* (New York, 1941), p. 96.

16 **I arrived two days** EC letter, September 1907, quoted in Ryder, *Cavell*, p. 63.

16 **One house had been** EC, *Nursing Mirror*, 25 April 1908, quoted in Judson, *Cavell*, p. 152.

17 **Our hospital** EC quoted in Judson, *Cavell*, p. 152.

18 **It is not enough** Gahan Memorandum, IWM/Cavell.

19 **My darling mother** EC letter to family, quoted in Ryder, *Cavell*, pp. 82–3.

20 **sinister tales of** EC letter to *Nursing Mirror*, quoted in ibid., p. 83.

20 **wildest rumours are current** EC letter to mother, 30.8.1914, IWM/Cavell.

20 **I shall never** Jacqueline van Til, *With Edith Cavell in Belgium* (New York, 1922).

21 **In the afternoon** EC in *Nursing Mirror*, quoted in Ryder, *Cavell*, p. 84.

22 **We are busy** EC letter to mother, 14.9.1914, IWM/Cavell.

22 **scarcity in the poor** EC letter to mother, 19.10.1914, IWM/Cavell.

22 **Germans all over** Extract from diary of Ernst Symons, September 1914, quoted in Ryder, *Cavell*, p. 102.

22 **on September 26th** Van Til, *With Edith Cavell*.

23 **To us it seemed** Ibid.

25 **At first I hid** EC signed confession in Prison de St Gilles, October 1915, written in German, translated into English and published in Ambroise Got (ed.), *The Case of Miss Cavell* (London, 1920).

25 **I am writing** Sergeant Jesse Tunmore letter to EC, 20.1.1915, quoted in Ryder, *Cavell*, p. 128.

26 **I am a wounded** Lance Corporal J. Doman letter to EC, 22.2.1915, quoted in ibid., p. 132.

26 **What do you think** EC letter to mother, 22.12.1914, IWM/Cavell.

27 **Indeed, at this time** Judson, *Cavell*, p. 226.

28 **My darling Mother** EC's last letter to reach her mother, 14.6.1915, quoted in Ryder, *Cavell*, p. 83.

28 **Are there any more** Marie de Croy recalling EC, quoted in ibid., p. 168.

29 **My dearest Gracie** EC letter to Grace Jemmett, quoted in ibid., p. 178.

30 **My dear old Jack!** EC letter to Sister Wilkins, 23.8.1915, quoted in ibid., p. 186.

30 **The money from** Subsequent letter from EC to Sister Wilkins, ibid.

30 **Your delightful letter** EC letter to nurses from prison, 14.9.1915, IWM/Cavell.

31 **I indeed labour** EC marked extract from the Bible: 'Book of Revelation', quoted in Ryder, *Cavell*, p. 208.

31 **How happy and prudent** EC marked extract from Thomas à Kempis, *The Imitation of Christ*, quoted in ibid.

32 **She presented herself** Gahan Memorandum, IWM/Cavell.

32 **wished all her friends** Ibid.

32 **I have no fear** Ibid.

32 **My dear sisters** EC from Prison de St Gilles, 11.10.1915, IWM/Cavell.

33 **My dear girl** EC to Grace Jemmett quoted in Judson, *Cavell*, p. 280.

34 **I thought I had** Wilhelm Behrens, 'The Truth', quoted at www.edithcavell.org.uk.

34 **die as women** EC letter quoted in Ryder, *Cavell*, p. 83.

34 **I am but a looker-on** EC, 'A Friend Within The Gates', *Nursing Mirror*, April 1915, IWM/Cavell.

35 **Why have you** Ryder, *Cavell*, pp. 198–99.

35 **I realise that patriotism** Gahan Memorandum, IWM/Cavell.

2. Dietrich Bonhoeffer

36 **There are people** Dietrich Bonhoeffer ('DB'), writing from prison, December 1942, quoted in Eberhard Bethge (trans. Rosaleen Ockenden), *Bonhoeffer: An Illustrated Introduction in Documents and Photographs* (London, 1979).

36 **If the test of tolerance** Ralph W. Sockman.

38 **set themselves up** DB radio broadcast, quoted in Dietrich Bonhoeffer, *No Rusty Swords*, ed. Edwin H. Robertson, (London, 1970).

38 **If the leader allows** DB radio broadcast, quoted in Bethge, *Bonhoeffer*, p. 60.

39 **Only he who cries** DB quoted in Bethge, *Bonhoeffer*, p. 512.

39 **The Church has** DB, 'The Church and the Question of the Jews', June 1933, quoted in Bethge, *Bonhoeffer*, pp. 62–3.

39 **jam a spoke in the wheel** Ibid.

39 **What happened to him** James Mark on DB, quoted in ibid.

40 **If these tempests** Marilynne Robinson, 'Dietrich Bonhoeffer: Watching with Christ in Gethsemane', in *The Death of Adam: Essays in Modern Thought* (Boston, 1998), pp. 108–25.

40 **It takes courage** Harry S. Truman, Address at the State Capitol, Raleigh, NC, 19 October 1948.

42 **I am at last writing** DB letter to Karl Barth, 24.10.1933, quoted in Bethge, *Bonhoeffer*.

43 **Bonhoeffer was very concerned** Ernest Cromwell interview with Koester.

44 **Perhaps those who** Horace Walpole, *Memoirs of the Reign of King George II*, ed. Lord Holland, vol. 2 (1846), p. 370.

44 **[In going back] he knew** Ernest Cromwell interview with Koester.

45 **The retreat in 1933** Quoted in Bethge, *Bonhoeffer*.

45 **Above all I miss** DB diary entry, 13 June 1939, quoted in ibid., p. 98.

46 **The decision has been taken** Ibid.

46 **It was a mistake** DB letter to Reinhold Niebuhr, quoted in ibid., p. 99.

47 **two roads diverged** Robert Frost, 'The Road Not Taken', in *Mountain Interval* (New York, 1916).

48 **It is easy** DB, Eberhard Bethge (ed.) and Neville Horton Smith (trans.), *Ethics* (London, 1955), p. 54.

49 **As a good Lutheran** Bethge, *Bonhoeffer*, pp. 62–3.

50 **During the next fall** Maria von Wedemeyer, 'The Other Letters from Prison', appendix in DB, *Letters and Papers from Prison* (London, 1953; 3rd ed. 1984), p. 413.

51 **You can imagine** Ibid., p. 22.

51 **She will be a** DB letter to parents, ibid.

51 **Dietrich often mentioned** Ibid, p. 414.

52 **My dear, dear Maria** Ibid.

52 **Both of us** Von Wedemeyer, ibid., p. 418.

53 **It helped him** Ibid., p. 415.

53 **The fact that I brought** Ibid., p. 416.

53 **We made a bet** Ibid., p. 417.

53 **Isn't it so** Ibid., p. 416.

53 **It is wiser** DB, 'Optimism', in *Letters from Prison*, p. 15.

53 **There is nothing in the world** Lucius Annaeus Seneca.

54 **I love the man** Thomas Paine, *The American Crisis*, 19 December 1776.

54 **All I really want** DB letter to mother, 28.12.1944, ibid., p. 399.

55 **cheerful and ready** Testimony of Captain Payne Best, quoted in Bethge, *Bonhoeffer*.

55 **in the principle** DB speaking to Payne Best, directed to Bishop George Bell. Quoted in ibid.

55 **In nearly fifty years** H. Fischer Hullstrung's words in 'A Report from Flassenburg IKDP', quoted in Bethge, *Bonhoeffer*, p. 831.

56 **In recent years** DB, 'Insecurity and Death', *Letters from Prison*, p. 16.

58 **Who would have thought** DB letter from mother, ibid., p. 27.

58 **There remains an experience** DB, 'The View from Below', ibid., p. 17.

59 **The Church must share** DB quoted in Bethge, *Bonhoeffer*.

59 **Life was not a question** Ernest Cromwell interview with Koester.

59 **It is not the critic** Theodore Roosevelt, 'Man in the Arena' speech, Paris, 23 April 1910.

60 **like a bull** DB, 'Who Stands Fast?', *Letters from Prison*, p. 4.

60 **responsible action** DB, 'Civil Courage', ibid., p. 6.

60 **At no point** Bethge, *Bonhoeffer*.

60 **(Discipline) If you set out** DB prose poem, 'Stations on the Road to Freedom', *Letters from Prison*, p. 371.

62 **Civil courage** DB, 'Civil Courage', ibid., p. 5.

62 **Jesus, the man** Bethge, *Bonhoeffer*.

63 **in recent years** DB, 'Civil Courage', *Letters from Prison*, p. 5.

64   **belong to the annals** Gerhard Liebholz, quoted in De Gruchy (ed.), *Cambridge Companion*, p. 45.

3. Raoul Wallenberg

65   **He remains the hero** Dr Jonathan Sacks, 'Thought for the Day', BBC Radio 4, 5 March 2004; transcript on www.chiefrabbi.org.

67   **Raoul was not** Lars Berg, quoted in Harvey Rosenfeld, *Raoul Wallenberg* (London, 1955), p. 84.

67   **not because I** Per Anger, *With Raoul Wallenberg in Budapest: Memories of the War Years in Hungary* (New York, 1981).

67   **He had come up against** Nina Lagergren interview with Koester.

68   **Poor people** RW letter to grandfather, 12.3.1936, quoted in *Raoul Wallenberg: Letters and Dispatches 1924–1944*, trans. Kjersti Board (New York, 1995), p. 171.

68   **only one source** Lars Berg, quoted in Rosenfeld, *Wallenberg*, p. 30.

68   **But I have no choice** Anger, *With Raoul Wallenberg*.

70   **He told me about** Nina Lagergren interview with Koester.

71   **We have to rid** RW dispatch, 29.7.1944, *Wallenberg: Letters*, p. 246.

71   **Raoul Wallenberg began** Lars Berg, quoted in Rosenfeld, *Wallenberg*, p. 30.

72   **He had a job to do** Lars Berg, quoted in ibid., p. 30.

72   **radiant sparks of humanity** US senator Tom Lantos, quoted in Lawrence Joffe, 'Modest Hero Who Defied the Holocaust', *Guardian*, 12 September 2002.

74   **a matter-of-fact style** Per Anger, Introduction, *Wallenberg: Letters*, p. 232.

74   **For many months now** RW in the introduction to a contingency plan for financing the reconstruction of Hungary after the war. This document was found in Budapest after the war, and was reproduced in a book by Fredrik von Dardel, *Raoul Wallenberg – Fakta Kring ett ode* (Stockholm, 1970), quoted in *Raoul Wallenberg* (People Who Helped The World series), edited by Michael Nicholson and David Winner (Watford, 1989), p. 22.

76   **Eichmann could scarcely** Lars Berg, quoted in John Bierman, *Righteous Gentile: the Story of Raoul Wallenberg, Missing Hero of the Holocaust* (London, 1981), p. 99.

77   **For me there will be** Adolf Eichmann, quoted in ibid.

78   **it was possible to rescue** RW dispatch, 12.12.1944, *Wallenberg: Letters*, p. 267.

78   **He stood out there** Account by Tommy Lapid, quoted in Bierman, *Righteous Gentile*, p. 87.

79   **I urgently asked him** Anger, *With Raoul Wallenberg*.

80   **to give myself courage** Per Anger quoting RW upon his arrival in budapest on 9 July 1944, in *Wallenberg: Letters*.

80　**when it was a question** Lars Berg, quoted in Rosenfeld, *Wallenberg*, p. 84.

80　**During the first night** RW dispatch, 22.10.1944, *Wallenberg: Letters*, p. 262.

81　**The work is unbelievably** RW letter to Kolomon Lauer, 8.12.1944, quoted in Bierman, *Righteous Gentile*, p. 93.

82　**To start with** Per Anger, quoted in Bierman, *Righteous Gentile*, p. 51.

82　**I get the impression** Ivar Olsen in a letter to John Pehle in Washington on 10 August 1944, quoted in ibid., p. 53.

82　**My birthday was** RW letter to mother, 6.8.1944, *Wallenberg: Letters*, p. 274.

82　**For the moment** RW letter to mother, 22.10.1944, ibid., p. 276.

82　**We hear the artillery** RW letter, 8.12.1944, ibid., p. 277.

84　**A person like me** Professor Hedenius recalls a conversation with RW dating back to 1930, when they were together during military service, as recorded in 1980, according to the notes in Bierman, *Righteous Gentile*, p. 25.

84　**He told me that** Tibor Baranski, quoted in Rosenfeld, *Wallenberg*, p. 83.

85　**To tell the truth** RW letter to grandfather, 12.3.1936, *Wallenberg: Letters*, p.171.

85　**I have come to know** RW quoted in Bierman, *Righteous Gentile*, p. 117.

86　**Raoul meant so much** Nina Lagergren interview with Koester.

87　**I think it so important** Ibid.

87　**He was definitely not** Nina Lagergren, quoted in Bierman, *Righteous Gentile*, p. 27.

87　**He was more of a hero** Palko Forgacz, quoted in ibid., p. 218.

4. Martin Luther King

89　**If a man hasn't discovered** MLK and Carson (ed.), *Autobiography*, p. 344.

89　**I will never forget** Ibid., p. 7.

89　**My mother confronted** Ibid., p. 3.

90　**Then she said** Ibid., p. 4.

90　**The African American church** Peter J. Ling, *Martin Luther King Jr* (London, 2002).

91　**the action had caught me** MLK and Carson (ed.), *Autobiography*, p. 56.

91　**there comes a time** Ibid., p. 60.

91　**From that moment on** Ibid., p. 7.

92　**Why does God** Journalist Glenn Smiley, quoted in Ling, *Martin Luther King Jr*.

93　**So often our experience** William Ian Miller, *The Mystery of Courage* (Cambridge, MA, 2000).

93　**With my cup of coffee** MLK quoted in David J. Garrow, *Bearing* *the Cross: Martin Luther King, Jr and the Southern Christian Leadership Conference* (New York, 1986).

94 **They err greatly** Thomas Carlyle, in Michael K. Goldberg, Thomas Carlyle, Joel J. Brattin and Mark Engel (eds), *On Heroes, Hero Worship, and Heroics in History* (New York, 1993).

94 **the quiet assurance** MLK and Carson (ed.), *Autobiography*, p. 77.

94 **Disappointment is part of** Clayborne Carson and Kris Shepard (eds), *A Call to Conscience: The Landmark Speeches of Dr Martin Luther King Jr* (London, 2001), p. 98.

95 **A religion that ends** MLK quoting Harry Emerson in 'Pilgrimage to Non-Violence', *Stride Towards Freedom* (New York, 1958).

96 **the glaring reality** MLK and Carson (ed.), *Autobiography*, p. 27.

97 **perfect love casteth out fear** The Bible: 1 John 4:18.

97 **I'd feel like** MLK in Garrow, *Bearing the Cross*, p. 607.

97 **Every now and then** Clayborne Carson and Peter Holloran (eds), *A Knock at Midnight: Inspiration from the Great Sermons of Reverend Martin Luther King, Jr* (New York, 1998).

97 **committed to unrelenting** MLK, Nobel Peace Prize acceptance speech, 6 December 1964, in Göran Liljestrand (ed.), *Les Prix Nobel en 1964* (Stockholm, 1965).

97 **civilisation and violence** Ibid.

98 **a very real contender** J. Edgar Hoover memo, quoted in Brian Glick, *The War at Home: Covert Action Against US Activists and What We Can Do About It* (Boston, 1989).

98 **Violence can destroy** Hannah Arendt, *On Violence* (New York, 1970).

98 **We had to make it clear** Martin Luther King, Jr, 'The Power of Non-Violence', address at UC Berkeley, 4 June 1957, quoted in *I Have a Dream: Writings and Speeches That Changed the World*, ed. James Melvin Washington (San Francisco, 1992), pp. 29–33.

99 **overflowing love which** Ibid., p. 192.

99 **the love of God** Ibid.

99 **you must go on** Ibid.

99 **occasionally in life** MLK, *Where Do We Go from Here: Chaos or Community?* (Harmondsworth, 1969).

99 **Remain committed** Carson and Shepard (eds), *A Call to Conscience*, p. 130.

99 **black and white together** From the song 'We Shall Overcome', which in the 1960s became the unofficial anthem of the civil rights movement.

100 **It is no longer** MLK quoted in James A. Colaiaco, *Martin Luther King Jr, Apostle of Nonviolence* (London, 1993), p. 180.

100 **Somewhere there has to be** Garrow, *Bearing the Cross*, pp. 496–97.

100 **One may well ask** Mahatma Gandhi, quoted in MLK in 'Pilgrimage to Non-Violence', *Stride Towards Freedom* (New York, 1958).

100 **Suffering is infinitely** Ibid.

101 **In the final analysis** MLK, *Chaos or Community?*

101 **We have known the agony** MLK, 'A New Sense of Direction', 1968, first published in Worldview Magazine Archive, 1 April 1972.

102 **a stunning political drama** Barbara A. Holmes in Lewis V. Baldwin, *The Legacy of Martin Luther King, Jr: the Boundaries of Law, Politics, and Religion* (New York, 2002).

102 **The way of acquiescence** MLK and Carson (ed.), *Autobiography*.

103 **Now the plain, inexorable fact** Ibid.

103 **The problem with hatred** MLK, *Chaos or Community?*

104 **forces from all faiths** Stanley Levison, quoted in Garrow, *Bearing the Cross*, pp. 418–19.

104 **Non-violent democratic action** Ibid.

105 **There comes a time** Carson and Shepard (eds), *A Call to Conscience*, p. 140.

105 **America's soul becomes** MLK and Carson (ed.), *Autobiography*, p. 338.

105 **broken and eviscerated** Ibid., p. 337.

105 **a reluctant leader** Garrow, *Bearing the Cross*.

105 **his leadership role** Ibid.

105 **No, I'm not** MLK quoted in David Garrow, 'Martin Luther King Jr and the Spirit of Leadership', in Peter Albert and Ronald Hoffman (eds), *We Shall Overcome* (London, 1990), p. 21.

106 **In many of his sermons** Ling, *Martin Luther King Jr*.

106 **We know through painful** MLK, 'Letter from Birmingham Jail', 16 April 1963.

108 **We are the beneficiaries** Ibid.

108 **I cannot agree** Ibid.

109 **It is no longer a choice** MLK and Carson (ed.), *Autobiography*, p. 360.

110 **The practical cost of change** Martin Luther King Jr, *Chaos or Community: Where do we go from here?* (Harmondsworth, 1969).

110 **The time has come** Ibid.

110 **We are all called upon** Ibid.

110 **I never intend to** Clayborne Carson, Susan Carson, Adrienne Clay, Virginia Shadron, and Kieran Taylor (eds), *The Papers of Martin Luther King Jr*, Volume IV: 'Symbol of the Movement, January 1957–December 1958' (Berkeley, 2000).

111 **We are engaged in** 'Letter from Birmingham Jail', Garrow, *Bearing the Cross*.

111 **All I have been doing** MLK, *Chaos or Community?*

112 **It will be a long time** Michael Eric Dyson, *I Might Not Get There With You: The True Martin Luther King Jr* (New York, 2000).

112 **I have a dream** Carson and Shepard (eds), *A Call to Conscience*.

112 **In the act of courage** Theologian Paul Tillich, *The Courage to Be* (New Haven and London, 2000).

113 **He found himself** Quoted in Richard H. King, *Civil Rights and the Idea of Freedom* (Oxford, 1992).

113 **On some positions** MLK and Carson (ed.), *Autobiography*, p. 342.

114 **When I first took my position** MLK and Carson (ed.), *Autobiography*, p. 342.

114 **I have a dream** Carson and Shepard (eds), *A Call to Conscience*.

5. Robert Kennedy

115 **your country can do** inaugural address of John F. Kennedy, 20 January 1961.

115 **As our case is new** Robert F. Kennedy ('RFK') quoting Abraham Lincoln, RFK, *To Seek A Newer World* (London, 1968).

116 **We will not find** RFK quoted in Mary Anne Reilley, *Newsday*, 5 June 1988.

116 **to leave yesterday** Bill Clinton at Memorial Mass for RFK, Arlington Cemetery, reported by R. W. Apple Jr, *New York Times*, 7 June 1993.

116 **to strive, to seek** Edward Kennedy quoting from 'Ulysses' by Alfred Lord Tennyson, Memorial Mass for RFK, ibid.

116 **he was a man** Michael Harrington quoted in Ronald Steel, *In Love with Night: The American Romance with Robert Kennedy* (New York, 2000).

117 **He was obsessed** *Esquire*, March 1963.

118 **the story of an unpromising** Evan Thomas, *Robert Kennedy: His Life* (New York, 2000).

118 **Nothing came easy** Lem Billings, quoted in James W. Hilty, *Robert Kennedy: Brother Protector* (Philadelphia, 1997), p. 20.

118 **Bobby felt he was weak** Chuck Spalding, quoted in ibid., p. 39.

118 **A paratrooper** Thomas, *Robert Kennedy*.

119 **I thought there was** RFK quoted in Evan Thomas, 'Bobby: Good, Bad and In Between – Robert F Kennedy', *Washington Monthly*, October 2000.

120 **like a man on the rack** Thomas, *Robert Kennedy*, p. 21.

120 **kind of floundering** Don Wilson, quoted in ibid.

120 **impotent and frustrated** Wilson, quoted in ibid.

120 **He literally shrank** Ibid.

120 **The innocent suffer** RFK quoted in ibid.

120 **to explore new worlds** Richard Goodwin, quoted in ibid., p. 344.

120 **When the world is** Extract from Edith Hamilton, *The Greek Way*, quoted in David Brooks, 'The Education of Robert Kennedy', *New York Times*, 28 November 2006.

121 **based on the conviction** Ibid.

121 **Ladies and gentlemen** 'I have bad news for you' speech; see www.jfklibrary.org.

122 **This isn't really such** RFK quoted in James DiEugenio, Lisa Pease (eds), *The Assassinations: Probe Magazine on JFK, MLK, RFK, and Malcolm X* (Los Angeles, 2003), p. 606.

122 **resist the danger of futility** RFK, Day of Affirmation Address, Cape Town University, 6 June 1966; transcript of speech at www.americanrhetoric.com/speeches/rfkcapetown.htm.

122 **Perhaps we cannot prevent** RFK writing in his daybook, Thomas, *Robert Kennedy*, p. 319.

123 **I'm sure there will be** RFK quoted in Romain Gary, 'Courage in Death', *Times of India*.

123 **You've just got to give** RFK quoted in Arlene Schulman, *Robert F. Kennedy: Promise for the Future* (New York, 1997).

123 **It was a high counsel** Ralph Waldo Emerson, quoted in Thomas, *Robert Kennedy*, p. 18.

123 **doom was woven** Robert Lowell, 'R.F.K.'; full text published at www.thefreelibrary.com.

123 **They lived dangerously** Arthur Schlesinger, *Robert Kennedy and His Times* (London, 1978).

124 **courage is the first** A quote made famous by Churchill, but thought to be adapted from Aristotle.

124 **Not only were we** Kathleen Kennedy Townsend, quoted in Jack Sirica, 'The RFK Legacy', *Newsday*, 3 June 1993.

125 **not love as it is** RFK quoted by Edward Kennedy in tribute at St Patrick's Cathedral, New York City, 8 June 1968.

125 **a tenderness so rawly** Robert Goodwin, quoted in Hilty, *Brother Protector*, p. 497.

126 **I believe that** RFK, *To Seek A Newer World*.

126 **If I had grown up** RFK quoted in Thomas, *Robert Kennedy*, p. 305.

127 **It was total immersion** Marcy McGrory, quoted in Thomas, *Robert Kennedy*, p. 339.

127 **always saw poverty through** Peter Edelman, *Searching for America's Heart: RFK and the Renewal of Hope* (Boston, 2001).

127 **and found it distended** Thomas, *Robert Kennedy*, p. 339.

128 **children with swollen bellies** www.rfkmemorial.org/lifevision/ biography

128 **rat bites on the faces** Ibid.

128 **his children say he** Edelman, *Searching for America's Heart*.

128 **I have seen these other** RFK speaking at University of Kansas, 18 March 1968. For a full transcript of the speech visit the JFK Library and Museum website at www.jfklibrary.org.

128 **have been a revolutionary** Alice Roosevelt Longworth, quoted in Jean Stein and George Plimpton, *American Journey: The Times of Robert Kennedy* (New York, 1970).

128 **to see the world** Jack Newfield, quoted in Schlesinger, *Robert Kennedy and His Times*, p. 756.

129 **that previously just made** Robert Goodwin, quoted in ibid., p. 802.

129 **Tell him to bring** Recounted by Marian Wright Edelman in Commencement Address to Tulane University, 19 May 2001.

129 **I'm not for a guaranteed** Peter Edelman quoting conversation

with RFK in Edelman, 'The Big Picture', *Boston Review*, Oct/Nov 2000.

130 **the pathology of the ghetto** Quote borrowed by RFK from Kenneth B. Clark, *Dark Ghetto: Dilemmas of Social Power* (London, 1965).

130 **a besetting sin** Schlesinger, *Robert Kennedy and His Times*, p. 784.

130 **the destruction of thousands** Ibid.

130 **The whole history** Ibid.

130 **the violent youth** Schlesinger, *Robert Kennedy and His Times*, p. 785.

131 **coming to terms with** RFK, *To Seek a Newer World*.

132 **idealism, high aspirations** Ibid.

134 **Kennedy: Hawk, Dove** Thomas, *Robert Kennedy*.

135 **Kennedy taught us** Mario Cuomo quoted in Josh Getlin, 'The Cult of Bobby', *Los Angeles Times*, 20 October 1992.

135 **A mission of national reconciliation** Edelman, *Searching for America's Heart*.

136 **Kennedy was a man** Edelman, *Searching for America's Heart*.

136 **sums up best** Edward Kennedy, St. Patrick's Cathedral, 8 June 1968.

137 **The future does not belong** Edward Kennedy quoting RFK, Day of Affirmation Address.

137 **the driving power** Lord Beveridge, 1948 report 'Voluntary Action'.

137 **sail beyond the sunset** From 'Ulysses', Alfred Lord Tennyson.

6. Nelson Mandela

140 **He's good, and people's** Desmond Tutu of NM, BBC documentary, *Mandela: The Living Legend*, March 2003.

140 **You'd expect that** Joel Joffe interview with Cathy Koester, 2003.

141 **I dedicated my life** Ibid.

141 **He symbolises a** Graça Machel, quoted in Gordon Brown, 'Nelson Mandela', *Time*, 2 November 2006.

141 **When he says** Desmond Tutu of NM, *Mandela: The Living Legend*.

141 **He is so respected** Joffe interview with Koester.

143 **I was not born with** Nelson Mandela ('NM'), *Long Walk to Freedom* (London, 1994), p. 616.

143 **I came across few whites** Ibid.

144 **At first, as a student** Ibid.

144 **That is when I joined** Ibid.

145 **As a leader I have** Ibid., p. 20.

145 **It was at Mqhekezweni** Ibid., p. 21.

146 **The education I received** Ibid.

147 **amateur archaeological interest** Ibid., p. 285.

147 **It is important** Ibid., p. 285

148 **The principal of Healdtown** Ibid., p. 35.

148 **The government, in order** Ibid., p. 71.
148 **Alexandra, despite its problems** Ibid.
149 **In those days** Ibid., p. 33.
149 **Despite the university's** Ibid., p. 83.
150 **She was embarrassed** Ibid.
150 **I cannot pinpoint** Ibid., p. 89.
151 **To be an African** Ibid.
151 **Marriages between tribes** Ibid., p. 36.
151 **Seeing [the teacher]** Ibid.
152 **Suddenly the door opened** Ibid., pp. 38-9.
153 **I was beginning** Ibid., p. 82.
153 **Like all Xhosa children** Ibid.
154 **Because of the universal respect** Ibid.
154 **Even as I left Clarkebury** Ibid., p. 34.
154 **And that's just what happened** *Mandela: The Living Legend.*
155 **Lembede's Africanism** NM, *Long Walk*, p. 94.
155 **I was sympathetic** Ibid.
156 **I was wary of white influence** Ibid., p. 101.
157 **I am fundamentally an optimist** Ibid., p. 375.
157 **Here, I believed** Ibid., p. 110.
158 **The often haphazard** Ibid., p. 103.
159 **Mandela criticised apartheid** Anthony R. DeLuca, *Gandhi, Mao, Mandela and Gorbachev: Studies in Personality, Power, Politics* (Westport, CT, 2000).
159 **In my speech** NM, *Long Walk*, p. 245.
160 **Our dream for the Congress** Ibid., p. 159.
161 **I saw non-violence** Ibid., p. 119.
162 **Because it did not involve** Ibid., p. 271.
162 **I had chosen traditional** Ibid., p. 311.
163 **Many years ago** Ibid., p. 312.
165 **The trial was very much** Joffe interview with Koester.
165 **We lived in the shadows** NM, *Long Walk*, p. 334.
165 **What was so remarkable** Joffe interview with Koester.
166 **It was a very emotional** Ibid.
167 **During my lifetime** Ibid.
168 **We were face to face** NM, *Long Walk*, p. 372.
168 **Prison . . . is designed** Ibid., p. 375.
169 **For myself, I have never** Ibid., p. 615.
169 **I wondered – not for the** Ibid., p. 198.
169 **It added to my grief** Ibid., p. 431.
170 **The break-up of any marriage** Ibid., p. 192.
171 **This was one of the** Ibid., p. 334.
171 **What can one say** Ibid., p. 431.
171 **The pettiness, the meanness** *Mandela: The Living Legend.*
171 **Prison and the authorities** NM, *Long Walk*, p. 375.
172 **I was now** Ibid., p. 375.
172 **Our survival depended** Ibid.

172 **There are victories** Ibid., p. 376.

173 **I thought that once** Ibid., p. 215.

174 **They were almost** Ibid., p. 471.

174 **Mandela brought the policy** Ahmed Kathrada, *Memoirs* (Cape Town, 2005).

174 **As a leader in our time** DeLuca, *Gandhi, Mao, Mandela*.

175 **If he had come out** Graça Machel, quoted in Gordon Brown, 'Nelson Mandela'.

175 **humble servant of you** NM, *Long Walk*, p. 555.

175 **I admire him personally** Bill Clinton in *Mandela: The Living Legend*.

175 **It's almost as if** Zelda Le Grange in ibid.

175 **I wanted to be regarded** NM in *Mandela: The Living Legend*.

176 **The policy of apartheid** NM, *Long Walk*, p. 614.

176 **More than any other** Lyn S. Graybill, *Truth and Reconciliation in South Africa: Miracle or Model?* (Boulder, CO, 2002).

177 **If we don't forgive** NM in *Mandela: The Living Legend*.

177 **man's goodness is a flame** NM, *Long Walk*, p. 614.

7. Cicely Saunders

178 **Through her, dying** Shirley du Boulay, *Cicely Saunders* (London, 1993), p. 231.

178 **A society which shuns** CS quoted in David Clark (ed.), Introduction, *Cicely Saunders: Founder of the Hospice Movement: Selected Letters 1959–1999*, (Oxford, 2002).

178 **A dignified death** Dr Robert Fulton, quoted in Clark (ed.), *Cicely Saunders*.

178 **It is dignifying** Quoted in Du Boulay, *Cicely Saunders*, p. 233.

178 **Suffering is only intolerable** Quoted in Foreword, ibid.

179 **To talk of accepting death** CS quoted in ibid., p. 84.

179 **the woman who changed** Quoted in Foreword, CS, *Beyond all Pain – a Companion for the Suffering and Bereaved* (London, 1983).

179 **Fools rush in** CS interview with Cathy Koester, August 2003.

180 **She stayed her ground** Du Boulay, *Cicely Saunders*, p. 224.

180 **In a sense, I was an outsider** CS interview with Cherie Booth, 'I Didn't Set Out to Change the World', *Daily Telegraph*, 5 September 2002.

180 **Young patients dying** CS, 'A Personal Therapeutic Journey', *Into the Valley of the Shadow of Death* (London, 1996).

181 **I knew then the truth** CS, *Hospice: the Living Idea* (London, 1981).

182 **David's influence** CS quoted in Lynda Lee Potter, 'I've met kings, prime ministers . . .' *Daily Mail*, 26 February 2000.

182 **It is the action** Mahatma Gandhi.

183 **almost like social** CS interview with Booth.

183 **David Tasma was** Introduction, Clark (ed.), *Cicely Saunders*.

183   **love is certainly as** Diane Taylor, 'Love Is Stronger than Death', *Independent*, 23 August 2001.

183   **There can be something** CS interview with Booth.

184   **For the first time** CS quoted in Helena Katz, 'A Career of Compassion', *McGill Reporter*, 6 November 1997.

185   **It appears to me** CS quoted in Clark (ed.), *Cicely Saunders*.

185   **an ambition of singular** Introduction, ibid.

185   **Go and read medicine** Unnamed surgeon quoted in CS interview with Koester.

186   **There was a revolution** CS interview with Koester.

186   **the very high mortality** Sir Douglas Black, quoted in Du Boulay, *Cicely Saunders*.

187   **The dying are thus** August Kaspar writing in *The Meaning of Death*, ed. Herman Feifeld (New York, 1959).

188   **It is difficult to remain** Gerald Aronson, initially quoting Marguerite Yourcenar, in Du Boulay, *Cicely Saunders*.

188   **We emerge deserving** John Hinton, *Dying* (London, 1967).

189   **Introducing the regular** CS quoted in Sheryl Gay Stolberg, 'Her Life's Work Is Caring for the Dying, *Chicago Tribune*, 2 June 1999.

189   **There can be little doubt** Clark (ed.), *Cicely Saunders*.

190   **I started lecturing** CS interview with Booth.

190   **I learned to listen** CS interview with Koester.

190   **I experienced a lot** CS interview with Koester.

190   **I have tucked in a copy** CS letter to unnamed recipient, 30.8.1960, cited in Clark (ed.), *Cicely Saunders*.

191   **Time isn't a question** CS quoted in Du Boulay, *Cicely Saunders*, p. 140.

191   **When I told him** CS interview with Koester.

191   **There are so many things** Extracts from CS's diary, ibid., p. 140.

192   **Went over [to see Antoni]** Ibid.

193   **the hardest, the most peaceful** Ibid.

194   **Cicely was so happy** Ibid.

194   **In the midst of death** Ibid.

195   **I missed him quite** CS interview with Booth.

196   **a community of the unlike** CS interview with Koester.

196   **I think that you know** CS letter to Jack Wallace, 29.10.1959, quoted in Clark (ed.), *Cicely Saunders*.

197   **I didn't set out to change** CS interview with Booth.

197   **There are many reasons** CS quoted in Du Boulay, *Cicely Saunders*, p. 148.

197   **Somehow we will get it** CS letter to Captain T. L. Lonsdale, 10.7.1966, quoted in Clark (ed.), *Cicely Saunders*.

198   **I kept the faith** CS interview with Koester.

198   **We [St Christopher's]** CS quoted in Du Boulay, *Cicely Saunders*, p. 148.

198   **There was a sense** Introduction, Clark (ed.), *Cicely Saunders*.

199 **Looking after the dying** CS quoted in Du Boulay, *Cicely Saunders*.

200 **The realisation that life** CS, *The Management of Terminal Malignant Disease* (London, 1993).

201 **I think that God** CS interview with Koester.

202 **He was a wild, mad artist** CS quoted in Lee Potter, 'I've met kings, prime ministers . . .', *Daily Mail*.

202 **I know when Marian dies** CS quoted in Du Boulay, *Cicely Saunders*.

202 **complementary colour** CS quoted in Lee Potter, 'I've met kings, prime ministers . . .', *Daily Mail*.

203 **Loving inevitably means loss** Introduction to CS (ed.), *Beyond all Pain*.

203 **The movement for palliative care** CS quoted in Katz, 'A Career of Compassion'.

204 **Within a very few** Clark (ed.), *Cicely Saunders*.

204 **The twentieth century saw** Balfour Mount in Foreword, Clark (ed.), *Cicely Saunders*.

205 **As impressive as the statistics** Balfour Mount in Foreword, Clark (ed.), *Cicely Saunders*.

205 **The requirement is that** Sir Douglas Black in Foreword, Du Boulay, *Cicely Saunders*.

205 **Some biographies are** John Taylor in Foreword, Du Boulay, *Cicely Saunders*.

206 **Death and I are only nodding** Poem by Sidney Reeman, 28 January 1975, quoted in CS (ed.), *Beyond all Pain*.

8. Aung San Suu Kyi

208 **It was a quiet evening** Michael Aris's Introduction to Aung San Suu Kyi ('ASSK') and Michael Aris, *Freedom From Fear: And Other Writings* (London, 1991).

208 **She, like the whole country** Ibid.

209 **I could not, as my father's** ASSK speech, Rangoon, 26 August 1988.

210 **Fearlessness may be a gift** ASSK and Aris, *Freedom From Fear*, p. 184.

212 **Always one to practise** Ibid., p. 137.

212 **as there is an inevitable sameness** Ibid., p. 184.

212 **The greatest gift** ASSK quoting Nehru, ibid., p. 184.

212 **When I first decided** ASSK and Alan Clements, *The Voice of Hope: Conversations with Alan Clements* (London, 1997).

212 **On the other hand** Ibid.

213 **She always used** Aris, Introduction, *Freedom From Fear*.

214 **Not every day, no** ASSK in Clements, *Voice of Hope*.

214 **revolution of the spirit** ASSK and Aris, *Freedom From Fear*, p. 183.

214 **the quintessential revolution** Ibid., p. 183.

215 **Some have questioned** ASSK, 'Seed of Democracy Flowers in

Rural Burma, the Road to Tha Ma Nya', *Mainichi Daily News*, 27 November 1995.

216 **The total picture** ASSK in a biographical essay on her father, quoted in *Freedom from Fear*.

217 **a certain inevitability** Aris, Introduction, *Freedom From Fear*, p. ibid.

217 **what binds the father** Aris in ibid.

217 **By dedicating her life** Václav Havel, Foreword.

217 **She knew she would** Aris in ibid.

218 **Military coups** ASSK in Clements, *Voice of Hope*.

218 **All that Suu had to** Aris, Introduction, *Freedom From Fear*.

219 **The days I spent alone** Ibid.

220 **Sometimes I didn't even** ASSK in Clements, *Voice of Hope*.

221 **Very obviously the plan** Aris, Introduction, *Freedom From Fear*.

221 **Two years is a long time** ASSK in Clements, *Voice of Hope*.

222 **With my sons, I was always** Ibid.

222 **Sometimes I am beset** Aris, Introduction, *Freedom From Fear*.

223 **I was informed today** Ibid.

224 **Did the authorities** ASSK and Clements, *Voice of Hope*.

225 **Throughout the years** Ibid.

226 **I do not think** Ibid.

226 **People who think** Ibid.

227 **When you reflect upon** Ibid.

227 **That we ought to** Ibid.

227 **This is the eighth** ASSK, *Letters from Burma* (London, 1997).

228 **A couple of weeks ago** Ibid.

229 **How many can be said** Ibid.

229 **Actually, I didn't miss anything** ASSK, quoted in Mark Baker, 'Serenity and Steel: Suu Kyi Will Not Waver', *The Age* (Melbourne), 7 May 2002.

230 **Both have a stoic capacity** Fergal Keane, 'Suu Kyi's Release Is a Tribute to Her Courage and the Value of Sanctions', *Independent*, 11 May 2002.

231 **when the Burmese regime** Ibid.

232 **We only hope that** ASSK quoted by Mark Baker, *The Age*, 7 May 2002.

232 **I've always said** ASSK, *The Nation*, 12 August 2002.

232 **I don't think my** ASSK quoted in Amy Kazmin, 'Burma's symbol of hope steps out . . .', *Financial Times*, 7 May 2002.

232 **The NLD has always** ASSK quoted by Baker, *The Age*.

232 **everybody who cares** ASSK as reported in 'Suu Kyi Tape', *The Nation*, 7 August 2002.

233 **When Aung San Suu Kyi** *The Nation*, 8 August 2002.

234 **I attribute the award** Kimina Lyall, *The Australian*, 7 August 2002.

Conclusion

239 **We're going to do something** Todd Beamer, quoted in Toby Harnden, 'The quiet exectutive who defied hijackers', *Daily Telegraph*, 18 September 2001.

Bibliography

INTRODUCTION

Books and articles

King, Martin Luther, *The Autobiography of Martin Luther King Jr*, ed. Clayborne Carson (London, 2000)

Other

Edith Cavell's ('EC') last interview with Rev. H.S.T. Gahan, Gahan Memorandum, issued by Press Bureau and reprinted in the *Manchester Guardian*, 23 October 1915, Cavell Papers, Imperial War Museum, London ('IWM/Cavell')

1. EDITH CAVELL

Books and articles

Clark-Kennedy, A. E., *Edith Cavell: Pioneer and Patriot* (London, 1965)
Got, Ambroise (ed.), *The Case of Miss Cavell* (London, 1920)
Judson, Helen, *Edith Cavell* (New York, 1941)
Ryder, Rowland, *Edith Cavell* (London, 1975)
Van Til, Jacqueline, *With Edith Cavell in Belgium* (New York, 1922)

Cavell, Edith, 'A Friend within the Gates', *Nursing Mirror*, April 1915 (IWM/Cavell)

Other

EC collected letters (IWM/Cavell)

EC last interview with Rev. H.S.T. Gahan, Gahan Memorandum, issued by Press Bureau and reprinted in the *Manchester Guardian*, 23 October 1915 (IWM/Cavell)

EC letter to cousin, cited by Rev. Phillip McFadyen and Rev. David Chamberlain, 'Edith Cavell, 1865–1915 – A Norfolk Heroine', on http://www.edithcavell.org.uk.

Wilhelm Behrens, 'The Truth', quoted on http://www.edithcavell.org.uk

2. DIETRICH BONHOEFFER

Books and articles

Bethge, Eberhard, *Bonhoeffer: An Illustrated Introduction in Documents and Photographs*, trans. Rosaleen Ockenden (London, 1979)

Bonhoeffer, Dietrich, *Ethics*, ed. Eberhard Bethge, trans. Neville Horton Smith (London, 1955)

Bonhoeffer, Dietrich, *Letters and Papers from Prison* (London, 1953; third edition 1984)

Bonhoeffer, Dietrich, *No Rusty Swords*, ed. Edwin H. Robertson (London, 1970)

De Gruchy, John (ed.), *The Cambridge Companion to Dietrich Bonhoeffer* (Cambridge and New York, 1999)

Frost, Robert, 'The Road Not Taken', in *Mountain Interval* (New York, 1916)

Paine, Thomas, *The American Crisis* (19 December 1776)

Robinson, Marilynne, 'Dietrich Bonhoeffer: Watching with Christ in Gethsemane', in *The Death of Adam: Essays in Modern Thought* (Boston, 1998)

Other

Ernest Cromwell interview with Cathy Koester, 2002

Harry S. Truman, Address at the State Capitol, Raleigh, NC, 19 October 1948

Theodore Roosevelt, 'Man in the Arena' speech, Paris, 23 April 1910

3. RAOUL WALLENBERG

Books and articles

Anger, Per, *With Raoul Wallenberg in Budapest: Memories of the War Years in Hungary* (New York, 1981)

Bierman, John, *Righteous Gentile: the Story of Raoul Wallenberg, Missing Hero of the Holocaust* (London, 1981)

Nicholson, Michael, and David Winner (eds), *Raoul Wallenberg*, People Who Helped the World series (Watford, 1989)

Rosenfeld, Harvey, *Raoul Wallenberg* (London, 1995)

Wallenberg, Raoul, *Raoul Wallenberg: Letters and Dispatches 1924–1944*, trans. Kjersti Board (New York, 1995)

Joffe, Lawrence, 'Modest Hero Who Defied the Holocaust', *Guardian*, 12 September 2002

Other

Dr Jonathan Sacks, 'Thought for the Day', BBC Radio 4, 5 March 2004; transcript on www.chiefrabbi.org

Nina Lagergen interview with Cathy Koester, 2002

4. MARTIN LUTHER KING

Books and articles

Arendt, Hannah, *On Violence* (New York, 1970)

Baldwin, Lewis V., *The Legacy of Martin Luther King Jr: the Boundaries of Law, Politics and Religion* (New York, 2002)

Carlyle, Thomas, *On Heroes, Hero Worship and Heroics in History*, ed. Michael K. Goldberg, Joel J. Brattin and Mark Engel (New York, 1993)

Colaiaco, James A., *Martin Luther King Jr, Apostle of Nonviolence* (London, 1993)

Dyson, Michael Eric, *I Might Not Get There With You: The True Martin Luther King Jr* (New York, 2000)

Garrow, David J., *Bearing the Cross: Martin Luther King Jr and the Southern Christian Leadership Conference* (New York, 1986)

Glick, Brian, *The War at Home: Covert Action Against US Activists and What We Can Do About It* (Boston, 1989)

King, Martin Luther, *A Call to Conscience: The Landmark Speeches of Dr Martin Luther King Jr*, ed. Clayborne Carson and Kris Shepard (London, 2001)

King, Martin Luther, *Chaos or Community: Where do we go from here?* (Harmondsworth, 1969)

King, Martin Luther, *I Have a Dream: Writings and Speeches That Changed the World*, ed. James Melvin Washington (San Francisco, 1992)

King, Martin Luther, *A Knock at Midnight: Inspiration from the Great Sermons of Reverend Martin Luther King Jr*, ed. Clayborne Carson and Peter Holloran (New York, 1998)

King, Martin Luther, *Stride Toward Freedom* (New York, 1958)

King, Martin Luther, *The Autobiography of Martin Luther King Jr*, ed. Clayborne Carson (London, 2000)

King, Martin Luther, *The Papers of Martin Luther King Jr, Volume IV: Symbol of the Movement, January 1957 – December 1958*, ed. Clayborne Carson, Susan Carson, Adrienne Clay, Virginia Shadron and Kieran Taylor (Berkeley, 2000)

King, Martin Luther, *Where Do We Go from Here: Chaos or Community?* (Harmondsworth, 1969)

Liljestrand, Göran (ed.), *Les Prix Nobels en 1964* (Stockholm, 1965)

Ling, Peter J., *Martin Luther King Jr* (London, 2002)
Miller, William Ian, *The Mystery of Courage* (Cambridge, MA, 2000)
Tillich, Paul, *The Courage to Be* (New Haven and London, 2000)

Garrow, David, 'Martin Luther King Jr and the Spirit of Leadership', in Peter
Albert and Ronald Hoffman (eds), *We Shall Overcome* (London, 1990)

Other

MLK, 'A New Sense of Direction' speech, 1968, first published in Worldview Magazine Archive, 1 April 1972; see
www.cceia.org/resources/articles_papers_reports/4960.html
MLK, 'Letter from Birmingham Jail', 16 April 1963. Full text is available
at www.thekingcenter.org/prog/non/letter.html

5. ROBERT KENNEDY

Books and articles

DiEugenio, James and Lisa Pease (eds), *The Assassinations: Probe Magazine
on JFK, MLK, RFK and Malcolm X* (Los Angeles, 2003)
Edelman, Peter, *Searching for America's Heart: RFK and the Renewal of Hope*
(Boston, 2001)
Hilty, James W., *Robert Kennedy: Brother Protector* (Philadelphia, 1997)
Kennedy, Robert F., *To Seek A Newer World* (London, 1968)
Schlesinger, Arthur, *Robert Kennedy and His Times* (London, 1978)
Schulman, Arlene, *Robert F. Kennedy: Promise for the Future* (New York, 1997)
Steel, Ronald, *In Love with Night: The American Romance with Robert Kennedy*
(New York, 2000)
Stein, Jean and George Plimpton, *American Journey: The Times of Robert
Kennedy* (New York, 1970)
Thomas, Evan, *Robert Kennedy: His Life* (New York, 2000)

Brooks, David, 'The Education of Robert Kennedy', *New York Times*, 28
November 2006
Edelman, Peter, 'The Big Picture', *Boston Review*, Oct/Nov 2000
Getlin, Josh, 'The Cult of Bobby', *Los Angeles Times*, 20 October 1992
Reilly, Mary Anne, *Newsday*, 5 June 1988
Sirica, Jack, 'The RFK Legacy', *Newsday*, 3 June 1993
Thomas, Evan, 'Bobby: Good, Bad and In Between – Robert F Kennedy',
Washington Monthly, October 2000

Other

Inaugural address of John F. Kennedy, 20 January 1961
RFK, Day of Affirmation Address, Cape Town University, 6 June 1966;

transcript of speech at www.americanrhetoric.com/speeches/rfkcape-town.htm

Marian Wright Edelman, Commencement Address to Tulane University, 19 May 2001

www.rfkmemorial.org/lifevision/biography

www.jfklibrary.org

Available at this site are trancripts for the following:
– President Clinton's remarks for Robert F. Kennedy, Memorial Mass, Arlington National Cemetery, 6 June 1993
– Remarks of Robert F. Kennedy at the University of Kansas, 18 March 1968
– Tribute to Senator Robert F. Kennedy by Senator Edward M. Kennedy, St Patrick's Cathedral, New York City, 8 June 1968

6. NELSON MANDELA

Books and articles

DeLuca, Anthony R., *Gandhi, Mao, Mandela and Gorbachev: Studies in Personality, Power and Politics* (Westport, CT, 2000)

Graybill, Lyn S., *Truth and Reconciliation in South Africa: Miracle or Model?* (Boulder, CO, 2002)

Kathrada, Ahmed, *Memoirs* (Cape Town, 2005)

Mandela, Nelson, *Long Walk to Freedom* (London, 1994)

Other

Joel Joffe interview with Cathy Koester, 2003

Mandela: The Living Legend, BBC documentary, March 2003

7. CICELY SAUNDERS

Books and articles

Du Boulay, Shirley, *Cicely Saunders* (London, 1993)

Feifel, Herman (ed.), *The Meaning of Death* (New York, 1959)

Hinton, John, *Dying* (London, 1967)

Saunders, Cicely, *Beyond all Pain – a Companion for the Suffering and Bereaved* (London, 1983)

Saunders, Cicely, *Cicely Saunders: Founder of the Hospice Movement: Selected Letters 1959–1999*, ed. David Clark (Oxford, 2002)

Saunders, Cicely, *Hospice: the Living Idea* (London, 1981)

Saunders, Cicely, *Into the Valley of the Shadow of Death* (London, 1996)

Saunders, Cicely, *The Management of Terminal Malignant Disease* (London, 1993)

Booth, Cherie, 'I Didn't Set Out to Change the World', *Daily Telegraph*, 5 September 2002

Katz, Helena, 'A Career of Compassion', *McGill Reporter*, 6 November 1997

Potter, Lynda Lee, 'I've met kings, prime ministers and movie stars – but I've never felt so honoured to interview anybody as this inspirational, glorious woman', *Daily Mail*, 26 February 2000

Stolberg, Sheryl Gay, 'Her Life's Work Is Caring for the Dying', *Chicago Tribune*, 2 June 1999

Other

Cicely Saunders interview with Cathy Koester, August 2003

8. AUNG SAN SUU KYI

Books and articles

Suu Kyi, Aung San, and Michael, Aris, *Freedom From Fear: And Other Writings* (London, 1991)

Suu Kyi, Aung San, *Letters from Burma* (London, 1997)

Suu Kyi, Aung San, and Alan Clements, *The Voice of Hope: Conversations with Alan Clements* (London, 1997)

Baker, Mark, 'Serenity and Steel: Suu Kyi Will Not Waver', *The Age* (Melbourne), 7 May 2002

Kazmin, Amy, 'Burma's symbol of hope steps out into the sunlight: Fresh from 19 months' house arrest, Aung San Suu Kyi met the media at her opposition party's Rangoon headquarters. Amy Kazmin was there', *Financial Times*, 7 May 2002

Keane, Fergal, 'Suu Kyi's Release Is a Tribute to Her Courage and the Value of Sanctions', *Independent*, 11 May 2002

Suu Kyi, Aung San, Letter from Burma (No.1), in 'Seed of Democracy Flowers in Rural Burma, the Road to Tha Ma Nya', *Mainichi Daily News*, 27 November 1995 – made available on the Daw Aung San Suu Kyi website: www.dassk.com/letters.htm

Other

www.dassk.com

CONCLUSION

Toby Harnden, 'The quiet executive who defied hijackers', *Daily Telegraph*, 18 September 2001

Index

Permissions

The author and publishers would like to acknowledge and thank the following for their permission to quote from copyrighted material:

Dietrich Bonhoeffer, *Letters and Papers from Prison*, The Enlarged Edition, SCM Press 1971 © SCM-Canterbury Press Ltd; Dietrich Bonhoeffer, Ethics, SCM Press 1955 © SCM-Canterbury Press Ltd; *With Raoul Wallenberg in Budapest: Memories of the War Years in Hungary*, by Per Anger, originally published by the Holocaust Library in 1981, reprinted by the U.S. Holocaust Memorial Museum in 1996, is used by permission of the U.S. Holocaust Memorial Museum, Washington, DC; *Righteous Gentile: The Story of Raoul Wallenberg, Missing Hero of the Holocaust* by John Bierman (Allen Lane 1981, Penguin Books 1982). Copyright © John Bierman, 1981. Reproduced by permission of Penguin Books Ltd.; excerpts from *The Autobiography of Martin Luther King, Jr.* (edited by Clayborne Carson) reproduced by kind permission of Little, Brown Book Group, © 1998 by the Heirs to the Estate of Martin Luther King, Jr.; excerpts from *Long Walk To Freedom* by Nelson Mandela © 1994 Nelson R. Mandela. Reproduced by kind permission of Little, Brown Book Group; extracts from *Mandela: The Living Legend*, are reproduced with the permission of the BBC; *Cicely Saunders* by Shirley du Boulay, reproduced by permission of Hodder and Stoughton Limited; Cicely Saunders, *The Management of Terminal Malignant Disease*, is reproduced by permission of Edward Arnold (Publishers) Ltd; Beyond All Pain by Cicely Saunders, by permission of SPCK; *Selected Letters* by Cicely Saunders, reproduced by permission of Oxford University

Launched in 2004, the Jennifer Brown Research Laboratory, led by Professor Andrew Calder, was created to help solve pregnancy difficulties and save newborn lives. The Jennifer Brown Research Fund currently supports four separate research projects at the laboratory, looking at pre-eclampsia, early labour problems, curing blindness in babies and reducing incidences of brain damage in premature babies. The fundamental objective of the project is to maximise the potential for all babies to embark on life fully endowed both physically and intellectually. This can only be obtained if we understand and are able to prevent the death and long-term handicap which can sadly still result from impaired development, premature birth and the neonatal complications which may afflict such babies. Based in the prestigious Queen's Medical Research Institute at the Royal Infirmary in Edinburgh, the four research fellows are progressing extremely well with the scientific work, and significant outcomes look increasingly likely over the coming years.

For more information please contact:

The University of Edinburgh Reproductive and Development Sciences Departments at www.rds.mvm.ed.ac.uk
or
PiggyBankKids at www.piggybankkids.org

Anyone who wishes to organise a fundraising event or make a personal donation should contact either:

PiggyBankKids on 020 7936 1293
or:
The Jennifer Brown Research Laboratory
c/o Professor A. A. Calder
Room S7108, Simpson Centre for Reproductive Health
51 Little France Crescent
Edinburgh
EH16 4SA